Publications of the
National Bureau of Economic Research, Inc.
Number 56

The Trend of Government Activity in the
United States since 1900

Relation of the Directors
to the Work and Publications
of the National Bureau of Economic Research

1. The object of the National Bureau of Economic Research is to ascertain and to present to the public important economic facts and their interpretation in a scientific and impartial manner. The Board of Directors is charged with the responsibility of ensuring that the work of the National Bureau is carried on in strict conformity with this object.

2. To this end the Board of Directors shall appoint one or more Directors of Research.

3. The Director or Directors of Research shall submit to the members of the Board, or to its Executive Committee, for their formal adoption, all specific proposals concerning researches to be instituted.

4. No report shall be published until the Director or Directors of Research shall have submitted to the Board a summary drawing attention to the character of the data and their utilization in the report, the nature and treatment of the problems involved, the main conclusions and such other information as in their opinion would serve to determine the suitability of the report for publication in accordance with the principles of the National Bureau.

5. A copy of any manuscript proposed for publication shall also be submitted to each member of the Board. For each manuscript to be so submitted a special committee shall be appointed by the President, or at his designation by the Executive Director, consisting of three Directors selected as nearly as may be one from each general division of the Board. The names of the special manuscript committee shall be stated to each Director when the summary and report described in paragraph (4) are sent to him. It shall be the duty of each member of the committee to read the manuscript. If each member of the special committee signifies his approval within thirty days, the manuscript may be published. If each member of the special committee has not signified his approval within thirty days of the transmittal of the report and manuscript, the Director of Research shall then notify each member of the Board, requesting approval or disapproval of publication, and thirty additional days shall be granted for this purpose. The manuscript shall then not be published unless at least a majority of the entire Board and a two-thirds majority of those members of the Board who shall have voted on the proposal within the time fixed for the receipt of votes on the publication proposed shall have approved.

6. No manuscript may be published, though approved by each member of the special committee, until forty-five days have elapsed from the transmittal of the summary and report. The interval is allowed for the receipt of any memorandum of dissent or reservation, together with a brief statement of his reasons, that any member may wish to express; and such memorandum of dissent or reservation shall be published with the manuscript if he so desires. Publication does not, however, imply that each member of the Board has read the manuscript, or that either members of the Board in general, or of the special committee, have passed upon its validity in every detail.

7. A copy of this resolution shall, unless otherwise determined by the Board, be printed in each copy of every National Bureau book.

(Resolution adopted October 25, 1926
and revised February 6, 1933 and February 24, 1941)

The Trend

of Government Activity

in the United States since 1900

by Solomon Fabricant
New York University

assisted by Robert E. Lipsey

National Bureau of
Economic Research, Inc.

NEW YORK 1952

KRAUS REPRINT CO.
Millwood, New York
1975

Library of Congress Cataloging in Publication Data

Fabricant, Solomon, 1906-
    The trend of government activity in the United
States since 1900.

    Reprint of the ed. published by National Bureau of
Economic Research, New York, and issued as v. 56 of its
publications.
    Includes bibliographical references.
    1. United States—Politics and government—1901-
1953.   2. United States—Economic co..ditions.
I. Lipsey, Robert E., joint author.   II. Title.
III. Series: National Bureau of Economic Research.
General series ; no. 56.
JK421.F18   1975   320.9'73'091   75-6547
ISBN 0-527-03017-1

Library of Congress catalog card number: 52-7402

Reprinted with the permission of the
National Bureau of Economic Research
KRAUS REPRINT CO.
A U.S. Division of Kraus-Thomson Organization Limited

Printed in U.S.A.

Preface

THE RESOURCES DIVERTED TO GOVERNMENT bulk so large — even apart from the effects of Korea — and government touches so many sides of our economic life that proper understanding of government's activities is imperative. To contribute to this understanding we shall review changes since 1900 in the scope and character of government activities in the United States and ask how these changes have come about.

We set off (Chapter 1) by contrasting the role of government in the economy of 1900 with its role in the economy of 1950. Having posed our problem in this way, we begin the detailed review with a study (Chapter 2) of the changing aggregate volume of resources — labor, capital assets, and purchases of goods and services from private industry — utilized by all governmental bodies in the United States; and pause to compare the input so measured with the usual figures on government expenditures, which include relief, subsidy and other "transfer" payments and exclude the "use value" of government capital assets. Then (Chapter 3) we take note of the input by each type or level of government — federal, state, and local. Shifting our attention from resources used to services performed, we review the functional classification of input (Chapter 4). We then consider (Chapter 5) the factors that may have altered the relation between input and output in government, that is, the trend in the efficiency of government; determine change in government output, as well as we can; and ask how much government output has grown at the expense of private output. Interstate differences in government activity — measured by expenditure and employment of state and local governments —

are next considered and an attempt made to analyze statistically some of the measurable factors determining these differences (Chapter 6). We conclude (Chapter 7) with a summary and analysis of the influences underlying the trend of government activity, set against the background of the general economic development of the United States during the past half-century, and with a glance at the future. The appendices describe and assess the available statistics and the gaps in them; we keep that kind of discussion down to a minimum in the text.

A few other remarks may be directed to the reader. First, our emphasis will be on the trend of government activity and the factors that have caused it. Of course, government is itself a cause of change, and many government activities and policies have far-reaching effects on the economy. These we shall not attempt to evaluate; we deal with only part of the problem of understanding the role of government in economic life. Second, we shall try to be as objective as possible in treating our subject. We trust the reader, too, will make the same effort, for it is a subject on which people have very decided — and divided — opinions. Finally, if the reader has no time for our entire report, he should read the first and last chapters and glance at the charts in the rest of the text.

SOLOMON FABRICANT

ACKNOWLEDGMENTS

THIS REPORT, like others in the series, profited from the guidance of a National Bureau staff committee consisting of Thor Hultgren, F. C. Mills and Leo Wolman. Helpful suggestions were made also by Arthur F. Burns, Director of Research; by M. A. Copeland, Lawrence Klein, R. J. Saulnier and George J. Stigler, members of the National Bureau Research Staff; by Frank W. Fetter and Harry W. Laidler, of the Board of Directors of the National Bureau; and by Allen D. Manvel, R. A. Musgrave and George Wharton Pepper.

I am deeply indebted to Robert E. Lipsey for assistance in all phases of the study, including supervision of the checking of the manuscript; to Belle C. Nathan, for valuable help, especially in assembling the material on employment and productivity; and to Arnold Oliphant, Donald J. Kilian and Sylvia Schlachter, for most of the calculations and checking. I owe the excellence of the charts to H. Irving Forman. The difficult task of editing the manuscript was performed by Martha Anderson and Louise Cooper.

The study upon which this volume is based was made possible by funds granted by The Maurice and Laura Falk Foundation of Pittsburgh. The Falk Foundation is not, however, the author, publisher or proprietor of this publication, and is not to be understood as approving or disapproving by virtue of its grant any of the statements made or views expressed therein.

S. F.

CONTENTS

Appendices

Text Tables

xv

Appendix Tables

Charts

The Trend of Government Activity
in the United States since 1900

CHAPTER 1

Government Activity in 1900 and 1950: A Contrast

One out of every eight persons employed in the United States today is a government worker.[1] One out of every five dollars of the nation's capital assets — even excluding public roads and streets and most military and naval equipment — is government property. One out of every twenty dollars of the consolidated net sales of business is made to government. Are these proportions merely a holdover from the war, which may be expected in time to diminish substantially, or were they large before the war too? If large before the war, do they reflect a changed concept of government's functions brought into being under the New Deal, or are they part of a trend already established before the great depression? If part of a long-term trend, what accounts for it?

To answer these questions we must study changes in government activities and in the volume of resources devoted to these activities. Then, with the totals reviewed, we need to go on to distinguish the national, state, and local levels of government and ask how each has grown; and we must consider which functions at each of these levels advanced most rapidly, which lagged, and why. Before we approach the details of the story, however, let us throw the spotlight on some of the differences in the role of government between 1900 (the year with which we choose to start) and the present day.

The Economy of 1900

The twentieth century dawned on a United States in which farming was the leading industry. The world's greatest railroad net,

[1] By "today" we mean the period just before Korea. Our figures usually stop with 1949; but there was little change between 1949 and the first half of 1950.

stimulated into being by huge government land grants, was now substantially complete and at the disposal of the farmer. Rural free delivery had just been established. The Department of Agriculture had recently been raised to Cabinet status and, with the state colleges of agriculture and experiment stations already in existence, was providing farming with various services: the farmer's almanac could be supplemented by Weather Bureau reports and Department of Agriculture booklets.

However, few roads leading to the rail lines were hard surfaced or even graded. Although the Interstate Commerce Commission was already thirteen years old, it was not yet able to regulate railroad rates effectively. Farm mortgages were held only by private investors and institutions — not including national banks, which could not lend on real property — at interest rates frequently exceeding 6 percent. Farmers complained that they paid an unfairly high share of taxes. When disaster struck, the farmer could rely only on his own resources or on what local aid he might secure: not long before, President Cleveland had vetoed an appropriation of $25,000 to buy seed corn for Texas farmers ruined by a drought. Government tariffs raised the prices the farmer paid, but the prices he received fluctuated in a free market. Farm prices were above the low levels of the dark 1890's and were going higher; but this was not the fruit of the farmers' fight for "cheap money": the bitter greenback and silver campaigns had been lost and the latter officially closed by the passage of the Currency Act of 1900.

While farming was still growing somewhat as a source of employment, the swarming population — a million and a half persons were being added each year on the average — found no unlimited virgin territory over which to spread. Nonagricultural pursuits were already being followed by over 60 percent of the labor force — the halfway mark had been reached two decades before — and it was to these pursuits that the vast majority of new workers turned for a living. Unlike the situation in agriculture, most of the young people entering nonagricultural industries did not work for themselves or their parents. In 1900 well over half the entire labor force consisted of workers earning a wage or salary in a nonfamily, nonfarming business. Yet the number of workers affiliated with trade unions accounted for no more than 5 or 6 percent of these. Collective bargaining, except for some skilled trades, was negligible. The attitude of government toward labor organization was at best one of tolerance — the great Pullman strike was only six years past. The Department of Labor, not of Cabinet rank, was essentially a bureau devoted to statistics.

Labor legislation to protect the employed worker was being discussed extensively. The Industrial Commission named by President McKinley in 1898 was just beginning to issue its 19-volume report, some important parts of which were focused on labor questions. But the labor legislation of those states that had any — the federal government had virtually none — related mainly to methods of wage payment, safety in hazardous industries, hours of certain classes of workers, and child labor, and was usually of limited scope and in what Elizabeth Brandeis has called "the pre-enforcement stage".[2] If the unemployed worker and the chronically indigent were cared for by organized charity, the funds came largely from private sources. The first workmen's compensation act was yet to be passed. The severe depression of the middle 1890's, with its makeshift direct and primitive work relief, was fresh in memory. But 1900 itself stood at the center of a period of prosperity for labor as well as the farmer. And this was prosperity at levels exceeding those of earlier decades. Hours of work were lower: the ten-hour day was fairly well established. Average income was higher, indeed, higher than in most countries including Britain.[3]

The battle for free public schools had been won half a century before. The income of parents enabled them to send 80 percent of children ten to fourteen to school. But only 42 percent of the children fifteen to seventeen were able to continue in school.

The death rate still exceeded 160 per 1,000 in the first year of life. The few food inspection and other public health measures were poorly enforced. Public (and private) hospitals provided perhaps no more than three beds per thousand population.

[2] John R. Commons, et al., History of Labor in the United States, Vol. III, "Labor Legislation", by Elizabeth Brandeis (Macmillan, 1935), p. 625.

[3] Colin Clark, The Conditions of Economic Progress (London, Macmillan, 2nd ed., 1951), Ch. 3.

The problem of "big business" had already thrust itself upon the attention of the people. The Sherman Act was ten years old. But few cases had been tried or even started under it, and the country was in an industrial combination boom of major proportions. However, the Industrial Commission was holding hearings on this question also, and the muckrakers were preparing to spread the iniquities of the "trusts" under the noses of the people.

These enterprising journalists drew attention also to the "shame of the cities". Local government, untrammeled by a civil service, was frequently corrupt and inefficient. This was a serious defect in a government system operating largely through the county and municipality. State governments played a minor role in providing public services, and the federal government confined its activities largely to the traditional ones of postal service, defense, and conduct of foreign affairs. There was no central bank. The United States had just endorsed the gold standard, but Secretary Gage noted that there was still "no assurance whatever that the volume of bank currency will be continuously responsive to the country's needs".[4] Government transfers to the public consisted mainly of veterans' pensions.

Even defense and foreign affairs occupied the attention of few. The Civil War had occurred 35 years before; the Spanish War had been a quick and easy kill. Only recently had the United States acquired a colonial empire. Substantial foreign capital was still flowing to the United States. The country was only just beginning to turn its eyes back to the outside world, after almost a century of near isolation.

It was the Republican party that had won in 1896 and 1900, and on the whole the people still thought in terms of "the less government, the better". Even a Democratic president, vetoing the appropriation for seed corn referred to above, could state: "I can find no warrant for such an appropriation in the Constitution, and I do not believe that the power and duty of the general government ought to be extended to the relief of individual suffering which is in no manner properly related to the public service or

[4] *Annual Report of the Secretary of the Treasury, 1900,* p. LXXXIII.

benefit. A prevalent tendency to disregard the limited mission of this power and duty should, I think, be steadfastly resisted, to the end that the lesson should be constantly enforced that, though the people support the government, the government should not support the people."[5]

Yet efforts were constantly being made by every group "seriously dissatisfied with the results of private enterprise, or of private enterprise as regulated by local or state governments," to use the federal government as an agency for attaining what it desired. "The conquerors of the continent" were often "full of complaints concerning their economic plight, and insistent with the full force of their rugged personalities that government come to their aid".[6] And as the record will show, even before 1900 such efforts often succeeded when the group was of considerable size. By 1900 government already held something like 7 percent of the nation's capital assets (exclusive of roads and streets and most military and naval equipment), and employed something like 4 percent of the nation's labor force.

The Economy of 1950

Despite the spate of births during the 1940's children are relatively scarcer than they were at the beginning of the century and if the trend persists, will become still scarcer. We look to municipal and state government to protect our children's milk and to give them care before and after they are ill. The infant death rate is down to about 35 per 1,000 and we are seeking to reduce it still farther. More children are in school and stay in school longer, and these

[5] Veto of the Texas Seed Bill, Feb. 16, 1887, *The Writings and Speeches of Grover Cleveland,* edited by G. F. Parker (Cassel Publishing Co., 1892). (The veto message was drawn to our attention by a reference in W. J. Shultz, *American Public Finance* [Prentice-Hall, 1942], p. 19.) Almost identical words appear in Cleveland's second inaugural address, March 4, 1893: "The lessons of paternalism ought to be unlearned and the better lesson taught that while the people should patriotically and cheerfully support their Government its functions do not include the support of the people." *Grover Cleveland, Addresses, State Papers and Letters,* edited by A. E. Bergh (Sun Dial Classics Co., 1908).

[6] W. C. Mitchell, "Intelligence and the Guidance of Economic Evolution", in *The Backward Art of Spending Money* (McGraw-Hill, 1937), p. 119.

are largely public schools. They play more in government-operated parks and recreation centers and less in the streets. And programs for these purposes continue to be added.

Old people are more numerous. A substantial fraction — and we are expanding the fraction — now receive government pensions, as do many widows and others. A larger fraction of the helpless needing special care reside in better government institutions. And for the population at large, there are now 10 hospital beds per 1,000, of which almost three-quarters are provided by government.

More of us live in cities and demand and receive more and better municipal services. Six-sevenths of the labor force, instead of six-tenths, are occupied outside of farming. And the trend is still away from the farm. Agriculture is in substantial part a subsidized industry, which it was not in 1900.

Business enterprise is bigger and we try harder to control it. More people work for a large impersonal corporation. A higher percentage of the labor force is unionized and the unions receive government support and protection. Working conditions are more effectively patrolled by government as well as trade unions.

When depression hits, a bigger fraction is likely to be unemployed since fewer work on farms. Many of these may now receive unemployment compensation as a matter of right rather than charity. And we are expanding the coverage. We get more facts sooner about our economic troubles than we used to; and we are trying to use government agencies to prevent or alleviate them. We talk less about punishing criminals and more about slum clearance; and not only about slum clearance but also about subsidies for housing the lower middle class as well as the poor.

We are and feel more interdependent with those across our borders and are acting accordingly. We have endured two world wars and fear a third which will be greater than the second, as the second was greater than the first; and we spend money, through government, for old and new wars more freely.

Average incomes are higher and so are standards of welfare and responsibility for ourselves and others. We feel more able and more obligated to make long-term investments in human and natural resources and do so. We argue less about old age pensions and unemployment relief than about health security; not about the Tennessee Valley Authority but about the Missouri Valley Authority. We look more to government to prevent, remove, or alleviate the economic and social evils we see about us; we think of government as "an affirmative agency of national progress and social betterment", not "a mere organized police force, a necessary evil".[7]

Today government holds 20 percent of the nation's capital assets (exclusive of roads and streets and most military and naval equipment), not 7 percent as in 1900; and employs 12 percent of the nation's labor force, not 4 percent as in 1900. Today, through transfer payments, government adds $12 billion, or 6 percent, to the income of individuals, and through income taxes, subtracts $18 billion, or 9 percent; in 1900 transfer payments were well under 1 percent of total income, and income taxes could not be levied.

Before 1900 a bill to appropriate $25,000 for seed corn for Texan farmers hit by a drought could be vetoed. In 1949 a federal disaster-relief measure, started to aid snowbound ranchers in the Dakotas and Wyoming, could mushroom in little more than a year into 26,000 loans totaling $31 million, made by the Farmers Home Administration to farmers in 35 states, to mitigate the effects of factors ranging from boll weevil damage in the South to wind storm damage in New England.

Even with this brief contrast between 1900 and 1950, we begin to grasp the great changes that half a century saw in the role of government in our economic life, and to understand some of the factors that brought them. Let us now move up to a closer examination of the changes, taking note of what happened during the years between 1900 and 1950.

[7] Henry L.Stimson and McGeorge Bundy, *On Active Service in Peace and War* (Harper, 1948), p. 63.

CHAPTER 2

Resources Absorbed in Government Activity

Measurement of the scope and trend of government activity must be approached through the drafts it makes upon the productive resources of the nation — its labor force and its capital. We shall give attention later to the output of government, but no thoughtful reader will doubt the difficulties in reaching even the broadest judgments on output. With inputs it is otherwise: the men and other resources required in government activity are not of a type different from those employed in private industry. We begin with the most important input, manpower.

Number of Government Workers

In 1900 our federal, state, and local governments employed somewhat more than one million persons. Each decade thereafter saw a substantial net increase: over a half-million in 1900-10, almost a million in 1910-20, three-quarters of a million in 1920-30, over a million in 1930-40, and close to three million in 1940-49. By 1949 the total reached around seven million. Today's huge government employment, then, is the latest figure in a series with a pronounced upward trend.

The impatient reader — refusing to wade through the detailed description in Appendix B — will want to know immediately how reliable this series is. He should look at Chart 1. Estimates based on two virtually independent sources show substantially the same expansion in government employment. Whether the estimates are derived from reports by government workers (census data) or from reports by governments (payroll data), each decade records a lengthening of government payrolls. Both estimates show total net increases, for the last five decades, of close to six million.

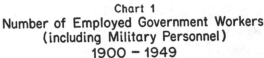

Chart 1
Number of Employed Government Workers
(including Military Personnel)
1900 – 1949

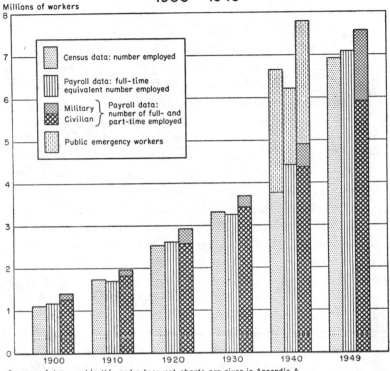

Sources of data used in this and subsequent charts are given in Appendix A.

The figures cited include all ordinary employees of all types of government unit — federal, state, local, including school and other "districts", and government enterprises and corporations.[1] Among these employees are members of the armed forces as well as civilians, and unclassified and temporary employees as well as civil service appointees. Practically all part-time workers are covered

---

[1] All government corporations are considered within the scope of government as the term is used here. A question arises about corporations — Federal Land Banks are an example — of whose stock government holds only a part. But for our purpose these borderline cases are negligible since they account for only a very small fraction of government input. When attention is centered on credit and finance, however, these cases are more troublesome.

by the payroll data.[2] Exclusion of most part-time workers from the census data helps to explain some (but not all) of the differences in the chart.

The glance at Chart 1 will have disclosed, also, the large number of public emergency employees in 1940, an extraordinary class of government worker we ignored when describing the trend. Scarcely any appear in the record for 1930, and none at all for the other years covered by the chart. This fact and the special nature of emergency employment justify showing it separately.

Because the numbers we report are so large, it is well to emphasize that certain groups that conceivably might be included are omitted. We exclude government contractors and their employees; volunteer firemen, members of school boards, and other citizens who occasionally lend a hand in various government activities at nominal or no compensation; farmers and others required as part of their civic duties to assist in road maintenance and similar work; and inmates of prisons and other institutions. The services of conᴛctors' employees are covered by our estimates of government purchases from private industry, to be given below. Some of the groups omitted, volunteer firemen, for example, declined in relative importance as urbanization proceeded. But their exclusion does not appear to bias to any important degree the trend shown by our figures: the *full*-time employees required to replace them in the few functions in which they may have been of significance constitute only a fraction of all government workers today (see Table 12, below).

The expanding host of public pensioners and recipients of welfare, subsidy, and similar government payments are all, of course, excluded from our figures.

Government in Relation to Total Employment

In a country where population is at a standstill or changing only slightly, the trend in the absolute number of government workers would be enough to give the picture. But our population — and

---

[2] In the calculation of "full-time equivalents", two half-time workers, for example, are counted as one full-time worker.

with it, total employment — has been growing rapidly. How does the growth of government compare with the growth of total employment?

It will be no surprise to find that the rate of growth in total employment, substantial though it has been, was far short of the very high rate of growth in government employment (Chart 2).

Chart 2
Government and Total Employment, 1900-1949
(Full-time equivalent number)

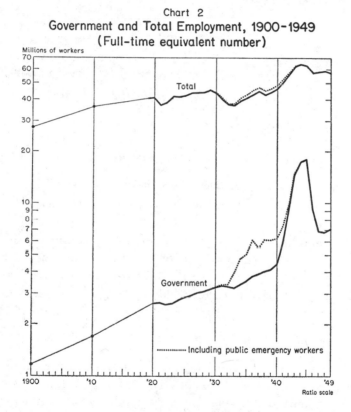

Total employment also rose each decade (on net balance), but the percentage increase was always less than in government employment. For 1900-49 as a whole, total employment increased about 120 percent, government employment 500 percent or more. The contrast is still more striking when the 500 percent increase

in government workers is compared with the 100 percent increase
in privately employed workers.[3]

Another way to describe the growing importance of government
workers in the total is to compare the present proportion with that
of earlier years. In 1900 one out of 24 workers was on a government payroll, in 1920, one out of 15, and in 1940, one out of 11.
The current ratio, as has been said, is one out of 8. The trend is
sharp and clear (Table 1).

Table 1

EMPLOYED GOVERNMENT WORKERS (INCLUDING MILITARY PERSON-
NEL) AS A PERCENTAGE OF ALL EMPLOYED WORKERS, 1900-1949

	1900	1910	1920	1930	1940	1949
Census data[a]	4.1	4.9	6.3			
Payroll data, full-time equivalent number			6.5	7.4	9.5 (12.9[b])	12.4

[a] Corresponding percentages for earlier years are: 1870, 2.7; 1880, 3.1;
1890, 3.5.
[b] The figure in parentheses includes public emergency workers.

Sources of data in this and subsequent tables are given in Appendix A.

That this trend is a continuation of one already apparent in the
nineteenth century is suggested by rough data that go back to
1870. Over the 80 years since 1870 the percentage of all workers
on government payrolls quadrupled.

Stock of Government-Owned Capital Goods

Government is obviously a big employer when an eighth of the
labor force is on a government payroll. But government is even
bigger, compared to private industry, as a holder of capital goods.
Of the vast stock of capital goods in existence in the United States
today — movable equipment, rolling stock, and improvements to
fixed property, but excluding roads and streets, the national arma-

[3] There are also interesting differences between government and private employment with respect to the effect of war and changes in business conditions;
but we shall be better prepared to take notice of these in the next chapter.

ment, and consumers' personal property, as well as business inventories — something like a fifth is publicly owned. What has been the trend in government's share of this important class of the nation's resources?

In 1902, the closest we can get to the opening of the century, government nonmilitary capital assets on which definite values can be put totaled somewhat under $4 billion. By 1946, the most recent year for which data are available, these assets were valued at over $50 billion. The increase reflects, of course, a low price level in 1902 compared with 1946, as well as growth in the "real" stock of capital goods. Expressed uniformly in 1929 prices, government-owned nonmilitary capital assets amounted to about $8 billion in 1902 and over $50 billion in 1946, a rise of $40-odd billion.

Almost every year added something to the government's stock of capital goods. Indeed, with one exception during the 1930's, declines seem to have come only after the two great wars, when surplus federal property was sold or scrapped. In each period marked off by the years in Table 2, a substantial net increase occurred. Some $6 billion were accumulated in 1902-12, about $5

Table 2

GOVERNMENT-OWNED NONMILITARY CAPITAL ASSETS, 1902-1946
(billions of dollars)

	1902	1912	1922	1929	1939	1946	1922	1929	1939	1946
			Excl. Roads and Streets				*Incl. Roads and Streets*			
Book values										
Incl. defense corporations	3.8	7.3	15.4	21.1	30.9	51.4	20.5	31.9	47.8	68.8
Excl. defense corporations	3.8	7.3	13.0	21.0	30.7	36.1	18.1	31.8	47.6	53.6
1929 prices[a]										
Incl. defense corporations	8.4	14.3	18.9	23.3	33.8	50.9				
Excl. defense corporations	8.4	14.3	15.9	23.2	33.6	35.8				

[a] Conversion of book values to 1929 prices changes the 1929 book values because the assets of 1929 are valued on the books at the prices prevailing in the years when the assets were acquired.

billion in 1912-22, $4 billion in 1922-29, around $10 billion in 1929-39, and $17 billion in 1939-46 (all in terms of 1929 prices).

We show only "nonmilitary" assets because lack of data compels us to exclude assets held by the military establishment. Included,

however, is a considerable amount of property acquired by the
federal government to carry on the two world wars, notably war
plants and shipping. On a somewhat narrower definition of "nonmilitary" these might be excluded. This would reduce the 1922 and
1946 figures, and the net increase from 1902 to 1946 would
amount to some $27 billion in 1929 prices.

Inclusion of all military assets would, of course, raise the levels
and changes shown in Table 2 substantially. The value of military
assets at the end of 1946 has been estimated at $58 billion in terms
of depreciated original cost.[4] Still other omissions are caused by
lack of information. Most notable is the omission of roads and
streets in the earlier years. Their importance is indicated by the
difference between the two sets of figures in the table.[5]

Quality as well as quantity of government assets was heightened.
More roads were surfaced, for example, one-room schoolhouses
gave way to larger and better equipped buildings, and trucks and
motorized fire apparatus displaced horse drawn equipment. Many
improvements are reflected in the deflated figures cited. Some,
however, are not, because the deflators used are in part derived
from the prices of commodities of improving quality. On this account, too, growth in the capital stock held by government is
understated.

Capital Goods Compared with Employment

Some four million full-time equivalent workers were employed by
government in 1946, excluding the military and civilians directly
engaged in national defense. Government-owned nonmilitary assets amounted to $36 billion, excluding defense plants, war surplus

---

[4] In terms of depreciated replacement value, the estimate is $80 billion. See
J. E. Reeve, and others, "Government Component in the National Wealth",
Studies in Income and Wealth, Volume Twelve (National Bureau of Economic
Research, 1950), p. 502.

[5] Sewage systems, nonschool assets of small municipalities and of certain townships and special districts, equipment of several federal agencies, and federal
property outside the continental United States are excluded in all years. Although less important than highways, these items are not negligible. In 1939
the depreciated cost of the Panama Canal was half a billion dollars.

and other quasi-military assets held by federal corporations, and roads and streets. Capital assets per worker therefore reached $9,000 in this year. Including roads and streets, they would be $13,000 per worker.[6] While labor is the biggest single resource used by government, government "property, plant, and equipment" is not of minor significance even in relation to labor.[7]

Chart 3
Government Employment, 1900–1949
and Capital Assets, 1902–1946
(Employment on a full-time equivalent basis, assets in 1929 prices)

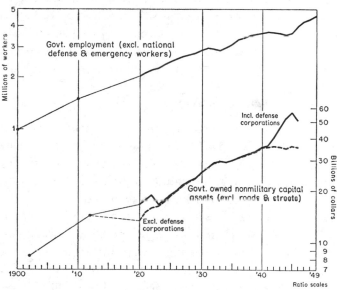

In 1902 corresponding capital assets (excluding roads and streets) per worker were surprisingly similar when figured in 1946 book values — perhaps about $7,500 or $8,000. Indeed, within

[6] These are 1946 "book values", which are based largely on prewar costs. In prices current in 1946 or today, the amount would be considerably greater.

[7] This may be put also in terms of a comparison of net rental values and salaries. Government's capital assets were worth some $750 per year per worker (figuring net rent at a rather arbitrary rate of 4 percent of 1946 net replacement cost). The average government employee received some $2,400 in 1946. The proportion is thus about 1 to 3.

the allowances that must be made for inevitable margins of error, the rise per worker may be insignificant. The rise in government employment has kept pace with the rise in government-owned capital assets (Chart 3). Inclusion of roads and streets and other missing nonmilitary assets, however, would not only raise the level, but probably also tilt up a bit the trend of assets per worker. Addition of all military items to both assets and employment would probably push up the rate of growth even more, as well as further raise the level of assets per worker.

This comparison of assets and workers leads to an important conclusion. The trend of government employment, rapidly upward though it has been, does not overstate the rate of increase in government input. But before we may accept this conclusion we must wait to learn something of the importance and trend of government purchases of materials and services from private industry.

Government's Share in the Nation's Stock of Capital Goods

Like government's current share in employment, government's share of the nation's capital goods is the latest in a series with an upward trend (Table 3). Indeed, there is great similarity in the average rate of change although not in the level of the two series, as one could infer from information already given.

Government owned one-fifteenth of the nation's capital goods in 1902; by 1946 its share was up to one-fifth. If roads, streets, and other important omitted items were included, government's share would be higher in both periods. If military property were included, government's share in 1946 would be still higher, and the rise to 1946 still sharper.

As in the case of employment, there is some evidence that the rising trend in government's share in the nation's property goes back into the nineteenth century. In 1890 the share was smaller than in 1900; and in 1880, smaller than in 1890.[8]

The differences between growth in government and in total

---

[8] For the earlier years we have figures only on tax-exempt real estate, largely but not entirely government property. Tax-exempt real estate, as a percentage of total national wealth, was 5.9 in 1880, 6.4 in 1890, and 7.3 in 1900. (*Studies in Income and Wealth, Volume Twelve, op. cit.,* p. 538.) This series probably

Table 3

GOVERNMENT-OWNED AND TOTAL CAPITAL ASSETS, 1902-1946
EXCLUDING MILITARY ASSETS, ROADS AND STREETS, AND LAND
(in 1929 prices)

Billions of Dollars	1902	1912	1922	1929	1939	1946
Government property	6.7	11.7	15.9 (13.4)	18.9	27.7	45.3 (31.9)
Total wealth (real estate improvements & equipment)	101	155	163 (160)	210	208	220 (207)
%, government of total	6.6	7.5	9.8 (8.4)	8.8	13.3	20.6 (15.4)

Percentage Changes	1902-12	1912-22	1922-29	1929-39	1939-46
Government property	+75	+36 (+15)	+19 (+40)	+47	+64 (+16)
Total wealth (real estate improvements & equipment)	+53	+5 (+3)	+29 (+31)	−1	+6 (0)

The figures include the assets of defense corporations; only the 1922 and 1946
figures would be substantially affected by their exclusion, as is indicated by
the figures in parentheses, which exclude defense corporation assets. Total
wealth includes residential buildings but excludes consumers' equipment.

wealth are striking enough to warrant viewing them from another
angle. Put in terms of absolute changes in property values (expressed in 1929 prices), and contrasting government with private
(instead of total) investment, we have Table 4, on p. 20.

These net investment figures reveal how great a participant in
the investment process government has been during the last half-
century. In a good many years government was the major net
investor. In the period that includes World War I, government net
investment equaled private net investment; and if some addition
be made for roads and streets, exceeded it. In two periods, one
including the great depression and the other World War II, government investment was at an exceptionally high level while aggre-

---

overstates the level of government's share of property because it includes property held by private tax-exempt institutions; and probably understates the
slope of the trend because it excludes government-owned equipment.

gate private net investment was negative. Annual figures available for 1919-43 show that government net investment in construction exceeded private net investment in plant and equipment combined in 1919, 1921, 1931-39, and 1942-43, inclusive, i.e., in 13 of the 25 years covered.[9]

Table 4

PUBLIC AND PRIVATE NET INVESTMENT IN CAPITAL ASSETS 1902-1946, EXCLUDING MILITARY ASSETS, ROADS AND STREETS, AND LAND

(in 1929 prices)

	1902-1912	1912-1922	1922-1929	1929-1939	1939-1946	1902-1946
Change in government-owned capital assets, billion dollars	5	4	3	9	17	39
Change in private capital assets (real estate improvements & equipment), billion dollars	49	4	44	−11	−5	80
Change in total capital assets, billion dollars	54	8	47	−2	12	119
%, government of total	9	50	6	*	140	32

* Denominator is negative.

If defense-agency assets were excluded, the increments in government-owned assets would be changed to: 1912-22, $2 billion; 1922-29, $5 billion; 1939-46, $4 billion; 1902-46, $25 billion.

The government figures, it must be emphasized, exclude strictly military investments, as well as several other government investments for which data are not available. In another respect, however, they overstress government's role in durable goods investment. Because most depreciation charges and retirements are deducted, the figures in Table 4 relate largely to net investment, that is, to net capital formation rather than gross capital formation. Government's share in *gross* investment is smaller because its assets include more construction items and are therefore longer lived.

Beginning with 1946 private investment was maintained at a

[9] Simon Kuznets, *National Product Since 1869* (National Bureau of Economic Research, 1946), Part I, Tables I6, I10, I16; 1929 prices.

high rate. It therefore seems likely — though figures comparable with those cited in Table 4 are lacking — that for the full period 1939-49 the story would be different from that for 1939-46 alone: private net investment would be positive and substantially greater than government net investment exclusive of investment in armament. But if armament were included, government net investment would still exceed private investment.

Government Purchases from Private Industry

In 1939, before the defense program got far underway, the government units of the United States paid out over $5.5 billion for the services of persons regularly employed by them, and held nonmilitary capital goods the services of which were worth perhaps $2 billion per year.[10]

These figures measure the value of the services of resources resident, so to speak, in the governmental sector of the economy. For some purposes their sum is the value of government's total input. It is this sum that, combined with corresponding inputs in other sectors, yields national input (or, its equivalent in money terms, national income);[11] and we might, therefore, conclude our review of government's input with this total. For other purposes, however — for example, to get at the total flow of resources through the governmental sector or to check on the displacement of one type of resource by another — it is desirable to go farther: to include also, before totaling the account, resources acquired by purchase from private industry. Among these are such items as new construction by private contractors, repairs, equipment, materials, supplies, transport, rents, and telephone services.[12]

---

[10] This is the imputed net rent, calculated at the rate of 4 percent of $48 billion, the 1939 book value of government capital assets including roads and streets.

[11] More accurately this *should* yield the correct measure of national input. Current calculations of national input either make shift with interest on the public *debt* as the measure of the services of government capital, or ignore these services; see the text below.

Net profits on public enterprises are taken to be covered by the rental value of the capital assets.

[12] Included also are contributions to UNRRA and ECA grants, which tend to swell the federal figures in recent years.

Resources purchased by government from private industry also must be reckoned in large figures. In 1939 they amounted to $5.5 billion (Table 5), to which might be added $1 billion of purchases by government enterprises omitted from the figure. Most recently,

Table 5

TOTAL GOVERNMENT PURCHASES AND PAYROLLS, 1903-1949

	1903	1913	1929	1939	1949
			Millions of Dollars		
Outlays on capital assets	324	680			
New construction			2,391	2,346	6,403
Other purchases	429	752	1,786	3,170	18,467
Payrolls	721	1,341	4,295	5,667	18,729
Total purchases & payrolls	1,473	2,773	8,472	11,183	43,599
			Percentage of Total		
Outlays on capital assets	22.0	24.5			
New construction			28.2	21.0	14.7
Other purchases	29.1	27.1	21.1	28.3	42.4
Payrolls	48.9	48.4	50.7	50.7	43.0
Total purchases & payrolls	100.0	100.0	100.0	100.0	100.0

Compensation of public emergency workers, of importance in 1939, is excluded. Including such compensation in 1939 payrolls alters the percentages of that year to the following: new construction, 18.0; other purchases, 24.3; payrolls, 57.8.

The figures for 1903 and 1913 are National Bureau of Economic Research estimates for fiscal years. Those for 1929-49 are Department of Commerce estimates for calendar years. While conceptually somewhat different, the two sets of estimates are sufficiently comparable to indicate broad trends. The differences between them are described in Appendix D. The appendix also contains National Bureau estimates for 1932 and 1942 and DC estimates for each year between 1929 and 1949.

1949, they have been well over four times as much. About 1903 they were only a seventh of the 1939 level. In money terms, then, purchases currently run about 33 times what they were in 1903.

Perspective on the level and growth of these purchases is provided by the payroll figures in Table 5 and Chart 4. Except during war years, the cost of goods and services purchased from private business has been about as large as payrolls. That is, measured by dollar expenditure, resources purchased have grown over the last half-century at about the same rate as government payrolls. As we shall see below, this means that the physical volume of goods and

Chart 4
Government Outlays on Capital Assets, Other Purchases, and Payrolls
1903–1949
-----NBER (fiscal years)
────Dept. of Commerce (calendar years)

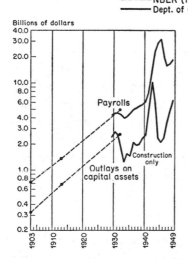

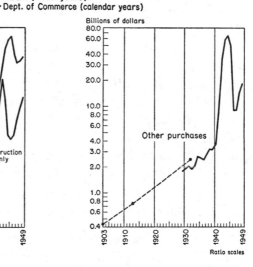

services acquired by purchase has grown *more* rapidly than the number of workers employed by government.

Another way to judge the relative importance of government purchases from private industry is to compare them with the total consolidated net sales of private industry as calculated by the Department of Commerce. This aggregate includes sales to consumers, to foreigners, and (of capital goods only) to business, as well as to government. In 1929, the first year for which we have the aggregate, the ratio of government purchases to it was 4.4 percent; in 1939, 6.7 percent; and in 1949, 8.7 percent.[13] These twenty years saw a doubling of the fraction of the business sector's sales of goods and services going to government.

The unstable part of government purchases has of course been outlays on capital assets, among which construction is the largest item. This can be seen in the annual figures plotted in Chart 4. The trend in these outlays, however, has roughly paralleled that in

[13] *Survey of Current Business,* National Income Supplement, 1951, p. 153. These government purchases exclude purchases from abroad; and the consolidated net sales are those of domestic business concerns only.

other purchases, at least before World War II. It is likely that the
large construction programs of state and local governments would
soon have brought outlays back to something approximating their
prewar relation to other purchases had not trouble started in
Korea.

To get some sense of the flow of *real* resources into government
it is necessary to go behind the current dollar values of the goods
and services purchased. The rough deflation we have been able to
make (Table 6) suggests that the physical volume of goods and
services purchased by government from private industry went up
more than a thousand percent between 1903 and 1949. This increase is far above the corresponding rises in government employment and real capital assets held by government.

Total Resources Put into Government Activity

The combined input of all real resources into government operations may be measured, as indicated earlier, inclusive or exclusive
of purchases from private industry (Table 6).

Table 6

GROWTH IN VOLUME OF RESOURCES USED BY GOVERNMENT
1900-1949

		Percentage Change over Period Shown	Average Annual Percentage Rate of Change
All Functions			
Number of workers	(1900-49)	509	3.8
Purchases, in constant prices	(1903-49)	1,156	5.6
Excluding National Defense			
Number of workers	(1900-49)	357	3.1
Purchases, in constant prices	(1903-49)	453	3.8
Capital assets, in constant prices[a]	(1902-46)	326	3.4
Total			3.4[b]

[a] Includes land, excludes roads, streets, and related assets, and assets of defense
corporations.
[b] This is an arithmetic mean, weights being payrolls, expenditures, and imputed
net rent (at 4 percent of book value) on capital assets at the opening of the
century. An harmonic mean, with weights based on values in 1946 or 1949,
also yields an estimate of 3.4.

Including only labor and capital, and omitting input for national defense, the total rose a little more than 350 percent between 1900 and 1949.[14] Including national defense, the rise was much greater, although lack of data on assets used by the military prevents its calculation. It was surely well over 500 percent. In contrast, national input somewhat more than doubled between 1900 and 1949: total employment went up from about 27 million in 1900 to 60 million in 1949 (Appendix B), and the nation's wealth (in 1929 prices) rose from $101 billion in 1902 to $220 billion in 1946 (Table 3). The rise in government input, therefore, was more than twice the rise in the nation's total input.[15]

When current resources acquired by purchase from private industry are also included, both rises are pushed up substantially. Total resources put into nondefense activity, so measured, rose over 400 percent between 1900 and 1949; and into all activities, probably over 700 percent.

At least one conclusion from these estimates is safe. The sixfold rise in government employment between 1900 and 1949, and the similar increase in capital assets, great as they are, understate the rise in the total volume of resources used in producing government services.[16]

[14] Precise figures for this total, and the other cited later, cannot be given because our data on capital assets and purchases do not cover the full period. The figures given represent the aggregate changes implied by the average annual changes for the available periods (Table 6, last column).

[15] Input of labor and capital in government (valued in terms of price prevailing either at the opening of the century or today — it matters little which "weight-base" is used) can be combined and expressed as a percentage of national input (in prices of the same period). The percentage was about 5 in 1900, is 14 today.

[16] Some readers may be puzzled by the treatment of depreciation of government capital assets that is implied by our calculations of total input. Capital assets used up in producing government services may be taken into account in either of two ways. If capital consumption is treated as part of the input of capital assets, input will cover the net rental value of the assets *and* their depreciation. But capital consumption may also be treated as part of the goods and services acquired from private industry: some of the purchases from private industry are used to maintain the real capital used by government. We follow the second procedure. Total input of all resources, including purchases, is not affected by the choice. However, if total input is measured by the input of labor and capital alone, the first procedure will give more weight to capital

Government Expenditures

Our measure of input does not include, even at its broadest, all items of government expenditure. On the other hand, it includes one item not ordinarily included in estimates of government expenditures. As expenditures are frequently used to measure government's absorption of resources, it is worth digressing a moment to indicate what the differences are.

Government expenditures ordinarily cover (1) payrolls (and pension payments); (2) purchases of goods and services from private industry;[17] (3) interest on the public debt; and (4) transfer items of various sorts, such as relief payments and subsidies. Sometimes they are defined to include also (5) transfers to other governments, such as grants-in-aid and shares of taxes; (6) loans; and even (7) other debt transactions, particularly repayments of the public debt. Our measure of input includes only the first two items plus (8) an imputed rental on government-owned capital goods. Item (8) is, in a sense, a substitute for the interest item.

It is clear, then, that our estimate of input $[(1) + (2) + (8)]$ will fall short of the usual estimate of expenditures $[(1) + (2) + (3) + (4)]$ by the amount of transfers (4) and by the difference between interest and imputed rent $[(8) - (3)]$.

Before World War I the estimate of imputed rent (at 4 percent) somewhat exceeded interest payments, and transfers to the public were quite small (Table 7). The war brought a big rise in interest

---

assets, and the result will be somewhat different from the one in the text. The difference will not be much, because real capital assets rose only slightly more than employment; giving the former more or less weight will therefore not affect the combination very much. (The difference in procedures involves only a difference in weights because we lack an adequate measure of depreciation on government capital. In effect, we measure the depreciation by taking a constant percentage of real capital assets. The weight of capital assets in the calculation of total input is then taken at 6.5 percent of the value of those assets — 4 percent for net rent, 2.5 percent for depreciation — rather than at 4 percent for net rent only. For the basis of the 2.5 percent see Solomon Fabricant, *Capital Consumption and Adjustment,* National Bureau of Economic Research, 1938, Ch. 7.)

[17] Ordinarily, purchases by public service enterprises are omitted entirely (we include them); instead, subsidies to public enterprises are included (we exclude them).

Table 7

TOTAL GOVERNMENT EXPENDITURES, 1903-1949

	1903	1913	1929	1939	1949
	Millions of Dollars				
Purchases & payrolls[a]	1,473	2,773	8,472	11,183	43,599
Transfer payments to the public[a]	155	183	912	4,397	11,610
Net interest paid	87	167	983	1,205	4,610
Total expenditures	1,715	3,123	10,367	16,785	59,819
	Percentage of Total				
Purchases & payrolls	86	89	82	67	73
Transfer payments to the public	9	6	9	26	19
Net interest paid	5	5	9	7	8
Total expenditures	100	100	100	100	100

[a] Purchases and payrolls inclusive of work relief, and transfer payments exclusive of work relief (Department of Commerce estimates), are as follows for 1939: purchases and payrolls, $13,068 million; transfer payments, $2,512 million.

The figures for 1903 and 1913 are National Bureau of Economic Research estimates for fiscal years, those for 1929-49 are Department of Commerce estimates for calendar years; cf. note to Table 5.

payments, however. Then the great depression and the legislation to which it led expanded transfer payments to the public, first in the form of relief, then in the form of social security and subsidy payments. World War II pushed interest payments up again. In 1903 expenditures exceeded input as we measure it by some 5 percent. In 1949 the excess was about 31 percent. Government expenditures rose more rapidly than our measure of input.[18]

Government expenditures, including interest and transfers, will therefore overstate the level and rate of growth of government's absorption of real resources. But even our measure of input is at a very high level today, and shows a very high average rate of growth, over the last half century, in government's use of resources.

[18] As mentioned earlier, 4 percent is a rather arbitrary figure. A lower imputed rental rate would reduce the level of input, as we measure it, in both 1903 and 1949, and thus increase both ratios of expenditures to input. If we assumed a declining secular trend in the appropriate imputed rental rate, the 1949 ratio would be increased more than the 1903 ratio.

Chapter 3

Shares of Federal, State, and Local Governments in Resource Input

The huge federal budget and large volume of federal employment have been discussed widely and often. Some readers may suppose, therefore, that the larger part of today's seven million government workers is on federal payrolls and that expansion of federal payrolls accounts for all or most of the six million persons taken on since 1900. And they may have similar impressions of the distribution of government-owned capital assets and government purchases from private industry. The facts show that these notions exaggerate the role of the federal government.

Distribution of Employment among Types of Government
Even today, when the uneasy peace keeps our armed forces at an unprecedented peacetime level, federal employment is barely larger than that of state and local governments. Of the seven million full-time equivalent workers on government payrolls, very close to half are employed by state and local governments. (The proportion before adjusting part-time work to a full-time equivalent basis is even higher because part-time work is more common in local governments.) In 1940, just before the big expansion in national defense activities, state and local governments accounted for almost two-thirds of the 4.4 million employees on government payrolls (excluding emergency workers). And at three of the four earlier decennial dates, the share of state and local governments was close to three-quarters.

Of the increase between 1900 and 1949, about three and a third million workers were additions to federal payrolls; two and two-thirds million, to state and local government payrolls. The biggest part of the increase in federal personnel, over two million, came in 1940-49. The jump in this decade accounted for well over half of all employees on federal payrolls in 1949. The next biggest rise, which came in 1930-40, was much smaller, under three-quarters of a million. Nevertheless, more federal workers were added in the 1930's alone than during the preceding three decades combined. State and local employment was much more consistent in amount of net growth during the five decades. But there were variations here too: the rise in the 1920's was substantially bigger than in other decades.

The changes in the distribution of government employees among the various types of unit from 1940 to 1949, and before and after 1920 as well (Table 8), reflect the effects of war, about which more will be said in a moment. The great depression, too, is re-

Table 8

GOVERNMENT WORKERS, DISTRIBUTION AMONG MAIN TYPES OF GOVERNMENT UNIT, 1900-1949

(payroll data, full-time equivalent number; public emergency workers excluded)

	1900	1910	1920	1930	1940	1949
			Thousands of Workers			
Federal	312	484	956	820	1,532	3,608
Armed forces	126	140	344	266	532	1,642
Civilian	186	345	613	554	1,000	1,966
State and local	852	1,209	1,654	2,436	2,883	3,478
States, nonschool	68	108	183	279	457	642
Cities, nonschool	194	336	429	702	754	933
Other local, nonschool	123	(189)	(235)	345	444	535
School	467	576	807	1,110	1,228	1,368
Total	1,164	1,693	2,610	3,256	4,415	7,086
			Percentage of Total			
Federal	26.8	28.6	36.6	25.2	34.7	50.9
Armed forces	10.8	8.3	13.2	8.2	12.0	23.2
Civilian	16.0	20.4	23.5	17.0	22.7	27.7
State and local	73.2	71.4	63.4	74.8	65.3	49.1
States, nonschool	5.8	6.4	7.0	8.6	10.4	9.1
Cities, nonschool	16.7	19.8	16.4	21.6	17.1	13.2
Other local, nonschool	10.6	(11.2)	(9.0)	10.6	10.1	7.6
School	40.1	34.0	30.9	34.1	27.8	19.3
Total	100.0	100.0	100.0	100.0	100.0	100.0

School employment cannot be distributed among the types of state and local governments in most years. Figures in parentheses are very rough estimates.

flected in the table. If we focus on the net change between 1900 and 1940, we find little alteration in the relative importance of the armed forces, municipal nonschool employment, and other local nonschool employment. The net change in the relative position of federal civilian employment was definitely upward. State non-school employment also expanded relatively. The share in the total of school employment (entirely a state and local matter, but not available by type of government unit in most years) fell rather consistently and very considerably.

Even the sectors of government that dropped in relative importance show substantial increases in absolute number. In the slowest growing sector, schools, the number of teachers and other employees tripled between 1900 and 1949.

Varied Impress of Wars and Business Cycles on Government Employment

The two major wars of our time are clearly reflected in the annual series plotted in Chart 5. In both wars, federal civilian as well as federal military employment rose to great heights, then fell sharply. After both wars, however, the decline halted at a level substantially above the prewar.

State and local government employment also felt the impact of war. But the effect was the reverse of what happened to federal employment. During World War II each nonfederal sector cut employment. After the war, each restored its personnel to prewar levels and pushed on to new heights. The effect of World War I is not so clear, partly because our information is scanty. Municipal nonschool employment did not increase from 1915 to 1920. Scattered information for one or two state governments suggests the war had the same effect on their employment. On the other hand, the rate of increase in school employment was not affected by World War I. On employment by other units of local government at that time we have no information.

Apart from the war periods, fluctuations in ordinary government employment are few, and none is really large. Employment in most private industries fluctuates closely and usually substantially with general business conditions, even when measured on an

Chart 5

Number of Government Workers Employed by Each Main Type of Government Unit, 1900 – 1949

(Payroll data, full-time equivalent number)

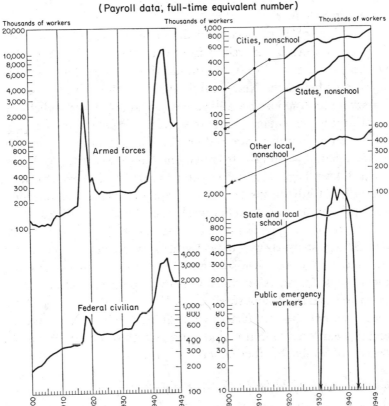

annual basis. Our annual series on government employment — with the notable exception of public emergency employment — shows hardly any such repercussions.

The sharp business contractions of 1920-21 and 1937-38, and the mild contractions of 1923-24 and 1926-27 seem to have caused scarcely a ripple in the series. Even the big contraction of 1929-32 made only a modest impression, certainly one much different from that stamped on the line for total employment, including private industry, plotted in Chart 2. All types of government employment except the armed forces continued to gain until 1931, some without slowing down much (Chart 5). Even the few declines after 1931 were over by 1933 or 1934. After 1933 federal civilian and state nonschool employment accelerated sharply, as did the armed forces after 1935.

The most striking reflection of the great depression, and of the 1937-38 contraction as well, is in the count of public emergency workers — those on WPA and similar rolls. Few persons were on work-relief before the New Deal in 1933. All through the preceding severe contraction in employment, additions to work-relief lists were large in percentage terms but small in absolute terms. The big expansion in number came after 1933 and continued through 1936, a period when private employment also was growing. Work relief did not begin to move counter to regular employment until after 1936. With the onset of the war, and the resulting labor shortages, the number of emergency workers declined, then vanished.

To return to a question posed at the outset of this report, these figures suggest clearly that the activities government took on under the New Deal were a very substantial factor in expanding government employment. After 1933 growth in both federal and state government employment speeded up. Yet, as we shall see, the New Deal was not the sole factor determining trends in government employment even in that period. And growth before 1933 is obviously attributable to other factors.

Capital Assets Held by Each Type of Government

Apart from military and quasi-military items, by far the larger share of government capital assets always has been held by state and local governments. Schools, roads, state hospitals, county courthouses, and the various municipal facilities — these make up the bulk of government property. Thus in 1902 federal nonmilitary assets accounted for only a sixth of the total not including streets and roads (Table 9). In 1939, before the sharp rise in national defense facilities began, the federal fraction was under a fifth. Including roads (almost entirely state and local property), the federal share was only an eighth in 1939.

Rapid growth usually has characterized the book value of capital assets held by every major type of government unit (Chart 6).

Table 9

BOOK VALUES OF CAPITAL ASSETS, DISTRIBUTION AMONG MAIN TYPES OF GOVERNMENT UNIT, 1902-1946

	EXCLUDING ROADS AND STREETS						INCLUDING ROADS AND STREETS			
	1902	1912	1922	1929	1939	1946	1922	1929	1939	1946
	Percentage of Total									
Federal, nonmilitary	16.1	13.4	24.6	9.7	19.1	45.2	18.4	6.4	12.4	33.7
States, nonschool	(14.4)	13.7	10.4	10.9	10.4	7.4	7.8	7.2	6.7	5.6
Cities over 2,500, nonschool	44.5	46.5	37.9	43.4	38.6	25.3	28.5	28.7	25.0	18.9
Counties, nonschool	7.1	6.5	(5.0)	(5.2)	(4.2)	(2.9)	(3.8)	(3.4)	(2.7)	(2.2)
State & local, school	18.0	19.9	22.1	30.7	27.7	19.1	16.6	20.3	17.9	14.2
Total, excl. roads & streets	100.0	100.0	100.0	100.0	100.0	100.0	75.1	66.2	64.7	74.6
Roads & streets							24.9	33.8	35.3	25.4
Total, incl. roads & streets							100.0	100.0	100.0	100.0
	Billions of Dollars									
Total	3.8	7.3	15.4	21.1	30.9	51.4	20.5	31.9	47.8	68.8

Figures in parentheses are very rough estimates.

Exclusive of defense corporations and roads and streets, the percentages for 1922 and 1946 (but not other years) are different enough to be noted:

	1922	1946
Federal, nonmilitary	10.8	22.1
States, nonschool	12.4	10.6
Cities over 2,500, nonschool	44.8	36.0
Counties, nonschool	(5.9)	(4.2)
State & local, school	26.1	27.2
Total	100.0	100.0

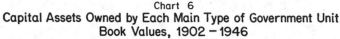

Chart 6
**Capital Assets Owned by Each Main Type of Government Unit
Book Values, 1902 – 1946**

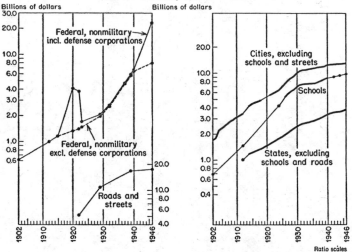

Apparently only during the depression of the 1930's and World War II did state and local governments increase their assets slowly; and if corrections for price changes could be made, this slow growth would probably also show up in the World War I period. But it was precisely during these periods that federal assets multiplied most rapidly.

The relatively high average rate of growth in school assets up to about 1929 and the relatively low average rate of growth in federal assets in the same period are outstanding in Chart 6. Indeed, the federal group of assets grew during 1902-29 at a rate below that of any other government unit except (probably) counties. It was after 1929 that federal assets grew more rapidly than the assets of other government units, including schools. This was a result first of a federal building program outside the District of Columbia to reduce the need for renting quarters for post offices and other field agencies, then of federal works stimulated by the depression, and finally the defense construction program.

There are wide differences between the distribution of capital goods among the various government units (Table 9) and the distribution of employment among them (Table 8). (This is true even after allowing for the lack of information on military assets and the crudity of the estimates.) Neither the levels nor the trends of the two sets of percentages are similar. The explanation is simple: the functions of the various government units differ, as we shall see in some detail in the next chapter, and capital goods and workers have differing roles in each function.

Purchases by Type of Government

Our information on government purchases from private business (Table 10) suggests that the story of the relative importance of the several types of government as users of labor and capital applies fairly well also to this third class of input. Thus, we noticed that

Table 10

PURCHASES, DISTRIBUTION AMONG MAIN TYPES OF GOVERNMENT UNIT, 1903-1949

| | NATIONAL BUREAU ESTIMATE (FISCAL YEARS) | | | | DEPARTMENT OF COMMERCE ESTIMATE (CALENDAR YEARS) | | | | |
	1903	1913	1932	1942	1929	1932	1939	1942	1949
				Percentage of Total					
Federal	29.0	22.1	20.5	88.9	11.3	17.1	32.5	92.9	65.1
Nonwar	14.4	13.2	14.5	4.1					
War	14.5	10.0	6.0	84.0					
State & Local	71.0	77.9	79.5	11.4	88.7	82.9	67.5	7.1	34.9
State, nonschool	6.0	8.2	24.9	3.5					
Local, nonschool	55.7	58.0	42.9	5.5					
School	9.3	11.8	11.7	2.1					
Total	100.0	100.0	100.0	100.0	100.0	100.0	100.0	100.0	100.0
				Billions of Dollars					
Total	.8	1.4	5.0	31.1	4.2	3.7	5.5	45.8	24.9

Compensation of public emergency workers is excluded. Higher education is excluded from the National Bureau school estimate.

at the opening of the century the federal government accounted for only a small fraction of the labor and capital resources used for public purposes; that its share rose during World War I but then fell back to approximately its prewar level, or lower, during the 1920's; that the New Deal pushed it up above that level; and, finally, that World War II and its aftermath further raised this share so that today the federal government uses half, or more than half, of all resources (including military equipment) devoted to public purposes. The federal government's share in goods and services obtained from private business has roughly the same history, at least during the period for which information is available.

There are, of course, some differences between the pattern of purchases and that of labor and capital, just as there are between the labor and capital patterns themselves. These differences also can be explained by differences in the scope and kind of activity of the several types of government. The relatively low proportion of purchases taken by schools and the high proportion taken by the military arm of the federal government during wartime, for example, are to be expected. Moreover, increase in the relative importance of the defense function explains the relatively rapid rise in the federal government's total share in purchases, even exceeding the rise in its share of workers and capital assets.

Table 11 adds further information (pp. 38-9). At the opening of the century, for example, purchases were much less important than payrolls in the costs of state government, more important in the costs of local government. And there is a striking difference between these two types of government in what happened later to these proportions. State payrolls fell sharply relative to purchases, while local nonschool government payrolls rose somewhat relative to purchases. Indeed, it is rather surprising, in view of the diversities shown by Table 11, that the various types of total government expenditure have such stable proportions (Table 5). Apparently the innumerable changes in relative importance of functions within each unit and of types of unit within the total, on the one hand, and in the distribution of expenditures among payrolls, outlays, and other purchases within each functional category, on the other, have offset one another. But the data at hand are not enough for a detailed description and analysis of these changes.

Dollar figures, annual when available, are given in Chart 7. Among other things, these show how the great depression and World War II distinctively marked the expenditures of the several

Chart 7

Government Outlays on Capital Assets, Other Purchases, and Payrolls by Level of Government, 1903–1949

-----NBER (fiscal years)
————Dept. of Commerce (calendar years)

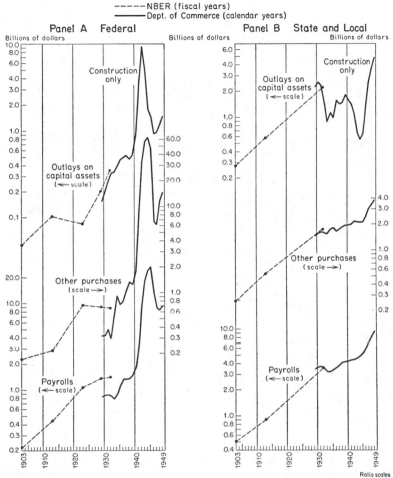

Panel A   Federal

Panel B   State and Local

Ratio scales

types of government. We have noted that government employment tends to be cyclically stable; now we can note that payrolls, too, show little reaction even to the business decline of the 1930's; and this is true also of purchases of other than construction items. Only construction outlays of state and local governments fell sharply with the business contraction of the early 1930's.

These various expenditures do not, of course, include the transfer

Table 11

RELATIVE IMPORTANCE OF GOVERNMENT PURCHASES AND PAYROLLS BY TYPE OF GOVERNMENT UNIT, 1903-1949

NATIONAL BUREAU ESTIMATE (fiscal year)	1903	1913	1923	1929	1932	1939	1942	1949
			Percentage of Total					
Federal, total								
Outlays on capital assets	11.0	13.5	4.5	9.0	14.6	25.7	30.8	
Other purchases	39.0	28.2	38.0	30.4	27.3	25.2	51.5	
Payrolls	50.0	58.2	57.5	60.6	58.1	49.1	17.7	
Total	100.0	100.0	100.0	100.0	100.0	100.0	100.0	
Federal, war								
Outlays on capital assets	21.2	14.7	9.0	15.0	15.3	32.2	32.4	
Other purchases	37.9	35.4	29.7	22.6	26.7	15.3	54.1	
Payrolls	40.9	49.9	61.3	62.4	57.9	52.5	13.6	
Total	100.0	100.0	100.0	100.0	100.0	100.0	100.0	
Federal, nonwar								
Outlays on capital assets	3.5	13.0	2.1	6.5	14.3	23.3	15.2	
Other purchases	39.7	24.6	42.5	33.6	27.5	28.9	26.2	
Payrolls	56.8	62.4	55.5	59.9	58.1	47.8	58.6	
Total	100.0	100.0	100.0	100.0	100.0	100.0	100.0	
State and local, total								
Outlays on capital assets	26.6	28.7			29.4		16.3	
Other purchases	25.0	26.7			23.3		28.0	
Payrolls	48.4	44.6			47.3		55.8	
Total	100.0	100.0			100.0		100.0	
States, nonschool								
Outlays on capital assets	17.4	19.2	39.7	46.0	50.5	34.5	33.6	
Other purchases	27.0	33.1	28.6	25.3	23.0	30.3	25.9	
Payrolls	55.7	47.7	31.7	28.7	26.5	35.1	40.5	
Total	100.0	100.0	100.0	100.0	100.0	100.0	100.0	
Local, nonschool								
Outlays on capital assets	30.7	35.2			30.2		13.8	
Other purchases	30.2	29.6			26.2		32.1	
Payrolls	39.1	35.3			43.6		54.1	
Total	100.0	100.0			100.0		100.0	

School							
Outlays on capital assets	18.8	16.4	19.9	18.3	10.4	11.3	6.2
Other purchases	9.6	16.7	16.0	17.7	18.3	20.6	22.8
Payrolls	71.6	66.9	64.1	64.0	71.3	68.1	71.0
Total	100.0	100.0	100.0	100.0	100.0	100.0	100.0
DEPARTMENT OF COMMERCE ESTIMATE (adjusted, calendar year)							
Federal, total							
New construction			11.8	22.5	16.4	18.0	5.8
Other purchases			24.2	19.8	38.2	64.7	57.7
Payrolls			64.0	57.7	45.5	17.3	36.4
Total			100.0	100.0	100.0	100.0	100.0
State and local, total							
New construction			31.2	22.2	22.9	14.2	27.1
Other purchases			20.5	24.4	24.3	28.1	20.8
Payrolls			48.3	53.4	52.8	57.7	52.1
Total			100.0	100.0	100.0	100.0	100.0

Millions of Dollars

NATIONAL BUREAU ESTIMATE (total purchases and payrolls)							
Federal, total	437	758	1,882	2,245	2,423	4,294	33,556
Federal, war	185	253	667	652	707	1,179	30,486
Federal, nonwar	251	505	1,215	1,593	1,716	3,115	3,070
State and local, total	1,037	2,015	809	1,343	7,493	2,024	7,786
States, nonschool	102	224			1,681		1,822
Local, nonschool	689	1,282			3,779		3,750
Schools	246	509	1,537	2,092	2,034	2,117	2,213
DEPARTMENT OF COMMERCE ESTIMATE (total purchases and payrolls)							
Federal, total	1,311	1,480			3,282	51,447	25,473
State and local, total	7,161	6,505			7,901	7,695	18,126

Compensation of public emergency workers is excluded. Higher education is excluded from the N.B.E.R. school estimate.

items and grants mentioned in Chapter 2. We measure the input of any type of government by the real resources it absorbs. Money granted by state governments to local governments (or state government receipts shared with local governments), for example, are spent for real resources at the local level, and we account for these expenditures at that level. However, input at the local government level has been financed increasingly by grants from state governments; and input at the state government level (and grants-in-aid by state to local governments) have been financed increasingly by grants from the federal government. Thus, grants received by state governments accounted for less than 2 percent of their total revenues in 1903 and 13 percent in 1942. Grants-in-aid received by local governments amounted to 7 percent of their revenues in 1903 and 26 percent in 1942. As for transfers to the public, these too have grown at all levels of government. The figures for each type of government are given in Appendix D.

Factors Affecting the Distribution of Input among Types of Government

Before we take the next step in our review of government activity, we may note the factors that have determined the distribution of input among types of government. This is useful preparation even if our list is skeletal and rather formal.

First, the several types of government increased their input at diverse rates because the functions performed by them at the opening of the century grew at diverse rates. The federal government's input, for example, expanded more rapidly than that of state and local governments partly because of the increased importance of the functions constitutionally allocated to the central government. National defense is the outstanding illustration of the last decade.

Second, while all levels of government have taken on new functions, as we shall see in detail in the next chapter, the speed of acquisition has differed. The rapid growth of federal functions under the New Deal explains, at least in part, the relatively rapid growth of federal input during the 1930's.

Third, functions or parts of functions have been shifted from one level of government to another. Centralization at the state level of functions formerly undertaken by local governments, for example, is one reason why state employment has grown more rapidly than local government employment. Centralization of a different kind has occurred through the expansion of the grant-in-aid. The uses to be made of grants are almost always specified by the grantor, and matching by the grantee is often required. In some degree, therefore, the power to decide what functions are to be undertaken has been taken away from the recipient of a grant and become centralized at a higher level of government. The rise of income taxation has contributed to this development.

Finally, different rates of change in the prices of resources used at the several levels of government have affected the distribution of input (in terms of cost) among them. For example, the average salary paid employees of schools rose much more rapidly than salaries paid by other government units (Appendix B and D).

Diverse trends in efficiency also may have had a part although, as we shall see in Chapter 5, there is little that can be nailed down in this area.

How the distribution of input among types of government has changed should not be over-emphasized. It is well to remember, too, that during the last half-century every level of government has substantially increased the volume of resources it uses. We shall want, therefore, to consider also how the basic factors underlying our economic development have caused expansion of activity at all levels of government; and how growth at one level of government has tended to stimulate growth at other levels: state roads are patrolled by county police and federal social security is administered by state governments.

CHAPTER 4

Functional Classification of Government Activity

To understand the big increase in government's input since 1900 we need to know more about the uses to which it has been turned. Government engages in activities as diverse as those of housewives, ministers, or handymen. Many are as well known, but the ordinary citizen's notion of their relative importance is likely to be shaped by his range of experience with them. To get a more balanced view, let us look at the pre-World War II functional distribution of government input, then consider major changes during the last half century.

Industries in Which Government Operates and Its Share in the Employment Offered by Each

Two-thirds of all government workers in 1940, although on government payrolls, were employed in producing goods and services also produced by nongovernmental industries. The largest part was in education, as the reader will have gathered from the preceding chapter: education occupied close to a third of all government workers in 1940. Medical and health services, transport and public utilities (including the postal service), construction, and shipbuilding also occupied considerable numbers of government employees. The rest were scattered over almost all other industries.

Only a third were in the group labeled, for want of a better title, "general government" (Chart 8). This group carries on functions rated in this country as peculiarly governmental — protection by the armed forces, police, and fire departments, regulation of business and other social relations, maintenance of roads, and similar functions.

That "general government" and education are entirely or largely

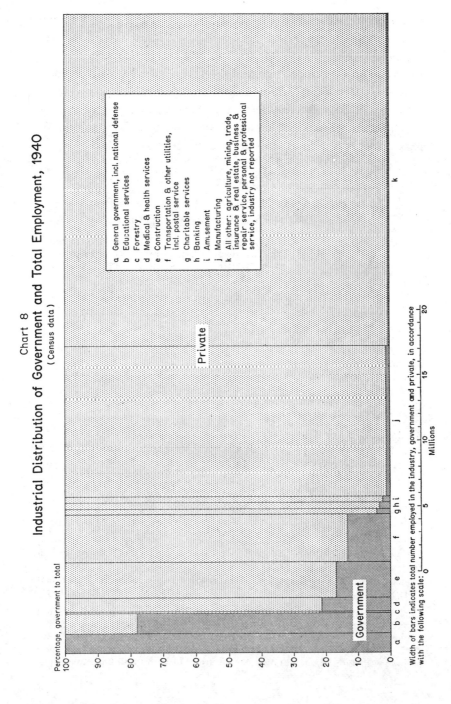

Chart 8

Industrial Distribution of Government and Total Employment, 1940

(Census data)

a General government, incl. national defense
b Educational services
c Forestry
d Medical & health services
e Construction
f Transportation & other utilities, incl. postal service
g Charitable services
h Banking
i Amusement
j Manufacturing
k All other: agriculture, mining, trade, insurance & real estate, business & repair service, personal & professional service, industry not reported

Percentage, government to total

Private

Government

Width of bars indicates total number employed in the industry, government and private, in accordance with the following scale:

Millions

manned by government workers is obvious. It is less well known
that government employees constituted a substantial fraction, over
10 percent, of workers in forestry, medical and health services, construction, and transportation and public utilities. In 1940, 21 percent of all persons performing health and medical services were on
government payrolls; the percentage was 22 for forestry, 17 for
construction, 24 for electric and gas utilities, and 37 for shipbuilding (classified in Chart 8 under manufacturing).

Table 12

MAIN FUNCTIONAL CLASSES OF GOVERNMENT INPUT JUST BEFORE WORLD WAR II

	FULL- AND PART-TIME WORKERS, 1940	CAPITAL ASSETS, 1939	EXPENDITURES, 1942 (1939 FOR NATIONAL DEFENSE)
	Percentage Distribution		
General control	9	11[a]	7
National defense	14	8	7
Public safety, other	7	1	5
Highways	10	32	10
Sanitation & waste removal	2	5	1
Health & hospitals	6	3	4
Public welfare	6	0.5	18
Correction	1	1	[b]
Development & conservation of natural resources	2	8	9
Recreation & parks	1	5	[b]
Schools	28	14	16
Other general functions	4	[a]	4
Public enterprises	10	12[a]	17
Total	100	100	100
	Absolute Numbers		
Total	4.8 million persons	$63 billion	$16 billion

[a] "Other general functions" and the postal system are included under general
control.

[b] Not shown separately but included in the figures for other functional
categories.

Capital assets include land, subsoil assets, construction, and equipment; and
cover items not included in other tables, such as property in the hands of the
armed forces and sewage systems. Expenditures cover costs of operation (including transfers to the public), outlays on capital assets, and enterprises; and
exclude grants-in-aid, interest, and contributions to trust funds and enterprises.

Major Functional Classes of Government Input:
the Prewar Pattern

Such government functions as administration, legislation, tax collection, and regulation[1]— which tend to bulk large in the eyes of some — actually accounted for only a small fraction of all government workers in 1940. When the third of all government employees classed under the heading "general government" in Chart 8 is broken down among specific functions, as in Table 12, the number of employees occupied in these administrative and regulatory activities is found to be only 9 percent of all government employment. Even the 9 percent or so shown in the table is an overstatement. Because "full-time equivalents" could not be computed for each functional group, the large number of part-time county, township, and village workers inflates the figure.

To judge by employment, the important functions of government were: schools, national defense (including the activities of civilian as well as military personnel), highways (in Chart 8 many highway workers are shown under construction), and public enterprises. Together these accounted for three-fifths of government workers. Police and fire departments ("other public safety"), health and hospitals, and public welfare, together with general control, employed most of the remaining employees.

The patterns of use to which government's property and expenditures are put differ in a number of ways from those which engage its employees.[2] Lines of communication — roads and streets, rivers

[1] Regulation is not shown separately in Table 12. The somewhat more detailed data which it summarizes indicate that fewer than one percent of government workers were assigned to this function; see Table B15.

[2] The three columns of Table 12 relate, it is true, to periods a year or more apart; the functional classes are not identical in content, partly because a good deal of government property is devoted to various uses (e.g., many customs houses also include a post office and provide space for the field operations of still other federal agencies); and the estimates, especially those of capital assets, are very rough. Yet these defects seem minor: even by 1942 (which relates mainly to the fiscal year ending June 30) the war could not have had any serious effect on any function except national defense, as is clear from information on the federal government, state governments, and large cities; see charts below and the detailed appendix tables. (However, transfers to the public were much smaller in 1942 than in 1939.) To show the expenditure pattern as

and harbors — are far more important as users of capital assets
than of workers. This is also true of other resource development,
including reclamation and flood control projects, recreation centers and parks, sanitation and waste disposal works (which cover
sewage systems), and public enterprises as a whole. Less important
as users of capital assets than of workers are education, social welfare, and protection (other than national defense).

Expenditures consist in part of payrolls and capital outlays, and
in this way overlap — and may confirm — our labor and capital
data. On the other hand, the expenditure data also include purchases from private industry and transfers to the public, which
explains some of the differences among the patterns in Table 12.
Because public welfare expenditures include heavy cash transfers
to the public, this class bulks larger in expenditures than in employment or capital assets; indeed, it leads all the other expenditure
classes. Public enterprises as well as natural resources are more
important judged by expenditures than by employment because of
the large proportion of purchases from private industry. Other
functions show much smaller percentages in the expenditure column than in the other columns: schools, because purchases and
outlays were small compared with payrolls (Table 11); and national defense, because rates of pay are low. These differences are
all to be expected; they are not due to inconsistencies in the data.
Since expenditure data are the usual source to which people turn
for information on government functions, it is well to remember
that they give only one view.[3]

The viewpoints provided by Table 12 are close enough to the

it was before the great expansion in war spending, we substituted the 1939
national defense figure in computing the percentage breakdown of government
expenditures. The other deficiencies do not account for the prominent differences we observe.

[3] For our present purpose, to determine the functional pattern of input, the
best single measure would be expenditures as in Table 12, adjusted, however,
to exclude transfers and outlays and include the rental value of capital assets.
Because this is not available, we need to make shift with all three measures in
Table 12.

The three do not merit equal weights. As we saw in Chapter 2, the cost of
labor is some three times the use value of capital assets; and it is possible to
impute weights accordingly. We cannot say anything as definite about the
weight of the expenditure data in relation to that of the others.

object of our interest for us to be able to discern major proportions. For finer details of the pattern, however, we need to move closer and scan the list of government activities included in each major functional group.

Kinds of Current Government Activities

The scope and variety of government services have become so wide as to require systematic stocktaking if we are to comprehend them. This is recognized in the appearance of *An Inventory of Governmental Activities in the United States*[4] listing some 400 broad activities classified into 15 major groups.[5] Under the major heading protection to persons and property, for example, "police protection and law enforcement" appears as one of eight items. And under police protection and law enforcement the inventory further shows records and statistics, crime control, vice and morals controls, detention and custody of prisoners, traffic control, control of international borders, and fish and game protection. Specific types of vice and morals control are the regulation of prostitution, liquor and narcotic distribution, dance halls, poolrooms, etc., censoring of motion pictures and books, and supervision of athletic contests and racing. Traffic control includes engineering and research, highway patrols, establishing and maintaining traffic signals, motor vehicle inspection, and conducting drivers' examinations.

But no formal listing can begin to convey a notion of the rich variety of government activities today. One must sit back and reflect upon the life cycle of an inhabitant of this country.[6] Note

[4] By Carl H. Chatters and Margorie Leonard Hoover (Municipal Finance Officers Association, 1947).

[5] The number of activities does not have any significance as a measure of the relative importance of the category. The activities of government, as of any operating unit, can be subdivided almost *ad infinitum* and the count extended beyond any specified limit. To measure importance we need a list of the services of government with the value of each. (In the absence of a market value for most government services, cost would do.) But no such detailed listing is available. In a sense, therefore, "inventory" is a misnomer, since no indication of relative importance — an essential characteristic of an inventory — is provided in the mere listing or even count of activities. We are thrown back on the rather broad functional groups of workers, assets, and expenditures.

[6] It would have to be the life cycle of a person born this year, assuming no further changes in the scope of government activity during his lifetime.

how and to what extent government activity impinges on every phase of his existence from before birth through death: prenatal clinics, birth certificates, maternal aid, milk inspection, inoculation, schools and playgrounds, protection at street crossings, working papers, factory inspection, minimum wages, conciliation and mediation of labor disputes, examination for licensed occupations, elections, marriage license, insurance of bank deposits, low rent housing, community planning, fire-fighting, hospitals, unemployment compensation, old age and survivors insurance, death certificates, and, when necessary, the morgue and surrogates court. A farmer would have a slightly different list, and a businessman still another. Or one could follow the cycle of day and night — with its round of police protection, time observation, radio programs, street cleaning, postal deliveries, traffic regulation, and subway service; or of the seasons — in the summer, for example, special school sessions, noxious weed, mosquito, and flood control, fish and game protection, crop insurance, highway construction, inspection of public bathing places, and auto and trailer camps.

We may also view the multitude of government services in terms of their ultimate objectives: (1) maintenance of order; (2) promotion of economic activity; (3) production to meet current needs; (4) development of the nation's capacity to defend itself and satisfy its needs; and (5) distribution of the nation's income.

Maintenance of order is an objective of national defense — usually so big an activity as to be designated separately as an objective in itself. Maintenance of a military establishment makes up the bulk of it, but covered also are many of the activities connected with our international relations, control of resident aliens, immigration regulation, and operation of arsenals.

Apart from national defense, maintenance of order involves the establishment and enforcement of many of the rules necessary when large groups live and work together. It is a basic objective of such activities as conducting elections, passing laws, administering courts, police protection, corrections, regulation of poolrooms and athletic contests, traffic control, protective inspections (buildings, elevators, banks, drugs, weights and measures), securities and exchange regulation, coinage and regulation of money, establishment and administration of standards.

Promotion of economic activity, including its stabilization, is the objective of activities such as planning, the work of the Council of Economic Advisers, banking regulation, crop insurance, "triple A" activities, price fixing, oil production control, public works in some part, and many informational and research activities.

Production to meet current needs is the prime objective of the operation of public enterprises (the postal service, subways, electric light and power plants, water works, liquor stores, airports, terminals, warehouses, harbor facilities, canals and waterways, toll bridges, municipal auditoriums), streets and roads, fire fighting, insurance, recreation facilities, schools, employment bureaus, sanitation, hospitals and clinics, serum and vaccine production, housing, banking. The consular service also might be included here.

Developmental activities are concerned with improving people and natural resources, and fostering education and the pursuit of private business. Schools, libraries, banks, recreation appear here as well as in other classes. Other items are antitrust regulation, patent laws, forestry, reclamation, irrigation, prescription of working conditions for women and children, agricultural experiment stations, geological surveys, statistics collection and analysis, control of disease, prenatal clinics, school lunches.

The distribution of income involves what are usually called "transfer" activities — e.g., public assistance, agricultural price support (in part), social insurance, veterans' aid, school lunches, disaster relief, and the host of productive services provided free or for a small fee.

The reader will have observed that this classification has the defect common to many: the classes are not mutually exclusive. For example, economic stabilization and income redistribution may themselves be viewed as a means of maintaining order. Indeed, since we have to look beyond the information supplied by the description of an activity or by its usual functional classification, there are great difficulties in identifying the specific objectives of any particular government activity. Many, if not all, of the individual activities of government are aimed at several ends. Public

education is justified as essential to the maintenance and development of the country, it produces a currently needed service, supervision of child play, and it is a vehicle by which national income is
transferred. Antitrust legislation has been supported as a means of
controlling the distribution of national income, of stabilizing business, of stimulating economic development, and of promoting the
nation's defense (recall the Congressional hearings on cartels).
The examples are endless. This means, of course, that the growth
of an activity is usually the result of several causes, a matter that
will concern us more closely in later chapters.

When we inquire into the relative importance of the several
activities and objectives, we encounter a related difficulty: many
an agency of government performs more than one function, but
only the total input of the agency can be ascertained.

For these and other reasons it is extraordinarily difficult to clas-
sify government input by objectives. Perhaps all that can be done
is to indicate how the various objectives rank by current expenditures. National defense is first today, as it has been since the onset
of World War II. Together with expenditures on police, general
control, and other public safety, it puts maintenance of order way
out front as the major product of government. Production of current services is next: highways, sanitation, health and hospitals,
and the activities of public enterprises. Some part of this expenditure might be allocated to development, but it is doubtful if that
objective, largely the aim of expenditures on schools and natural
resources, would move up past third place. Distribution of income,
the fourth, is chiefly furthered by public welfare expenditures
(which now include a considerable amount for veterans) but also
by some agriculture expenditures (included under natural resources). Promotion and stabilization of economic activity is
clearly last, being represented mainly by a small part of the
expenditure on general control and regulation.

Distribution of Functions among Types of Government

The several types of government unit do not all engage in each of
the activities mentioned. The differences among them are shown
in Table 13, where the structure of government is laid out in some

Table 13

FUNCTIONAL CLASSIFICATION OF GOVERNMENT EXPENDITURES, BY TYPE OF EXPENDITURE AND GOVERNMENT UNIT 1942 (1939 FOR NATIONAL DEFENSE)

	FEDERAL	STATE AND LOCAL	STATES	COUNTIES	CITIES	TOWNSHIPS AND TOWNS	SCHOOL DISTRICTS	OTHER SPECIAL DISTRICTS
			Percentage Distribution					
General control	7.1	7.5	6.6	19.3	6.9	12.7	.....	.....
National defense	17.7	.....	.....	.....	.....	.....	.....	.....
Public safety, other	.7	8.7	5.1	4.4	17.8	9.4	.....	6.8
Highways	2.1	16.1	30.4	22.6	8.9	29.8	.....	3.4
Natural resources	18.0	1.9	5.0	1.2	.....	.....	.....	16.2
Sanitation	.....	2.5	.....	.2	6.2	2.7	.....	14.2
Health & hospitals	.4	6.6	12.0	9.2	5.1	2.0	.....	.7
Public welfare	16.9	13.5	20.3	29.3	8.6	14.0	.....	.....
Veterans' services & benefits	8.4	.....	.....	.....	.....	.....	.....	.....
Schools	.3	27.7	11.6	6.4	16.1	20.1	100.0	.....
Miscellaneous operation	1.8	5.9	6.4	6.8	7.6	6.4	.....	14.9
Public enterprises	26.5	9.6	2.4	.6	22.9	3.3	.....	43.9
Total	100.0	100.0	100.0	100.0	100.0	100.0	100.0	100.0
			Millions of Dollars					
Total	6,647	9,106	2,591	1,326	3,177	299	1,564	148

Blank spaces indicate either zero or small amounts not shown separately but included in the figures for other functional categories. Expenditures cover operation and outlays, including all expenditures of enterprises, and include various kinds of transfer to the public. Aid paid to other governments, interest, and con-tributions to trust funds and enterprises are excluded. Data for the federal government are for the fiscal year ending June 30, 1942, except national defense, which is for the year ending June 30, 1939. State and local government data are usually for the fiscal year ending June 30 or December 31, 1942.

detail, together with the functional pattern of expenditures characteristic of each type of unit.[7]

When we list the three leading functions of each type of government unit, we find they accounted for the following percentages
of expenditures:

Type of Government Unit	Three Leading Functional Groups (in order of importance)	Percentage of Expenditures
Federal	Public enterprises, natural resources, national defense	62
State	Highways, public welfare, health & hospitals	63
County	Public welfare, highways, general control	71
Municipal	Public enterprises, public safety, schools	57
Township & town	Highways, schools, public welfare	64
School district	Schools (sole function)	100
Other special district	Public enterprises, natural resources, misc. general operation	75

A difference of emphasis is clear. In part, this reflects a "division
of labor" among the several levels of government stemming from
the nature of our government structure. The federal government
undertakes the national defense, regulates interstate commerce, and
operates the postal system; state and local governments provide
hospitals, roads, and other local services. State governments may
occasionally vote veterans a bonus, but the continuing burden of
veterans' services and benefits is carried by the federal government
and is large enough to warrant a separate line in the table.[8] The
distribution of functions reflects in part also assignments of responsibility by state to local governments and by one type of local
government to another, for example, city and county governments

[7] However, and this comment applies to later tables as well, not all the government units of a specific type provide each and every one of the services listed
for that type of unit. Further, of the units that do provide a certain class of
service, not all do it on the same level of adequacy or with the same qualitative
content.

Something is said in Chapter 6 about variation among government units in
service provided.

[8] We must remember that the federal government makes substantial contributions in support of state and, indirectly, local services, and state governments
help finance local services. These grants-in-aid are not distributed among the
expenditures of the grantor agency in Table 13; they are distributed only
among expenditures of the grantee, by whom the service is "produced" for the

to special school, sanitary, and other districts. These assignments vary from one state to another, and even within states. As a consequence, there is some seeming duplication of functions in Table 13.[9]

Differences in the degree of urbanization, and therefore the needs, of the people served by the several types of local unit also help determine the patterns in Table 13. Local transport and other utility services in cities but not counties account for the larger importance of municipal public enterprise expenditures. Park and recreation facilities are sufficiently important in cities for workers operating them to be shown separately; this class of employees is not distinguished in the records of the county governments (Table B15).

---

benefit of consumers, business, or society at large.

The following tabulation shows the purposes for which grants-in-aid were made in 1942:

FUNCTIONAL CLASSIFICATION OF
PAYMENTS FOR GRANTS-IN-AID, 1942
(millions of dollars)

	Federal	State	Local	Total
General control	......	....	....	......
National defense	101	....	....	101
Public safety, other	......	17	....	17
Highways	154	338	7	499
Natural resources	29	1	....	30
Sanitation	....	....	....	......
Health & hospitals	29	10	4	43
Public welfare	376	389	2	767
Veterans' services & benefits	......	....	....	......
Schools	29	766	24	819
Miscellaneous operation	119	230	11	360
Total	837	1,751	48	2,636

Grants by local governments are almost entirely to other local governments, for example, by counties to school districts. Federal and state data are from *Governmental Finances in the United States: 1942, Compendium of State Government Finances in 1949.* The local total is from the *Historical Review of State and Local Government Finances* and the breakdown by function is partly from that source and partly estimated from *City Finances,* 1944 and 1945. (These are all publications of the Bureau of the Census.)

[9] Another reason, already noted, for some of the apparent duplication arises from qualitative differences among the several types of government units in the services appearing in any particular class. What real duplications exist are likely to be of minor importance (Chatters and Hoover, p. 3). For example, when the federal government undertakes to regulate competition, state laws tend to become dead letters.

The complementary character of the several parts of our government structure is reflected also in employment and capital assets. Chart 9 shows the percentage which the federal government accounts for of total expenditures and employment, and the percentage which state governments account for of state and local expenditures and employment. For most functions, both expenditures and employment are divided among the government levels in the same pattern. Because of deficiencies in classification, capital assets are not charted. But when we allow for these deficiencies, capital assets show a distribution of functions consistent in most respects with that revealed by the other data.

Change in the Functional Distribution of Input

Ceaseless change in the relative importance of private industries seems to be characteristic of economic development. During the last half-century, relative declines in agricultural employment, relative rises followed by declines in mining, domestic service, and rail transport, and almost continuous relative rises in electric light and power, insurance, real estate, and personal and business service (other than domestic) are some of the changes revealed in the industrial distribution of private employment. And other types of input, and output as well, would show similar trends.

Within government, too, there have been changes. The pre-World War II functional pattern is that of a section cut across trends of varying slope. While total expenditures of government rose 9-fold between 1903 and 1942, the multiplications for individual major functions ranged from 4 to 76 (Table 14). The same wide variation is found on each of the two main levels of government distinguished in the table: a rise ranging from 4- to 375-fold for federal functions, and from 4- to 57-fold for state and local governments.

A look at the whole half-century, although it requires moving to less complete and somewhat different expenditure data, leaves the same general impression of wide variation, as the reader will see when he inspects later tables. Federal expenditures, including the grants-in-aid excluded from Table 14, were 68 times larger in 1949 than in 1900 (Table 16). The functional group with the smallest rise went up 19-fold; the biggest increase was over 2,000-

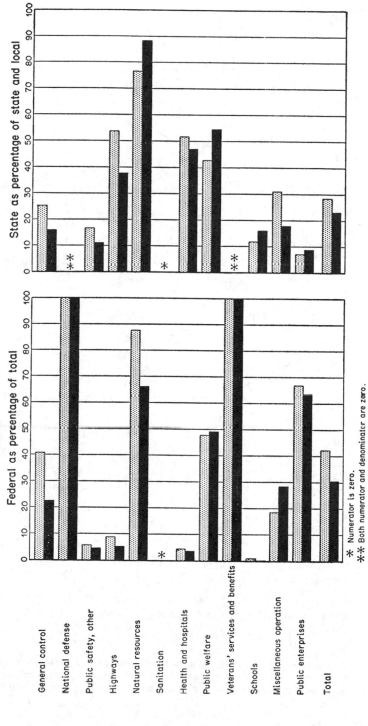

Chart 9

Division of Functions among Major Types of Government, Just Before World War II

Expenditures, 1942 (1939 for National Defense)
Employment, 1940

State as percentage of state and local

Federal as percentage of total

General control
National defense
Public safety, other
Highways
Natural resources
Sanitation
Health and hospitals
Public welfare
Veterans' services and benefits
Schools
Miscellaneous operation
Public enterprises
Total

* Numerator is zero.
** Both numerator and denominator are zero.

Table 14

FOUR DECADES OF CHANGE IN THE FUNCTIONAL DISTRIBUTION OF GOVERNMENT EXPENDITURES

MILLIONS OF DOLLARS

	1942 (1939 for National Defense)			1903		
	Federal	State & Local	Total	Federal	State & Local	Total
General control	471	686	1,157	73	186	259
National defense	1,179	......	1,179	176	......	176
Public safety, other	47	790	837	6	102	108
Highways	141	1,465	1,606	27	207	234
Natural resources	1,197	170	1,367	15	3	18
Sanitation	......	228	228	......	47	47
Health & hospitals	27	604	631	3	35	38
Public welfare	1,125	1,230	2,355	3	59	62
Veterans' services & benefits	556	......	556	144	......	144
Schools	23	2,520	2,543	2	268	270
Misc. & unallocable	122	538	659	2	71	73
Public enterprises	1,759	873	2,632	139	92	231
Grand total	6,647	9,106	15,753	589	1,069	1,658

PERCENTAGE OF COLUMN TOTAL

	1942 (1939 for National Defense)			1903		
	Federal	State & Local	Total	Federal	State & Local	Total
General control	7.1	7.5	7.3	12.4	17.4	15.6
National defense	17.7	......	7.5	29.9	......	10.6
Public safety, other	.7	8.7	5.3	1.0	9.5	6.5
Highways	2.1	16.1	10.2	4.6	19.4	14.1
Natural resources	18.0	1.9	8.7	2.5	.3	1.1
Sanitation	......	2.5	1.4	......	4.4	2.8
Health & hospitals	.4	6.6	4.0	.5	3.3	2.3
Public welfare	16.9	13.5	14.9	.5	5.5	3.7
Veterans' services & benefits	8.4	......	3.5	24.4	......	8.7
Schools	.3	27.7	16.1	.3	25.1	16.3
Misc. & unallocable	1.8	5.9	4.2	.3	6.6	4.4
Public enterprises	26.5	9.6	16.7	23.6	8.6	13.9
Grand total	100.0	100.0	100.0	100.0	100.0	100.0

Expenditures cover current operations and outlays on capital assets, including all expenditures of enterprises and transfers to the public; they exclude interest payments, grants-in-aid, and contributions to trust funds and enterprises.

Table 14 (concluded)

	1942 RELATIVE TO 1903 (1939 FOR NATIONAL DEFENSE)			% OF INCREASE IN GRAND TOTAL		
	Federal	State & Local	Total	Federal	State & Local	Total
General control	6.5	3.7	4.5	2.8	3.5	6.4
National defense	6.7	......	6.7	7.1	......	7.1
Public safety, other	7.8	7.7	7.8	0.3	4.9	5.2
Highways	5.2	7.1	6.9	0.8	8.9	9.7
Natural resources	80.	57.	76.	8.4	1.2	9.6
Sanitation	......	4.9	4.9	......	1.3	1.3
Health & hospitals	9.0	17.3	16.6	0.2	4.0	4.2
Public welfare	375.	21.	38.	8.0	8.3	16.3
Veterans' services & benefits	3.9	......	3.9	2.9	......	2.9
Schools	11.5	9.4	9.4	0.1	16.0	16.1
Misc. & unallocable	61.	7.6	9.0	0.9	3.3	4.2
Public enterprises	12.7	9.5	11.4	11.5	5.5	17.0
Grand total	11.3	8.5	9.5	43.0	57.0	100.0

fold (ignoring two relatively small functional groups that would show infinitely large increases, because nothing — or nothing important enough to be accounted for separately — was spent on them in 1900). So goes the story for state governments: while aggregate expenditures, excluding enterprises, multiplied 58 times between 1903 and 1949, the range for major functions was from 11 to 375 (Table 18); and similarly, too, for local governments (Table 19).

Because we deal with major groups, we are obviously limiting the extent of the dispersion: increasing the number of functional classes by subdivision would widen the range still further. But we need not labor the point. Expenditures on the various functions, and related employment and volume of capital assets as well,[10] rose at different rates. The great expansion in government input meant widely divergent, not substantially uniform, increases in all kinds of activity.

What is perhaps more surprising is that *every* major function grew in some degree. No function for which separate data are available failed to expand its input. Even the function that grew

[10] Tables B16-18 and C4-7.

least rapidly, during the 40 years covered by Table 14, multiplied its expenditures four times, more than enough to make up for the rise in prices.

Moreover, a general upward trend characterized the functions of every type of government. In not a single major function of the federal government, the state governments, or the several types of local government did expenditures fall, or even rise less than prices over the 40 or 50 years for which we have information.[11]

Our employment data show the same generality of increase. In not a single function of the federal government, the cities, or New York and Vermont, two states for which we have detailed records, did the number of workers actually decline.[12]

The results are almost as striking when the rates of increase in government functions are measured against growth in population. Thus, to continue with the employment data — the expenditure data run in the same direction — every federal function pushed employment up more than population grew. Every New York state and Vermont function pushed employment up more than the population of the state grew. As for the cities, all except three functions pushed employment up more than urban population grew.

If figures were available on *minor* functions, they would undoubtedly show more declines, relative to population or even absolute. Indeed, some minor functions must have been superseded by others and dropped entirely. It is noteworthy, however, that the detailed histories of state and local activities, cited below, fail to report any substantial number of activities dropped after 1900. Those mentioned include activities associated with expositions and similar temporary business, state bounties on coyotes, regulation

[11] Expenditures on two functions, general control and highways, in local governments other than cities and counties, are reported to have risen very slightly, even less than prices. But this seems to be due to defects in the data: cities of less than 8,000 are included in the "other local governments" group in 1903 but not in 1942; and in the case of general control, where the rise was least, inadequate accounts or reports in 1903 might well tend to inflate it by including items that should have been classified elsewhere. Increased specialization after 1903, as government activity expanded and small government units gave way to larger, also might have caused a transfer of activities from general control to other functions.

[12] Tables B16-18.

of midwives, and the servicing of police booths for foot patrolmen.

Which major functions were the laggards and which the leaders? The expenditure data in Table 14, being most complete, give a first view. Between the opening of the century and the period before the effects of World War II became serious, general control,[13] sanitation, and veterans' services and benefits rose at a percentage rate considerably below the average. The big percentage expansions of expenditures came in activities connected with the development and conservation of natural resources, public welfare, and health. The big *absolute* additions to expenditures came from expansion in public welfare, schools, and public enterprises. These, together with highways and natural resources, accounted for over two-thirds of the $14 billion increase in government expenditures.[14] The federal government provided the larger part of the increase in expenditures (excluding grants-in-aid) on natural resources and public enterprises; the state and local governments, the larger part of the increase in highways and schools; and the rise in public welfare expenditure was split between the two levels of government.

A closer view, to get inside the broad functional groups summarized in Table 14, and to consider fluctuations in rate of growth as well as changes during the last decade, requires dealing with fragmentary data. Because these do not lend themselves to easy combination, we must consider them piecemeal.

We may pause for a moment, however, to glance at the comprehensive employment data spanning the full period, insufficiently detailed though they are (Table 15). Unaffected by price changes and the swelling of transfers to the public, these figures confirm the importance of schools and enterprises in accounting for the rise during the four decades before World War II. With national defense, these functions contributed over half the increase in employment (excluding emergency workers). Over the full period, national defense is of course outstanding.

[13] Recall, however, the qualification mentioned in footnote 11.

[14] The larger part of the increase in welfare and a good part of the increase in natural resources (and veterans' services and benefits as well) represent, however, transfers to the public (under social security, relief, agricultural and other acts) and therefore the rise in input as we have defined it is exaggerated. We must keep in mind the estimates in Table 7.

Table 15

CLASSIFICATION OF GOVERNMENT WORKERS, BY MAIN FUNCTIONAL CATEGORY, 1900, 1940, AND 1949

	FULL-TIME EQUIVALENT NUMBER (1,000)			% OF TOTAL			RELATIVE TO 1900		% OF INCREASE IN TOTAL	
	1900	1940	1949	1900	1940[a]	1949	1940	1949	1900-1940	1900-1949
National defense	166	788	2,524	14.3	12.7	35.6	4.7	15.2	19.1	39.8
Schools	467	1,228	1,368	40.1	19.8	19.3	2.6	2.9	23.4	15.2
Public enterprises	129	531	721	11.1	8.5	10.2	4.1	5.6	12.4	10.0
All other regular employees	402	1,868	2,473	34.5	30.1	34.9	4.6	6.2	45.1	35.0
Total regular employees	1,164	4,415	7,086	100.0	71.0	100.0	3.8	6.1	100.0	100.0
Public emergency workers	0	1,800	0	0.0	29.0	0.0	*			
Grand total	1,164	6,215	7,086	100.0	100.0	100.0	5.3	6.1		

* Denominator is zero.
a Percentage of total excluding emergency workers: national defense, 17.8; schools, 27.8; public enterprises, 12.0; all other regular employees, 42.3.

Growth of Federal Activities

The percentages in Table 16 provide fuller functional detail for federal expenditures for enough years to mark the trends and important changes in trends up to World War II, and the net change since then. Here we can find information not given in our introductory survey of the expenditure data: the decline in the relative importance of national defense expenditures during the 40 years before World War II was the reflection of a trend; even after World War I expenditures on veterans bulked no larger in the budget than in the early 1900's — because the budget had swelled so much; there appeared in the 1930's and continued thereafter large new items for social security, unemployment compensation, and business loans and guaranties; at the same time aids to agriculture, already in existence before the depression, were greatly expanded; the heavy burden of work- and direct-relief was shouldered during the 1930's and virtually disappeared when war came; a highway program (by grants to the states) and a federal reserve system appeared after World War I; conservation expenditures began in the early 1900's; the merchant marine and housing programs brought by World War I were expanded during the 1930's; our current expenditures on international affairs took on a new character in recent years; and there was hopefully removed from the national defense budget and placed under "natural resources not primarily agricultural" a large item called "development and control of atomic energy".

The data plotted in Chart 10, for the broad groups available, show how federal expenditures fluctuated from year to year as well as in response to the great episodic events of world war and severe depression. What happened to federal employment and property over these years is shown in Charts 11 and 12, in which the functional classifications are somewhat different from those in Chart 10.[15]

The bits of information we have on capital assets add a few interesting details to our story. In 1902 federal nonmilitary property consisted almost entirely of waterway improvements and pub-

[15] See Table B16 for more details on employment than appear in Chart 11.

Table 16

Change in the Functional Distribution of Federal Government Expenditures, 1900-1949

	1900	1913	1923	1929	1939	1949	1949 Relative to 1900
			PERCENTAGE DISTRIBUTION				
National defense	32.1	26.4	24.6	23.1	12.2	33.0	70
Veterans' services & benefits	27.4	19.6	28.6	26.2	6.3	18.5	46
Pensions	26.7	18.7	15.8	14.4	4.7	6.0	
Insurance			3.6	8.9	.5	.3	
Readjustment benefits			5.6	*	.01	9.3	
Hospitals, other services, & administrative costs	.8	.9	3.6	2.9	1.1	3.0	
International affairs & finance	.6	.5	.6	.4	.2	18.0	2,153
Conduct of foreign affairs	.6	.5	.6	.4	.2	.5	
International recovery & relief						15.9	
Foreign economic development					.02	(−.1)	
Foreign military assistance						1.2	
Philippine war damage & rehabilitation						.5	
Social welfare, health & security	.9	1.4	1.5	1.6	44.7	5.3	381
Retirement & dependents' insurance					1.2	1.6	
Assistance to the aged & other special groups		.5	.2	.3	7.4	2.9	
Work & direct relief		.02	*	.01	35.2	.02	
Promotion of public health	.2	.3	.6	.4	.4	.5	
Crime control & correction	.8	.6	.6	.8	.3	.2	
Other			.1	.1	.06	.04	
Housing & community development			.04	.02	(−1.7)	.8	**
Education & general research	.6	.6	.6	.6	.4	.2	23
Promotion of education	.2	.3	.4	.4	.3	.1	
Educational aid to special groups			*	*	.01	.01	
Library & museum service	.1	.1	.02	.1	.06	.03	
General purpose research	.2	.2	.2	.2	.05	.05	
Agriculture & agric. resources	.6	1.6	2.3	2.1	13.6	7.0	837
Development & improvement of agric., excl. financial aids & conservation	.6	1.5	1.8	1.7	.8	.5	
Loan & investment program to aid agriculture			.4	.4	3.2	5.5	
Other financial aids					9.2	.9	
Conservation & development of agric. land & water resources		.1	.04	.03	.3	.2	

* Less than .005 percent.

** Denominator is zero.

Table 16 (concluded)

	1900	1913	1923	1929	1939	1949	1949 Relative to 1900
			PERCENTAGE	DISTRIBUTION			
Natural resources not primarily agricultural	1.7	2.4	1.2	1.8	2.6	4.2	168
Development & control of atomic energy						1.7	
Other conservation & development	1.7	2.4	1.2	1.8	2.6	2.5	
Postal service	20.4	28.0	22.4	26.5	8.9	6.0	20
Transportation & communication, other	4.7	10.1	10.6	9.0	5.2	3.2	46
Promotion of the Merchant Marine			3.1	.5	.5	.3	
Provision of navigation aids & facilities	4.5	9.8	3.1	4.6	1.8	.9	
Provision of highways		.02	3.2	3.2	2.0	1.3	
Regulation of transp. & communication	.1	.2	.2	.3	.2	.06	
Other		.1	.9	.2	.8	.7	
Finance, commerce, & industry		.2	.5	.6	.6	.3	**
Control of money supply & private finance			.2	.2	.1	.02	
Promotion or regulation of trade & industry							
Business loans & guarantees					.5	.2	
Other					(−.2)	(−.04)	
Labor	.04	.02	.1	.1	.8	.5	965
Unempl. compensation & placement activities				.01	.7	.5	
Other	.04	.02	.1	.1	.1	.08	
General government	11.0	9.0	7.0	7.8	6.3	3.0	19
Legislative	1.9	1.0	.4	.4	.2	.09	
Judicial	.6	.4	.6	.6	.1	.05	
Executive direction & management	.04	.02	.02	.02	.01	.02	
Federal financial management	4.3	2.8	3.1	2.5	1.2	1.1	
Govt. payment toward civilian employee general retirement systems					.7	.8	.7
Other	4.2	4.9	2.9	3.5	3.9	1.2	
Total expenditures	100.0	100.0	100.0	100.0	100.0	100.0	68
		BILLIONS	OF	DOLLARS			
Total expenditures	529	936	2,487	2,947	8,827	35,964	

Blank spaces mean zero or not identifiable. Expenditures include payrolls, current purchases, outlays on capital assets, loans and investments (which are negative when repayments exceed new loans), grants-in-aid, and transfers to the public, but not interest. For this reason they differ from expenditures reported in Tables 11 and 13.

Chart 10
Functional Classification of Federal Government Expenditures
1900 – 1949

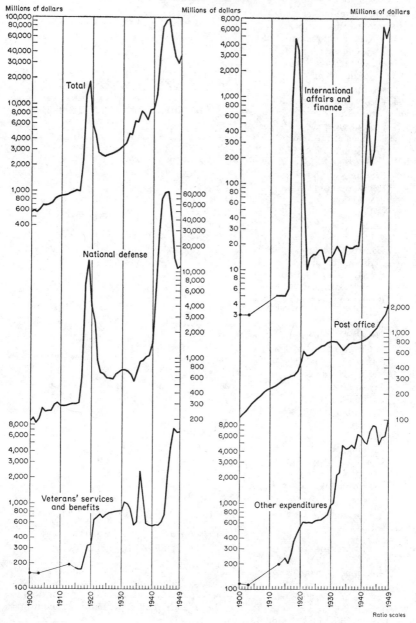

Ratio scales

Chart 11
Federal Government Workers, Major Functional Categories
1900 – 1949

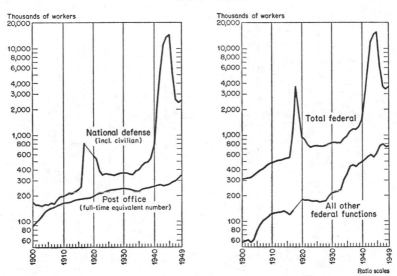

lic buildings, most of the latter in the District of Columbia. Reclamation projects were started in the first decade. Later, especially in the 1930's, other real property outside the District of Columbia — such as that of the Forest Service and the Farm Security Administration — and the assets of federal corporations — for example, the Tennessee Valley Authority and the U. S. Housing Authority — came to be substantial parts of the total (Chart 12). During the two war and immediate postwar periods the property of federal defense corporations, of course, assumed preponderant importance. Today, to judge from the 1946 data, the groups of assets important in 1902 make up little more than half when defense property (chiefly defense plants and the Merchant Marine) is excluded, only a fifth when defense property is included.[16]

[16] Like contract workers, property rented by government from private owners is excluded. We cannot be sure how much change in the proportion of rented to owned property has affected the trend we report in capital assets. At any rate, we take account of any change in rented property in our measure of purchases from private industry. In the case of federal property, the accelerated growth of federal building outside the District of Columbia, beginning in the late 1920's (Chart 12), apparently reflected a decision by Congress to turn to

(Footnote concluded on p. 67)

Chart 12

Federal Government Property, Major Categories, 1902–1946

(Reported or estimated values)

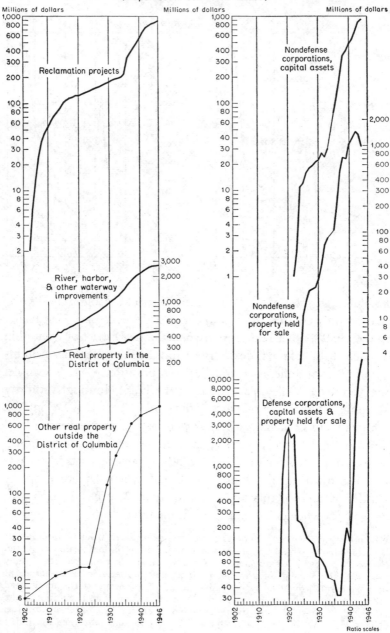

Ratio scales

The expansion of federal activities is also revealed in the new agencies established during the period with which we are concerned or as close to it as the records permit (Table 17).[17] Some agencies have since disappeared and others have been born, but taking our stand in 1939 we find almost 20 percent of federal employment — omitting emergency workers — in agencies that had come into existence since 1896. Exclusive of the two great federal services, national defense and the Post Office, over half the 1939 employment was in twentieth century agencies. Corresponding or even larger proportions characterize agencies associated with such functions as industrial and commercial development, labor, welfare, regulation, and public service enterprises (other than the postal system). The Women's Bureau, National Labor Relations Board, and Wage and Hour Division helped to swell the number dealing with labor. Welfare now includes the vast and various relief, social security, and other programs instituted under the New Deal, as well as the Veterans Administration. In 1896 the only "welfare" activities of the federal government we could identify as such were supervision of Indian affairs and operation of federal penitentiaries.

Measured by 1939 employment, the big additions to federal agencies came during the seven years beginning with 1933. Yet,

---

(Footnote concluded from p. 65)
government ownership of federally used buildings in lieu of renting private property.

Much property is still rented, partly because of small requirements in many areas, partly because of the rapid expansion of federal activity during the war. As of December 31, 1947, and not including space costing $2,000 a year or less, the federal government had under lease space, mostly for offices, for which it paid an annual rent of about $50 million, equivalent to a property value of perhaps $½ billion. (Survey of Space Leased by the Federal Government, 80th Cong., 2d Sess., *Senate Report 1617,* June 14, 1948.)

Some government property is rented to private lessees; e.g., municipal docks.

[17] Strictly speaking, the list of new agencies would include the Bureau of the Census and the Bureau of Labor Statistics, a substantial part of whose activities was carried over from predecessors. However, we excluded these from the list of new agencies, although much in the way of new activities was added even in these, as we shall illustrate below. The advantage of dealing with agencies, despite the difficulty caused by the fact that new agencies and new activities are not the same, is that we have employment figures: these provide a measure of importance superior to the simple enumeration of new activities.

Table 17

Growth of Federal Government Activities, 1897-1939

FUNCTION	AGENCIES IN EXISTENCE IN 1896		AGENCIES ESTABLISHED 1897-1939		
	Number Employed, Dec. 1939 (1,000)	% of Total Employment, Dec. 1939, in Old Agencies	Number Employed, Dec. 1939 (1,000)	% of Total Employment, Dec. 1939, in All New Agencies	% of Total Employment, Dec. 1939, All Agencies with Given Function
General control	89.8	8.7	7.6	2.7	7.8
Law enforcement	11.3	1.1	2.8	1.0	19.7
Highways & waterways	27.2	2.6	2.9	1.0	9.8
Conservation & development	32.6	3.1	34.3	12.0	51.3
Agriculture	8.3	.8	4.9	1.7	37.1
Industrial & commercial development	.2	[e]	23.2	8.1	99.1
Regulation	5.9	.6	33.2	11.6	84.9
Labor & industrial relations	.0	.0	3.1	1.1	100.0
Health & hospitals[a]	9.7	.9	.0	.0	.0
Welfare	3.3	.3	137.4	48.1	97.7
Veterans' services & benefits[b]	.0	.0	38.5	13.5	100.0
Other[c]	3.3	.3	98.9[d]	34.6	96.8
Indian affairs	13.8	1.3	.0	[e]	.1
Postal service[f]	249.0	24.1	35.4	12.4	99.8
Other public enterprises	.1	[e]	.7	.2	10.9
General information & research	5.8	.6	.0	.0	.0
Education & reference	2.5	.2	.1	[e]	[e]
National defense	575.8	55.6			
Total	1,035.3	100.0	285.7	100.0	21.6
Total excl. postal service & national defense	210.5		285.6		57.6

[a] Some hospitals are included under veterans' services and benefits.

[b] Separate data on employment connected with the payment of veterans' pensions in 1896 are not available. Growth in this category is therefore somewhat overstated.

[c] Includes correction.

[d] Fewer than 50 workers.

[e] Less than .05 percent.

[f] Full-time equivalent number.

Table 17 (continued)

AGENCIES IN EXISTENCE IN 1939 AND ESTABLISHED AFTER 1896, WITH DATE OF ESTABLISHMENT

General Control

Equatorial Islands (1898)
High Commissioner, Philippines (1899)
Governor of Hawaii (1900)
Governor of Alaska (1912)
Alien Property Custodian (1917)
Governor of the Virgin Islands (1917)
Bureau of the Budget (1921)
Board of Tax Appeals (1924)
Division of Territorial and Island Possessions (1934)
National Archives (1934)
Division of Savings Bonds (1936)
Temporary National Economic Committee (1938)
Federal Works Agency-Administrator (1939)
Public Works Administration (1939)

Law Enforcement

Federal Bureau of Investigation (1908)
Bureau of Narcotics (1930)

Highways and Waterways

Alaska Road Commission (1905)
Public Roads Administration (1939)

Conservation and Development

Bureau of Reclamation (1902)
Forest Service (1905)
National Park Service (1906)
Commission of Fine Arts (1910)
Bureau of Mines (1910)
National Capital Park and Planning Commission (1924)
Grazing Service (1934)
Soil Conservation Service (1935)
War Minerals Relief Commission (1939)

Industrial and Commercial Development

Bureau of Standards (1901)
Bureau of Foreign and Domestic Commerce (1912)

Industrial and Commercial Development

Tariff Commission (1916)
Mount Rushmore National Memorial Commission (1929)
Reconstruction Finance Corporation (1932)
Home Owners' Loan Corporation (1933)
Electric Home and Farm Authority (1934)
Export-Import Bank (1934)
Federal Housing Administration (1934)
Rural Electrification Administration (1935)
Golden State International Exposition Commission (1939)
New York World's Fair Commission (1939)
Federal Loan Agency Administrator (1939)

Agriculture

Bureau of Plant Industry (1902)
Extension Service (1914)
Bureau of Dairy Industry (1924)
National Agricultural Research Center (1934)
Bureau of Entomology and Plant Quarantine (1935)

Regulation

Board of Governors of the Federal Reserve System (1913)
Federal Trade Commission (1914)
National Advisory Committee for Aeronautics (1915)
Farm Credit Administration (1916)
Federal Power Commission (1920)
Food and Drug Administration (1928)
Federal Home Loan Bank Board (1932)
Federal Savings and Loan Insurance Corporation (1932)
Agricultural Adjustment Administration (1933)

Table 17 (concluded)

AGENCIES IN EXISTENCE IN 1939 AND ESTABLISHED AFTER 1896, WITH DATE OF ESTABLISHMENT

Regulation (concl.)

Commodity Credit Corporation (1933)

Federal Surplus Commodities Corporation (1933)

Federal Deposit Insurance Corporation (1933)

Securities and Exchange Commission (1934)

Federal Communications Commission (1934)

Consumers' Counsel (1935)

Federal Alcohol Administration (1935)

Petroleum Conservation Service (1935)

Commodity Exchange Administration (1936)

Maritime Commission (1936)

Civil Aeronautics Authority (1938)

Federal Crop Insurance Corporation (1938)

Agricultural Marketing Service (1939)

Bituminous Coal Division (1939)

Labor and Industrial Relations

Conciliation Service (1913)

Employees' Compensation Commission (1916)

Women's Bureau (1918)

Division of Labor Standards (1934)

National Mediation Board (1934)

National Labor Relations Board (1935)

Division of Public Contracts (1936)

Maritime Labor Board (1936)

Wage and Hour Division (1938)

Welfare

Children's Bureau (1912)

Veterans Administration (1930)

Prison Industries Fund (1934)

Farm Security Administration (1935)

Railroad Retirement Board (1935)

Social Security Board (1935)

National Youth Administration (1935)

Puerto Rico Reconstruction Administration (1935)

Works Projects Administration (1935)

Civilian Conservation Corps (1937)

Public Enterprises

Panama Canal (1912)

Alaska Railroad Commission (1914)

Tennessee Valley Authority (1933)

Alley Dwelling Authority (1934)

U. S. Housing Authority (1937)

Bonneville Project (1937)

General Information and Research

Bureau of Home Economics (1923)

International Labor Office (1934)

National Resources Planning Board (1939)

Office of Government Reports (1939)

Indian Affairs

Indian Arts and Crafts Board (1935)

National Defense

American Battle Monuments Commission (1923)

having stressed that important fact, we must not overlook another fact — in every decade the agencies and functions of the federal government were increased: the Bureaus of Reclamation, Mines, Standards, Plant Industry, and the FBI, among others, were set up in the first decade; the Tariff Commission, Extension Service, Federal Reserve Board, Federal Trade Commission, Children's and Women's Bureaus, and Panama Canal, for example, in the second decade; the Bureau of the Budget, Narcotics, Dairy Industry, and Home Economics, in the third decade; and in the fourth decade, the Reconstruction Finance Corporation and Federal Home Loan Bank Board before the New Deal, and a large group of temporary and permanent agencies with the New Deal.

And in almost every period the older agencies also expanded their functions and services. In 1940 the postal service, for example, transported and delivered 120 percent more letters, 1,200 percent more packages, and 100 percent more newspapers, magazines, and other printed material, than in 1908. In addition, in 1940 the postal system performed the extra services required by 35 percent more registered letters, 275 percent more money-orders, and 600 percent more special deliveries than in 1908; and in 1940 took care of millions of insurance transactions and postal savings accounts that were not its responsibility in 1908. Further, the postal system extended its delivery routes, increased the frequency and speed of its service, provided and serviced more mailboxes, chutes and branch offices, and introduced metered postage and the return envelope.

The Census Bureau is another example. Its product consists, of course, largely of the wealth of detailed information streaming out as releases, bulletins, and volumes, including material in the monthly *Survey of Current Business* and the annual *Statistical Abstract*.[18] Compared with 1900 we are provided today with information about a population twice as great. This information covers many more activities: the Census of Trade, Service Establishments, Construction, and Housing has become part of our

---

[18] "Bylines" do not tell the whole story. The Bureau of the Census is more and more frequently a fact-gathering and tabulatory agency for other federal departments.

statistical wealth only since 1929. Far more details and useful tabulations are available now than in 1900: the 1940 Census of Population was the first to give information on incomes, for example, and the 1930 Census was the first to cover unemployment adequately. The census information is available more promptly than in the past: some of the earlier censuses took many years to compile. Censuses have become more frequent (except for the interruption during World War II): the Census of Agriculture became quinquennial after 1919. Current information on a monthly, quarterly, or even annual basis hardly existed at the opening of the century; what we have today, notably the *Monthly Report on the Labor Force,* many monthly statistics on factory output, and quarterly reports on state and local government employment, is in substantial part the product of the Census Bureau. And the information has improved greatly in quality, based as it is on clearer concepts, questionnaires, and field procedures. The appendices to this report show in a number of ways how the Census Bureau's product has grown in volume and quality since 1900.[19]

Growth of State Activities

The outline of change in state government expenditures is easily drawn from Table 18.[20] Here we need only note the substantial rise in the relative importance of highways in the first half of the period covered, and of public welfare in the second half ("other general expenditures" were huge in 1948 and 1949 because they included

[19] The Bureau of the Census has added to the nation's real income in more than one way. Who does not enjoy reading that "all the beer consumed in the United States in a year would make a river 20 feet deep, 100 yards wide, extending from Washington, D. C., to Bridgeport, Conn."? (*Uncle Sam: How He Grew,* "150 Years of American History as Recorded in the U. S. Census", by Roscoe Wright, Chief of Public Relations for the Census Bureau. Bureau of the Census, 1943, p. 57.)

[20] Expenditures by state enterprises are not covered. However, in 1942 operating ex_ _ of all such enterprises amounted to only $38 million, and very much less in 1903.

Grants-in-aid to local governments also are excluded. Giving aid is itself an activity, of course, and one that has increased greatly, as we have noted: state aid in 1903 was well under $100 million; by 1949 it had mounted to over $3.5 billion. But for our present purpose the activity is not measured by the sums handled.

Table 18

CHANGE IN THE FUNCTIONAL DISTRIBUTION OF STATE GOVERNMENT
EXPENDITURES, 1903-1949

	1903	1915	1927	1939	1942	1948	1949	1949 Relative to 1903
	PERCENTAGE DISTRIBUTION							
General control	23.9	13.9	8.5	7.3	6.8	4.7	4.6	11.2
Public safety	6.0	8.3	5.2	5.0	5.2	3.7	3.5	34.0
Highways	4.3	18.1	42.0	32.6	31.1	26.1	27.6	375.4
Sanitation & health	2.6	1.7	1.5	1.9	2.2	1.9	1.7	38.3
Hospitals & instn. for the handicapped	45.3	15.3	11.5	10.7	10.2	9.8	10.4	41.2
Public welfare		9.4	5.0	20.4	20.8	16.7	19.3	
Correction		8.9	4.8	3.2	3.1	2.6	2.5	
Schools	13.7	16.4	14.5	10.9	11.9	14.2	14.3	60.9
Natural resources	4.3	5.0	5.5	4.3	5.1	4.8	4.9	218.6
Other general expenditures		3.1	1.4	3.7	3.6	15.5ᵃ	11.2ᵃ	
Total	100.0	100.0	100.0	100.0	100.0	100.0	100.0	58.1
	MILLIONS OF DOLLARS							
Total	117	360	1,309	2,562	2,531	5,776	6,799	

ᵃ Includes 10.7 percent, $616 million, veterans' bonus in 1948; 7.4 percent, $505 million, in 1949.

Expenditures cover current operations, outlays on capital assets, and transfers to the public, except interest payments; they exclude grants-in-aid and enterprises, and contributions to trust funds.

large bonuses to veterans), and the substantial declines through most of the period in the relative position of general control, hospitals, and correction. The chart gives the annual data, when available.[21]

When we peer within the broad groups presented in Table 18 and Chart 13 we find the big rise in public welfare to be due almost entirely to the recent provision of public assistance outside

[21] We need not stop to study the data on change in the functional distribution of employment, available only for New York 1900-40 and Vermont 1900-45, or the more complete information on capital assets, available, however, only for 1915-31; see Tables B17 and C5. The main trends seem to agree fairly well with those of expenditures, as far as we can judge from the disparate data.

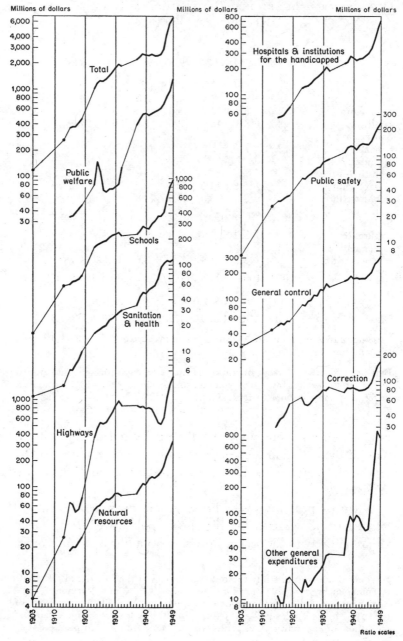

Chart 13
Functional Classification of State Government Expenditures
1903 – 1949

Millions of dollars

Total

Public welfare

Schools

Sanitation & health

Highways

Natural resources

Millions of dollars

Hospitals & institutions for the handicapped

Public safety

General control

Correction

Other general expenditures

Millions of dollars

Ratio scales

of institutions.[22] In 1915, the earliest year for which these details are available, the largest item of this kind was veterans' aid, accounting for $9 million; the rest — outdoor poor relief, care of the blind, deaf, and mute, mothers' pensions and gratuities, etc. — was only about $3.9 million. In 1949 aid to the blind alone amounted to $36 million and total public assistance — general relief, old-age, aid to dependent children, child welfare, and other items as well as aid to the blind — accounted for over a billion.

The increase in highway expenditures, especially between 1903 and 1927, reflects the meteoric rise of the motor vehicle. In addition, just before the turn of the century, the state governments began taking a hand in what hitherto had been entirely a function of the local agencies. It began with aid to the local governments, but then — especially under the stimulus of the Federal Highway Act of 1916, which extended federal aid to state (not local) highway departments — the states went on to assume direct responsibility for a large fraction of road building and maintenance. Thus Maine's first permanent participation in highway construction was undertaken in 1901, and its first comprehensive highway program formulated in 1913.[23] New York inaugurated its highway activity in 1898, and floated the first bond issue for the purpose in 1905. It took over the maintenance of state improved roads in 1906, and in 1907 launched a large scale state-county highway program.[24]

The rise in expenditures on natural resources includes, besides substantial increases in developmental functions related to forestry and fish and game, the development of farm extension services, experiment stations, and the like. The growth of activities of California illustrates some of these.[25] In 1900 the state government

---

[22] The details are taken from the Bureau of the Census annual reports, *Financial Statistics of States,* and related documents (see note to Table D9).

[23] F. E. Jewett, *A Financial History of Maine* (Columbia University Press, 1937).

[24] N. Y. State, Special Joint Committee on Taxation and Retrenchment, report on *State Expenditures, Tax Burden, and Wealth,* 1926.

[25] H. D. Anderson, *Our California State Taxes, Facts and Problems* (Stanford University Press, 1937), Ch. I.
It is tempting to *measure* the growth of state government activities in Cali-

carried on a few activities related to agriculture through several state boards, agriculture and forestry experiment stations, and a dairy bureau. Between 1900 and 1935 a poultry experiment station, pathology laboratories, dealers' exchange services, and similar agencies swelled the list of state agencies several-fold. And the state took on the regulation of strays and fertilizer salesmen, and of fertilizers, feeds, seeds, and other items purchased by farmers; the inspection of several types of fruits and animals; the control of various pests; and the application of standardization to several farm products.

The big increase in "other general expenditures" reflects two items: first, employment security administration, nonexistent before the great depression; and second, in 1948 and 1949, a very large bonus to veterans.

Even some of the functions relatively lagging in terms of percentage of total expenditures include some activities showing big rises. Examples are finance, reflecting the tapping of new sources of revenue and expansion of old, to meet the very great expansion in other state government expenditures; state police, expenditures for which were under a million in 1915, over $72 million in 1949; regulation of the sale of alcoholic beverages, health laboratories, and public utility regulation.[26] And when the so-called "enforcement stage" of labor law administration was reached in the 1900's, expenditures on factory and mine inspection and other labor law administration increased sharply.[27]

---

fornia between 1900 and 1935 by Anderson's counts of the number of activities. Thus in 1900 he lists 10 activities under agriculture and animal husbandry, and 66 in 1935, a rise of 460 percent. Unfortunately, it is impossible not to be arbitrary in defining an activity. The count will therefore necessarily depend on the judgment of the counter; e.g., is a new state hospital with a nursing school attached one new activity, two new activities, or merely the extension of an old activity? It must be admitted, however, that even simple description, as in the text above, inevitably conveys a sense of quantity by the mere number of items mentioned or space covered.

The difficulty is an exaggerated case of the one met when counting rising and declining functions.

[26] The Division of State Police of New York was created only in 1917. And state utility regulation did not begin until 1907 — in Wisconsin and New York.

[27] Elizabeth Brandeis, *op. cit.*, pp. 635 ff.

There came also additions to the enterprises operated by state governments. State liquor stores and workmen's compensation — outstanding today — appeared on the scene only after 1900.

In California, before 1900, state agencies dealing with public health and safety were few compared with the laboratories, stations, bureaus, and camps concerned with communicable diseases, foods and drugs, and sanitary engineering, among other things, added after 1900. Regulation, limited to dairy containers, olive oil, and renovated butter in 1900, was extended to drugs, condensed milk, fish dealers, elevators, imported meats, clothes cleaning establishments, auto camps, serum manufacturers, and other products, facilities, and industries. And as in the case of the federal government, these accretions to the state's activities came in every decade both before and after 1900.[28]

Growth of Local Activities

The big percentage increases in local government expenditures between the opening of the century and 1940 or 1942 were in hos-

Table 19

CHANGE IN THE FUNCTIONAL DISTRIBUTION OF LOCAL GOVERNMENT EXPENDITURES, 1903-1942

	1903	1942	1942 Relative to 1903
	PERCENTAGE DISTRIBUTION		
General control	20.7	9.4	3.6
Public safety	13.5	12.0	7.1
Highways	16.8	10.3	4.9
Sanitation & health	4.6	4.8	8.1
Hospitals, public welfare & correction	7.9	18.3	18.
Schools & libraries	33.0	40.1	9.7
Recreation	1.9	1.7	6.8
Misc. & unallocable	1.5	3.2	17.
Total	100.0	100.0	7.9
	MILLIONS OF DOLLARS		
Total	667	5,301	

Expenditures cover current operation and transfers to the public, except interest payments; they exclude enterprises and outlays on capital assets.

[28] Anderson, *op. cit.*

Table 20

CHANGE IN THE FUNCTIONAL DISTRIBUTION OF MUNICIPAL
GOVERNMENT EXPENDITURES, 1902-1940
(Cities with Populations over 100,000)

	1902	1912	1927	1940	1940 Relative to 1902
		PERCENTAGE DISTRIBUTION			
General control	8.7	8.3	6.4	5.8	6.2
Public safety	17.5	15.1	12.3	11.3	6.0
Highways		18.6	18.0	7.5	
Sanitation	24.2	8.8	9.4	4.9	5.2
Health		1.6	1.1	1.0	
Hospitals	1.5	2.3	2.6	4.1	26.2
Public welfare	3.5	2.2	2.0	11.5	32.7
Correction		1.0	.8	.7	
Schools	21.6	21.3	26.2	21.5	9.7
Libraries		1.0	1.0	.9	
Recreation	6.7	5.1	4.3	3.6	5.1
Misc. & unallocable	.9	1.3	1.0	.9	9.3
Enterprises	14.9	13.9	14.8	26.3[a]	16.5
Total	100.0	100.0	100.0	100.0	9.3
		MILLIONS OF DOLLARS			
Total	343	690	2,562	3,207	

[a] Including outlays on the New York City transit system, which amounted to 10.2 percent of total expenditures.

Expenditures cover current operations and outlays on capital assets, including enterprises and transfers to the public (except interest payments).

pitals, public welfare, and enterprises (Tables 19 and 20). The below average increases were in general control, highways, recreation, and sanitation. Similar trends characterize employment, to judge from the data for cities (Table B18).[29] (The three municipal functions whose employment failed to rise as rapidly as urban population, referred to earlier, are administrative, legislative, and judicial, included under general control.)

Chart 14 may help the reader see some of the very considerable changes that occurred, at least in municipal expenditures, in the years between the opening of the century and World War II.

[29] Data on change in the functional distribution of capital assets, exclusive of streets, schools, and sewage systems, are available for municipal governments only (Table C7). Pattern changes seem to have been rather slight, although they do show the relative increase in hospitals and decline in recreational facilities.

Chart 14
Functional Classification of Municipal Government Expenditures
Cities with Populations over 100,000
1902 – 1949

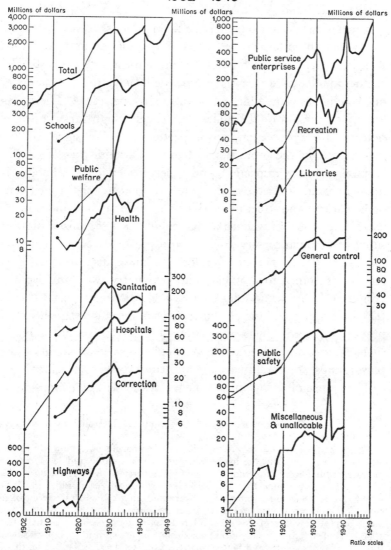

Millions of dollars

Millions of dollars

Millions of dollars

Ratio scales

There was a general tendency for the growth of all kinds of expenditures to slacken during World War I, the great depression,
and World War II; public welfare was an obvious exception in
the depression and World War I.

Much of the decline during these three periods, however, reflects
contraction in outlays on new construction and equipment rather
than in current service rendered. Through most of the last half-
century municipal services have expanded. In Detroit, for example,
many activities were added in all of the five decades.[30] There was
literary censorship by the police department, high pressure water
systems for fire protection, and inspection of smoke, signs, inflam-
mables, etc. in the protection category. Various types of clinics,
hospitals, sanitary inspection, and expert inspection of school children appeared under the health conservation category in the twentieth century; and street name signs and traffic lights, under highways. Expansion in welfare activities included organized old-age
support, ambulance service, family adjustment service, employment bureau, care of municipal lodging house, insurance advisory
service, assistance to mothers; and psychiatry was provided for
criminals. Listed as additions under education are special classes
for handicapped children, evening and summer high school, school
buses, continuation classes, branch libraries (including a book-
mobile), and an elephant ride. Various recreational facilities like
playgrounds, community centers and concerts were developed.

The course of events in Detroit was paralleled by expansion in

[30] L. D. Upson, "The Growth of a City Government", Detroit Bureau of Governmental Research, *Report No. 164, 1942.*

Numbers are given, but as was mentioned in an earlier note, they are rather
arbitrary measures. Thus the list of additions between 1900 and 1941, 256 in
number, is far longer than the list of activities carried on in 1900, only 140.
Yet it is fair to presume that the basic services already established in 1900,
such as streets, sewerage, water, elementary and high schools, police, garbage
collection, and street cleaning, were item for item at least as important (in
terms of cost or value of service rendered) as the *new* services added after
1900. (Table 20 shows very great expansion in expenditures, but this was
through wider coverage and better quality of old services, as well as addition
of new services.) The ratio of 256 to 140 therefore overstates the relative
importance of the additions. However, the impression made of wider scope of
activity, greater variety of services, and improvements in methods of satisfying
needs is reasonable, even though the measure lacks precision.

other cities. A survey of 34 cities for 1915-32[31] shows that every city added new activities — 21 installed traffic lights; 9, police teletypes; 9, venereal disease clinics; 10, classes for the deaf; 11, playgrounds.

The history of the Department of Health of New York City is a good illustration. At the time of the consolidation of the five boroughs in 1898 the Department devoted itself primarily to sanitary inspection and prevention of the spread of contagious diseases. School inspection, for example, consisted merely of a search for contagious diseases. Not one health clinic for the provision of medical care existed in 1898. By 1948 the Department visited schools systematically to check children's eyesight, teeth, and state of nutrition, produced and distributed vaccines and serums, and operated 170 clinics and 21 health centers. The diagnosis and treatment of venereal disease in particular had become largely a monopoly of the Department, since a means test was no longer applied.[32]

Changes in patterns of activity of counties, townships, and special districts are essentially like those of other types of government, after allowance is made for their different functions (recall Table

---

[31] C. H. Wooddy, "The Growth of Governmental Functions," Ch. 25, *Recent Social Trends in the United States* (McGraw-Hill, 1933). (The end-year of the period covered is not mentioned; we assumed it to be 1932.) Wooddy also makes the following interesting comparison, which is relevant to the point made in footnote 30:

| | RANK OF ABSOLUTE INCREASE IN | |
FUNCTION	*Expenditures (1915 prices), 1915-29*	*Activities, 1915-32*
Education	1	5
Highways	2	8
Protection	3	4
Miscellaneous	4	2
Health and sanitation	5	1
Recreation	6	3
Charities, hospitals, and correction	7	6
General control	8	7

For example, health and sanitation accounted for the largest number of new activities but ranked fifth in additions to dollar expenditures.

[32] We are indebted to Eugene Levine for a review of the annual reports of the New York City Department of Health and related material.

13).[33] In addition, there has been a partial transfer of the highway function from these local governments to state governments, and of the school function from counties and cities to special school districts.[34]

Change and Continuity

The major conclusions that we may draw from our review of change in functions can be put briefly.

First, hardly any function of any type of government actually declined over the last half-century. Whether measured by workers employed, capital assets, or expenditures (with allowance, naturally, for price changes), practically every function in every type of government expanded. The few apparent exceptions, namely certain functions in local governments other than counties and cities, are usually accounted for by known deficiencies in the figures. Even the loss of part of a function to another type of government meant slower growth rather than decline.[35]

This conclusion can be put almost as strongly in terms of input per capita. The exceptions are few.

Second, there was considerable variation among the several functions in degree of rise of input, however measured, and in all types of government. In the rear guard, among the types of government where these functions are significant, were general control, public safety, and sanitation; and in the van were public welfare, natural resources, and regulation of business and industrial relations (including factory legislation). Schools lagged in growth of employment, but not in growth of capital or expenditures.

Third, while the trend — or at least the net change — of input in every function was up, there were considerable fluctuations in rate of growth. Some functions were pushed up violently during the two wars and then down when they were over; many others

[33] Little separate information is available on counties, townships, and special districts beyond that included in Table 19. What there is is given in Tables D11 and D12 for those especially interested.

[34] Other functions as well have been transferred to special districts, to lessen costs or make possible the provision of services that could not otherwise be provided; cf. Ch. 5.

[35] It hardly seems necessary to note that some *individual* local governments had to cut input, when the population of the area served by them shrank enough.

declined during the wars, then rose; at least one, veterans' services, rose immediately after the wars, then began to decline. The great building booms centered at about 1909 and 1925 and the one current today pushed up outlays of cities; the two wars and the great depression pushed them down. The wars also reduced state government outlays and federal outlays on nonwar functions; but the great depression pushed them up. Peacetime functions in general, whether federal, state, or local, declined during World War II and probably also during World War I.

In addition to fluctuations involving positive and negative changes, there were changes in speed of rise, and these varied from function to function. To illustrate: conservation got its start in the early 1900's and rose most rapidly at that time; outlays on highways shot up until the 1920's, then continued to grow but at a slower pace in the 1930's; functions stimulated by the New Deal rose most rapidly during the 1930's.

Fourth, the biggest part of the half-century rise in total input came not from the spectacular appearance of "new" functions but, putting aside the effects of the cold war on national defense, from the more moderate but nevertheless substantial increase of functions already well established in 1900. Thus the big *percentage* expansions came in activities connected with public welfare, health, conservation of resources, public works, and, at the federal level, regulation. The big *absolute* additions to government input came, however, from those functions already important in 1900. Expansion in national defense, schools, and public enterprises accounted for over half the rise in government employment between 1900 and 1940; and for two-thirds between 1900 and 1949.

This leads us to our final conclusion. Many of the government functions relatively most important in 1900 were still very important in 1940 and 1950: schools, highways, municipal services, defense, public enterprises, are among these. A few, such as general control, declined; some new ones appeared. But measured by input the beginning and end patterns bear a distinct family resemblance to each other. Measured by input, though not necessarily also by impact on the economy's efficiency, there has been change, but no revolution, in the functional pattern of government activity: change, but also persistence.

CHAPTER 5

Productivity in Government and the Output of Government Services

The factors underlying the rising trend of government's use of resources may be put into two groups: first, those affecting the relation between these resources and the services into which they are transformed — that is, government's productivity; second, those affecting the volume of services rendered. We begin our exploration of these factors with a study of the changing relation between the input and output of government. Has government's productivity declined so that part of the rise in input reflects the need for more resources in order to maintain a given volume of services? Or has productivity risen, thereby causing government's output to rise even more rapidly than its input?

Declining Hours of Work

Changes in hours worked by government employees and in the rate of use of government's capital goods, as well as changes in the efficiency with which resources are used, influence the ratio of input to output. What can be said about the first factor? Since little is known about changes in the number of hours per week during which government capital goods are in use, except that they are probably associated with changes in hours of employment, we shall have to let the latter tell the tale for both.

In practically all industries in the private sector of the economy — the outstanding exception may be agriculture — hours of labor put in by workers declined between 1900 and 1940. The average reduction was probably about 20 percent including agriculture, perhaps 25 or 30 percent excluding agriculture. In such an environment should we not expect to find the hours of the average government worker also declining?

In some types of government work there is no specific work

week. The military and naval service is the prime example, and mention may be made also of the proverbial lighthouse keeper and the small-town chief of police on "continuous duty", subject to call at all hours of the day and night. In some others, hours per employee seem actually to have risen. The average public school year, for example, was lengthened. And the regular work week of federal employees in the District of Columbia today is little different from the 39 hours that prevailed in 1900-03.

Scattered reports on postal employees, prison guards, hospital attendants, firemen and policemen, New York City Health Department employees, and similar groups suggest, however, that hours in most government posts lessened after 1900, even without taking into account the extension and lengthening of the annual vacation.[1] That the decline has been as much as the 20 or 30 percent in private industry seems doubtful. Since government was already acting the part of the "ideal employer", setting standards of work and pay, at the opening of the century, it is likely that the strong pressures toward shorter hours in private industry, especially after 1929, were not matched by corresponding pressures in government.

Now, any fall in the hours of government work per week tends to push government employment up.[2] In some cases the effect of fewer hours might be partly offset by higher productivity induced by the reduction. But this offset could hardly be complete. There must be some government services which require a substantially fixed number of manhours per unit of service rendered. (Police protection provided by foot patrol may be an example.) In such cases, reduction of hours would tend to lead to corresponding rises in employees per unit of service rendered.

We have here, then, a factor making for increase in government employment. In some functions reduction in hours might conceivably have been the major factor. On the whole, however, it must be counted as contributing no more than 10 or 15 percent to the

[1] The data are from diverse sources: the U. S. Civil Service Commission, the Bureau of Labor Statistics, the Municipal Year Book, communications from the American Federation of Government Employees, and Paul Douglas' *Real Wages in the United States* (Houghton Mifflin, 1930), among others.

[2] Except when service is reduced as a consequence; but this is rare and usually only temporary

rise of government input — if we are right in our surmise that hours fell less than 20 percent.

We turn to what probably has been a more important factor: change in the efficiency of government's use of resources.

Improvements in Technology

Application of mechanical, electrical, and chemical devices in ever increasing quantity and quality is a major theme in the history of economic development. We may look, therefore, to technological advance as a potent cause of increased productivity in government activities as well as in private industry.

Developments in the postal system illustrate the increasing number, widening variety, and improving quality of mechanical devices put to use by government.[3]

Mechanical methods are not economically applicable in some phases of Post Office work, especially facing the mail preparatory to cancellation and sorting. But for handling a wide variety of other jobs, mechanical methods were devised and extended during the twentieth century to an extent seldom realized by patrons who use only the front entrance to the Post Office.

By 1940 improved machines were cancelling and postmarking letters at the rate of 600 per minute, as compared with hand cancellation of 1500 per hour. Letters were stacked mechanically and fed automatically into the cancelling machines. And the masses of mail were handled by automatic conveyors and other devices: chutes, floor wells, belt conveyors, bucket elevators, travelling hoppers with tripping devices, and floor trucks driven by hand or power. To use these devices the physical plant of the postal system has been modified by an extensive building and adaptation program. We have already seen the large investment in new federal facilities made during the 1930's, presumably in buildings technically better than older structures. And for carrying letters to and between post offices, motor trucks have displaced the earlier horse-drawn vehicles.

[3] Bureau of Labor Statistics *Bulletin 574*, "Technological Changes and Employment in the U. S. Postal Service", by Witt Bowden, December 1932, and annual reports of the Post Office Department.

Most of the new devices for handling the mail are not economical in smaller post offices, of which there are still a great many although their number has been declining.[4] The mere increase in average size must therefore have pushed up the percentage of mail handled mechanically, apart from the increase resulting from more and better machines in an office of a given size.

Mechanical devices have also speeded up the office work of the Post Office Department. Bookkeeping and calculating machines, introduced mainly during the period under discussion, save time and labor and reduce the number of errors — a further labor saver. Check-writing machines, signature devices, machines for computing the complicated rates on second class matter, time recorders, and many other appliances are now in use. Handling several hundred million postal money orders per year would be a burdensome task, indeed, without the aid of mechanical tabulating and summarizing equipment.

Census operations on the scale described in Chapter 4 would be quite impossible without these devices, to turn to another division of the federal government. The "three billion facts" said to have been collected in the 1940 Census would never have seen the light of day had hand operations been used; nor could the five million forms returned to the Census Bureau in 1938 (each containing an average of 44 entries) have been processed with the speed to which we have become accustomed.[5] The use of punch card tabulating equipment began, it is true, before 1900.[6] But there have been many improvements since the opening of the century. The first mechanical tabulator, for example, involved much labor in operation. Improvements in the Census Bureau laboratory reduced

---

[4] In 1900 there were 72,000 fourth class post offices out of a total of 77,000; in 1940, 29,000 out of a total of 44,000.

[5] See F. C. Mills and C. D. Long, *The Statistical Agencies of the Federal Government* (National Bureau of Economic Research, 1949), p. 34; and annual reports of the Department of Commerce (Department of Commerce and Labor until 1913). The remarkably short current lags between the period to which data refer and the date of their release are indicated on pp. 116-8 of the book by Mills and Long.

[6] Hollerith's "unit card" principle, the fundamental basis of all punch card tabulating systems, was embodied in equipment as early as 1890.

the amount of manual work, added a printing device, and a high speed feed system. Scores of columns can now be handled simultaneously. Part of the editing job, one of the most time consuming in census operations, has in effect been mechanized by a reject mechanism: cards failing to meet certain requirements (e.g., that all married people be over a certain age) are put aside for review. In addition, auxiliary equipment now moves the cards and duplicates information on two or more cards. Sorters, collators, summary punches, reproducers, multipliers, interpreters (which read the holes on a card and print the data read on the top of the same card) have been devised and extensively used.

Motorization spread quickly and widely throughout government. The horse-drawn vehicles once operated by city police departments, for example, had been entirely replaced by motorized vehicles in 1946.[7] Auto patrol has of course reduced the number of men needed for patrol duty. Its advantages are indicated by the fact that in 1938 close to two-fifths of all police officers on patrol duty rode in automobiles.[8] Mobilization of men and equipment has been expedited greatly by these means. Aided by modern signaling equipment (the telephone, teletype, and radio), motorization has made it possible largely to dispense with the reserve force.[9] Eleven years after Detroit had set up the first publicly owned police radio system (in 1928) over 700 municipal radio transmitters were in operation.[10]

In the growing portion of police duties relating to traffic control, also, mechanization has played a large part. Efforts to develop mechanical traffic signals began about 1910. But commercial development did not start until the 1920's. Today the number of

[7] Bureau of the Census, *Statistics of Cities Having a Population of over 30,000: 1905; Financial Statistics of Cities: 1915;* the International City Managers' Association, *Municipal Year Book, 1946,* p. 416.

[8] Federal Bureau of Investigation, *Uniform Crime Reports,* 2nd Quarter, 1939 (cited by Bruce Smith, *Police Systems in the United States,* Harper, 1940, p. 142).

[9] One consequence was a drastic cut in hours of policemen. This illustrates a way in which hours and efficiency — which we are treating as independent factors — are in fact inter-related.

[10] Bruce Smith, *ibid.,* p. 329.

intersections protected by traffic lights must be enormous compared with the 8,000 estimated for 1926.[11]

It is easy to multiply the examples:[12] automotive transport of fire-fighting equipment; use of construction equipment in road building and maintenance; use of the radio and motion picture in education; and widespread acceptance of office machines and calculators (federal employees today receive their pay in the form of checks printed on punch cards, and New York State income taxes are billed on punch cards). Even the simple listing of the special-purpose automotive equipment operated by the Sanitation Department of New York City is impressive: in 1947 there were 1,390 refuse collection trucks, 3 offal trucks, 193 flusher trucks, 68 mechanical brooms, 178 snow loaders, 556 cross walk snow plows, 49 rotary snow brooms, and 115 salt spreaders.[13]

Besides mechanization, other scientific advances have been used, of which two examples may be given. One is the technique of scientific sampling introduced in the Census Bureau's operations. A carefully devised small sample can be made to yield information of a specified level of accuracy at a fraction of the cost of a complete census, and to do it more quickly.[14] Thus by sampling only

[11] B. W. Marsh, "Traffic Control", *The Annals of the American Academy of Political and Social Science*, September 1927.

[12] Indeed, there is danger of giving too strong an impression of the benefits of mechanization. Some authorities feel, for example, that many police departments are overburdened with equipment. "Teletype systems are installed without regard to their specific local value as supplementary recording devices; and signal switchboards are provided with multicolored panels and decorative schemes of illumination which delight the eye of the beholder without contributing anything of value to the grim business of police protection. Ingenious contrivances have in truth become a special kind of police problem, both because they are costly and also because they serve to distract the attention of administrators and public alike away from . . . organization, personnel and procedure . . ." Bruce Smith, *op. cit.*, p. 144.

[13] *A Better Government for a Better City, A Study of Five Departments of the City of New York at the Request of Honorable William O'Dwyer, Mayor* (The Citizens Budget Commission, 1948), pp. 96-7.

[14] The increase in efficiency made possible can be determined with some precision. Suppose, for example, that an estimate of government nonmilitary employment within plus or minus 6 percent of the complete census figure is satisfactory. An estimate of such accuracy (or better) can be obtained, 19 times out of 20, from a sample of only 25,000 households — just 0.06 percent of the

25,000 households the Bureau of the Census can keep the country informed monthly of the national level of employment and unemployment only one month before. Further, when a small sample is taken, it is possible to use highly trained enumerators, more detailed instructions, and more elaborate schedules, at less than prohibitive cost, and thus reduce the possibility of errors that even censuses suffer from. The application of the scientific sampling method has multiplied the productivity in certain Census Bureau operations many-fold.

Adaptation and application of scientific methods and apparatus to the detection of crime and to judicial proof is another example.[15] Fingerprinting is especially noteworthy. The means of identification used about 1900, photographs and Bertillon anthropometric measurements, were complex and could not be found in any decisive records left at the scene of a crime. In addition, the use of photography for recording evidence, maintaining departmental records, and court presentation has spread widely, well beyond the point attained in 1900.[16]

In the past two decades, moreover, elaborate laboratories have been set up by many police forces, and the Federal Bureau of Investigation and state laboratories have placed their facilities at the disposal of smaller police units that do not operate their own.

---

population of 40 million households — using the same schedules, instructions, and enumerators. (See any of the Census Bureau monthly reports on the labor force.)

[15] *Municipal Police Administration,* 2nd ed., 1943, the International City Managers' Association, published for the Institute for Training in Municipal Administration.

[16] Most applications of "police science" are relatively new. Readers of detective stories will be surprised to learn that until well into the twentieth century, "the criminal identification unit of the Boston police had only one small table for taking fingerprints. . . . The bureau had no photographer of its own . . . no portable photographic equipment for taking pictures at the scene of crimes. There was no laboratory . . . no *modus operandi* system of records to identify the acts of crime in the metropolitan area, no equipment for photostating fingerprints or documents, or for taking plaster-of-paris impressions of footprints or other tell-tale marks, no comparison lenses for matching fingerprints, no enlargement apparatus for analyzing handwriting and no ballistics apparatus." A number of these deficiencies had been remedied by 1932. (L. V. Harrison, *Police Administration in Boston,* Harvard University Press, 1934, pp. 123-4.)

Changes in Public Administration

A major trend in public administration has been the spread of the merit system — the selection and promotion on a permanent tenure of public employees on the basis of specified standards of training, ability, effort, and experience rather than patronage. The merit system dates from its adoption by Congress and the State of New York in 1883. Yet at the close of the nineteenth century it was applied on only a limited scale.[17] Since 1900 there has been extensive expansion in three ways. First, the number of civil service commissions has increased greatly.[18] Second, the merit system has come to be applied by many government units without using the particular instrumentality of a civil service commission. Other personnel bodies, or a system without special administrative agencies or even without statutory provisions, have also provided the basis for a merit system. "City-manager" cities, for example, have merit systems although usually no civil service commission.[19] Third, the coverage of the various merit systems has grown. Often they at first included only certain specified classes of employees, for example, police officers and firemen, and were then gradually

[17] In 1900, civil service commissions — one indication of the existence of the merit system — had been established only by the federal government, two states, one county, and sixty-five cities. On this question see L. D. White, *Trends in Public Administration* (McGraw-Hill, 1933), and *Introduction to the Study of Public Administration* (Macmillan, 1939).

[18] By 1931, according to not quite complete data collected by White (see his *Trends*), there were civil service commissions in 12 states, 12 counties, and 250 cities. Further additions have since been made: in December 1944, e.g., 19 states had a service-wide merit system, one covered three classes of employees, and the system of the other 28 covered at least social security agencies. (*The Book of the States, 1945-6,* pp. 155-61; the inclusion of personnel in the social security agencies in the 28 states is the fruit of a subsidy provision of the federal Social Security Act.)

These numbers do not fully describe the trend, of course. Some commissions never become effective because of lack of funds or other handicaps, and some perform functions so limited as hardly to warrant accepting them as an indication of the existence of a merit system. On the other hand, the number of commissions understates the degree of coverage. For example, it is largely the bigger cities that have set up civil service commissions. Further, some commissions, such as that of New York State, cover county and certain other local government employees as well as state employees.

[19] Since about 1910 over 400 such city governments have been adopted, and along with this form of administration, the merit system.

widened to cover other classes of workers. The merit system of the federal government illustrates this trend, as well as the backsliding and forward spurts that have caused fluctuations about the trend.[20]

Current application of the merit system is by no means complete. Most counties, many states, and the smaller municipalities are still backward in this respect. But the coverage is far greater than it was at the opening of the century.[21] Even with considerable allowance for the nominal character of some existing merit systems, and the use of veterans' preferences and other exceptions, the trend away from patronage and toward an actual merit system is clear.

Some persons might question whether widening the scope of the merit system has tended to raise government's productivity. To them the merit system is merely a system for maintaining mediocrity.[22] But most informed opinion inclines to the view that the merit system tends to reduce corruption and waste in government. It increases efficiency by reducing turnover and creating a professional class of workers. Expressed in the terms we have been using, the merit system tends to reduce the number of government em-

[20] The basis for the expansion was the provision of the Pendleton Act (which set up the U. S. Civil Service Commission) conferring on the President the power to add to the Commission's jurisdiction. The initial coverage was rather small: in 1884 only 10 percent of all positions in the executive civil service were subject to examination; by 1900 the percentage was about 40; it grew to 80 in 1932, dropped sharply when the New Deal agencies came into being, then rose to 68 in 1939.

See *The Classified Executive Civil Service of the United States Government,* a pamphlet published by the U. S. Civil Service Commission, March 1933, for additions to the classified service made by executive order and Congressional action in each administration up to 1933. The percentages cited appear on p. 29; percentages for later years were computed from current Civil Service Commission data.

[21] Current data on merit systems will be found in the *Municipal Year Book* and *The Book of the States.*

[22] The civil service is "a unique system under which it is assumed that people are simple organic compounds, subject to laboratory methods. Examinations are given to these specimens, and on the basis of the results they are neatly catalogued and filed until needed. Orders are filled on the general understanding that short of an Act of God there will be no returns or exchanges. The finished product is a pale, quiet individual, faithful in a dim sort of way, disinclined to originality, but capable within a limited field of an insolence that makes one wonder why it is called 'civil'.

"The chief advantage of the civil service system appears to be that it offers regular, light employment at a moderate remuneration. This undoubtedly

ployees (and the quantity of other resources) required to produce a given volume of government services. On this view, expansion in the scope of the merit system has been a factor contributing to increased productivity in government during the last half-century.

Other developments in personnel management have tended to improve worker efficiency and thus increase productivity. Examples are: the raising of standards of qualification, the classification of positions and standardization of rates of pay, the introduction of pension systems, establishment of training programs, and the development of techniques for handling transfers, illness, and so on. All these tend to improve morale, reduce the rate of turnover, eliminate superannuated employees, and thus raise efficiency. These developments, largely a product of the more recent decades of the twentieth century, constitute a significant factor that we must count among those that have raised productivity in government since 1900.[23]

The merit system is a device for getting the most out of government's dollars when labor is purchased. Centralized purchasing — like the centralized civil service commission — is a means of getting the most out of each dollar spent in the purchase of goods. Thus centralized purchasing also must be considered in analyzing government's productivity.

Strictly defined, centralized purchasing is a form of organiza-

---

attracts large numbers of steady-going, unimaginative people, but I question whether their services are of any greater value to the public than the less routine but more lively efforts of patronage appointees who have a personal stake in the business. Andrew Jackson (said), 'I cannot but believe that more is lost by the long continuance of men in office than is generally to be gained by their experience.' " (William Turn, "In Defense of Patronage", *The Annals of the American Academy of Political and Social Science,* January 1937.)

[23] The *Report of the Congressional Joint Commission on Reclassification of Salaries,* March 12, 1920 (66th Cong., 2d Sess., House Doc. 686) describes the situation in the federal government before the introduction of the changes noted above. (An important factor in 1920 was the rise in the cost of living and other distortions caused by the war; nevertheless, the report provides a graphic picture of the influence on morale of lack of uniformity in pay for the same work and other factors of more immediate concern to us.) To cite one example, of the 3,000 employees 65 and older on Washington payrolls in 1920, it was reported that 1,800 would elect or could be compelled to retire if a retirement law were passed, and these could be replaced by a fourth the number of younger employees (Part 1, p. 125).

tion in which one office is delegated the authority to buy the supplies, materials, and equipment needed by all the branches of an organization.[24] It has many advantages over decentralized buying. Graft or favoritism tends to be reduced. The size of orders is materially increased. Excessive variety is eliminated. The use of trained buyers is enhanced. Central storage and distribution reduces the total volume of stocks held and the piling up of surpluses that become obsolete. These advantages are reflected in two ways: by reductions in the average price paid per unit and in the overhead cost of buying. (There are related benefits: the use of specifications and standardization, testing laboratories, and checking of bids against open market prices are noteworthy.) While it is easy to cite striking examples of the savings made by centralized purchasing,[25] no comprehensive measure is available except for such opinions as the following: "Experience has demonstrated beyond a doubt that by centralized purchasing the unit cost of supplies, materials, and equipment can be reduced, on an average, from 10 to 15 percent."[26] Duly discounting the enthusiasm of the proponent, there remains a factor of some substance.[27]

Like the merit system, centralized purchasing is a product

---

[24] Russell Forbes, *Governmental Purchasing* (Harper, 1929), p. 1.

[25] A number have been collected by Russell Forbes, *ibid.*, esp. Chapter 1 and Appendix A. See also various issues of the *National Municipal Review*.

[26] *Ibid.*, p. 4.

[27] It might be questioned that a mere reduction in the price paid for goods purchased — and the greater part of the advantages of centralized buying materializes in that form — enhances the productivity of government. Can the ratio of volume of government services to volume of resources used be raised by reducing the price paid for the resources? The answer is "no" only if an exceedingly narrow interpretation is placed on volume of resources used. But when goods are purchased, the resources acquired consist of more than just the goods themselves. The services involved in selling, packing, transporting, and billing the goods must also be counted. When centralization of purchases succeeds in reducing the volume of these services, as it does when it leads to larger purchases, a real reduction has occurred in the volume of resources used even though the total number of units purchased over the years remains unchanged. And this reduction is measured by the reduction in price.

mainly of the twentieth century.[28] It has spread not only with its acceptance in principle by various government units, but also through the growth of cooperative buying plans to provide the smaller government units with the advantages of centralized purchasing,[29] and through extension of a given system to cover more of the purchases of the government unit concerned.

Few government units have complete centralized purchasing even today. Exceptions for certain classes of specialized equipment or supplies, or a division among several central purchasing agen-

[28] In 1900 centralized purchasing is known to have been used only in the Navy Department of the federal government, in 4 states, and in 3 of the 41 cities having populations of 200,000 or more in 1930.

Since 1900, and especially since 1910, it has spread widely. In the federal government the organization of the General Supply Committee in 1909, and substantial extension of its powers in 1929, represent steps toward widening the scope of central purchasing. In 1933, upon the establishment of the Procurement Division, the full principle of central purchasing came to be applied to the majority of the federal government's purchases.

Of the 40 states with some degree of central purchasing by 1931, 19 set up the organization between 1910 and 1929.

As for cities with more than 10,000 inhabitants, by 1926 about 25 percent had centralized purchasing, the percentage being close to 100 for the very large cities, diminishing to about 15 for smaller cities. For cities under 10,000 in population the percentage was probably under 15. Centralized purchasing was instituted in cities chiefly between 1910 and 1919, to judge from data for cities of over 200,000 in 1930. Most city manager cities adopted central purchasing, just as they did the merit system and other improvements, along with the manager

Counties have been backward in this as in other respects. By 1930 centralized purchasing had been established in fewer than a hundred of the 3,000 counties in the United States.

The data are largely from Forbes, *op. cit.*, Chapters 1-3; A. E. Buck, "The Coming of Centralized Purchasing in State Governments", Supplement to the *National Municipal Review*, February 1920; L. D. White, *Trends in Public Administration*, Chapters 13, 14, and 15; L. D. White, *Introduction to the Study of Public Administration*, Chapter 5; John A. Fairlie and C. M. Kneier, *County Government and Administration* (Century, 1930), p. 404. Some rather different figures are given in a note in the *National Municipal Review*, June 1937, where it is reported that centralized purchasing, in one form or another, is found in 250 cities, 50 counties, and 36 states. No source is given.

[29] These have been set up in about 20 states, either by state legislation or by municipal leagues. The purchasing may be done through the state purchasing agent, through a large municipality or county, or through a cooperative organization. See the *National Municipal Review* for 1939, pp. 874-5, and other issues.

cies in the same unit are found.[30] And the system itself varies in effectiveness.[31] Yet on the whole the trend has been toward greater realization of the advantages of centralized purchasing, and this seems to have been another significant factor heightening government productivity.

The rise of the merit system and the spread of centralized purchasing are only two aspects of the reorganization of public administration that has been taking place in the United States (and other countries) during the last century. Since 1900 there has been a trend toward integrating internal administrative responsibility in city governments, and since about 1915, a corresponding development in state governments.[32] The reform of municipal government, which began with the commission plan and continued with the council-manager plan, illustrates the development toward internal integration. In the federal government also, efforts sprang up aimed at better internal organization. Recent Congressional approval of executive powers to improve the organization of the executive branch is the latest stage in this trend.

There also has been a trend towards better coordination between government units seeking the economies of large scale organization. This has involved absorption of counties by expanding cities, consolidation of school districts, setting up of authorities or special districts to perform functions required by participating governments, and contractual agreements whereby one unit performs for the others.

The expansion of state administrative power and influence at the expense of the cities and counties has also played a part. County functions, for example, have tended to be absorbed by the states,

[30] See A. M. Freiberg, "How Government Buys: An Appraisal", *Public Policy* (Harvard University Press, 1941), for a description of the pre-World War II organization of purchasing in the federal government.

[31] For example, out of 40 state purchasing acts analyzed in 1931, 22 did not specifically vest the power to modify a requisition in the central purchasing office (L. D. White, *Trends*, pp. 207-8). Lack of the power to modify lessens the degree to which purchasing is truly centralized. In effect, the purchasing officer is then merely a purchasing clerk, and the advantages of centralized purchasing are considerably less than they would be if control by the central office were strong.

[32] L. D. White, *Introduction to the Study of Public Administration*, Ch. 2.

and supervision of "the inefficient county"[33] by state governments has come to be recognized as a need and some steps taken to meet it. But this trend is still in its infancy.

There is a question whether efforts at better public administration have done more than to offset, perhaps only in part, the inefficiencies that tend to creep in as government units and procedures and organization become obsolescent. In a world of constant change, continual reorganization — especially difficult in government, whose structure tends to be static — is necessary even to maintain efficiency. Like the efforts of the Red Queen, changes in public administration may have succeeded only in preventing a decline in organizational efficiency, rather than in advancing it beyond the point it had reached at the opening of the century.

The rising scale of operations of federal, state, and city governments raises another question. Many of these units have expanded to huge proportions. Would not this tend to cause waste rather than reduction of resources per unit of service rendered by government? A tendency for unit costs to rise when the size of establishment goes beyond some optimum point, supposed to affect private operations (the evidence is ambiguous), may have affected government operations.

On the other hand, the same rather vague reasoning suggests that an increase in the scale of operations before the optimum size is reached reduces costs; and some of the growth in government operations may have had this effect. Some students of public administration think that many smaller units of government are obsolete and that consolidation into larger units would make for more efficiency.[34] Thus counties with small populations (because of

---

[33] "Like an octopus or a centipede, the county is a governmental unit which has to be seen to be believed. . . . Their junketory, thriftless, expensive, ramshackle, outmoded governments. . . ." Miriam Roher, "The Patient Lived", *National Municipal Review*, Feb. 1939, p. 120.

[34] See, e.g., William Anderson, *The Units of Government in the United States*, Public Administration Service, Publication 83, 1942. Professor Anderson suggests that larger units would attract more able men, could be more easily watched by voters, and would reduce overhead and waste. For an excellent discussion of the inefficiencies of local government and the problems its reconstruction would encounter, see L. W. Lancaster, *Government in Rural America* (Van Nostrand, 1937), Ch. 15.

small area or low population density) tend to have higher per capita county government expenditures than more populated counties.[35] These higher per capita expenditures presumably reflect higher costs for a given level of service per capita, rather than more services per capita, for service per capita is probably positively correlated with population size. Here, too, the evidence is inadequate;[36] nor is it possible to reach a firm conclusion by *a priori* reasoning.

It does seem fair to suppose, however, that a very rapid rate of expansion, such as occurred in the federal government during the two wars, and has sometimes occurred in other governments when population grew very rapidly, will tend to depress efficiency rather severely for a time. (A contraction after a war or because of loss of population might have a similar effect. Inflation also lowers morale and accelerates turnover.) Those familiar with the inside of the federal government's operations under the impact of the defense and war programs and the subsequent reconversion will appreciate this possibility. Yet adjustments of one kind or another ultimately take place, given time. Some of the changes in administration previously noted are intended to be adjustments of this kind. As far as the *trend* is concerned — and it is the trend in which we are interested — there is no clear case for expecting that change in the scale of operations will exert any large influence on efficiency.

Probable Trend in Government's Productivity

Review of some factors affecting the trend of government productivity — the use of improved technology and equipment, the spread of the merit system, the introduction of centralized purchasing, and various other advances in public administration — leaves the im-

[35] Clarence Heer, "Comparative Costs of County Government in the South", *Social Forces,* December 1932; J. Berolzheimer, "Influences Shaping Expenditures for Operations of State and Local Governments", *Bulletin of the National Tax Association,* March, April, May, 1947; and below, Ch. 6.

[36] Mabel L. Walker once made a valiant attempt to prepare objective measures of service per capita rendered by cities and compare them with size of city and government cost per capita (*Municipal Expenditures,* Johns Hopkins Press, 1930). No important, or even significant, relation appears between size of city and cost per capita, at a given level of service per capita.

pression that labor savings have been made. Indeed, it is hard to think of any factor tending in the opposite direction except possibly the very increase in the scale of government operations.[37] Nor does it appear that these savings of labor reflect merely increase in the volume of other resources — capital goods and other purchases — used per worker. *Total* productivity, output per combined unit of all resources, appears to have risen in government.

It is well to emphasize the uncertainties surrounding this conclusion. Unable to weigh all the factors affecting productivity, we cannot be sure what the net balance is. Yet, as has been suggested, government operations are not entirely unlike those of private enterprise, however different the objectives and means of financing; nor are government bureaus cut off from technological changes. Strong forces make for the development and spread of progressive ideas: organized research within government, the instinct of workmanship of officials, independent municipal research bureaus,[38] organizations of public officials and citizens, government commissions and legislative committees,[39] the press. For the few areas of

[37] The slow pace with which government structure and administration are adjusted to new needs and new situations might be thought to be another negative factor. But to cause increase in unit labor requirements, however, the lag would have to grow longer and longer.

Mention may be made, also, of the political power wielded by civil service workers, which might prevent the introduction of some new machines or methods. (See Sterling D. Spero's interesting account of the struggle over the Taylor system in the Ordnance Department of the Army, *Government as Employer*, Remsen Press, 1948, Ch. 19.) This could only lessen the advance in productivity, not cause it to fall.

[38] These are a product of the twentieth century. The first Bureau of Municipal Research was set up in New York in 1906. By 1944 there were 20 principal privately supported municipal research bureaus; see N. N. Gill, *Municipal Research Bureaus* (American Council on Public Affairs, Washington, 1944).

[39] In his discussion of the Post Office, Bowden (Bureau of Labor Statistics *Bulletin 574*) mentions the Penrose-Overstreet Commission, a joint congressional commission on second class matter created in the Appropriations Act for 1906-07; the Joint Commission on Business Methods of the Post Office Department and the Postal Service, created by act of Congress of 1907; the Hughes Commission, another commission on second class matter, 1911; four commissions consisting of Post Office inspectors and representatives of the Division of Post Office Service, making during 1913 and 1914 extensive studies of principal post offices; the Joint Commission on the Postal Service, composed of certain members of the Senate and House Post Office Committees, established in 1920 to investigate conditions and needs in detail; and important

government for which some sort of measure can be attempted, for example, the postal service (Chart 15),[40] there is clearer evidence of substantial advance in productivity. It seems reasonably safe to assume that, as in practically all private industry, a given volume of government production is turned out today with a smaller input of resources than at the opening of the century. The long term trend in government's productivity has probably been upward.[41]

Whether government productivity rose more or less rapidly than

---

surveys by Department officials during 1929-31 of 55 principal offices and various operations. The most recent example is the Hoover Commission.

The very charges that government agencies are slow to profit from technological advance, frequently made by investigating commissions and citizens' committees, and the accompanying recommendations for equipment pooling and better maintenance procedures, for example, themselves provide evidence that government's productivity has been advancing.

[40] Even the trend revealed, distinctly and sharply upward though it is, understates the true rise in output per worker or per manhour in postal operations. The measure of output fails to take into account an important element of quality improvement in postal service (recall Ch. 4). The index of output per manhour also may be biased downward because of a probable decline in overtime not caught by the figures on hours, which measure only the regular work week.

While for this government activity we can at least measure, if only conservatively, the trend in output per man and per manhour, we cannot measure the rise in output relative to the input of all resources. There is some evidence that the Post Office does more of its own work now than formerly. Local transfer or carriage of bulk mails, e.g., largely performed by contractors in 1908, is now done by the Post Office's own employees and equipment; and the story is the same for star routes, a class of contractual carriers that has declined in relative importance. As for capital assets, the earlier review may give the impression that some increase has occurred relative to employment and manhours and perhaps also relative to output. But we have no specific information on this; and we should not fall into the error of assuming that improvements in capital equipment, and least of all improvements in organization, necessarily mean increases in capital per worker.

[41] Our inability to obtain a more definite notion of what has happened arises not because statistical data are unpublished, but because government officials do not even collect or analyze such data. Nor can this failure, in turn, be ascribed entirely to conceptual difficulties in determining government product and government productivity. Suggested measures (e.g., the interesting list prepared by Clarence E. Ridley and Herbert A. Simon, *Measuring Municipal Activities,* International City Managers' Association, 1943, 2d ed.) seem hardly to have been applied. Since such data are needed for the information and education of the public and its representatives, for the more efficient control of government operations, and for sound government programming and budgeting, it is surely the responsibility of government officials to collect and analyze them.

productivity in private enterprise is another matter, and one on which lack of information makes it idle to speculate. Another disclaimer may be in order. To hold that government productivity probably has advanced does not imply an opinion about its abso-

Chart 15
Postal System
Indexes of Output, Employment, Manhours, and Output per Employee and per Manhour, 1908–1940

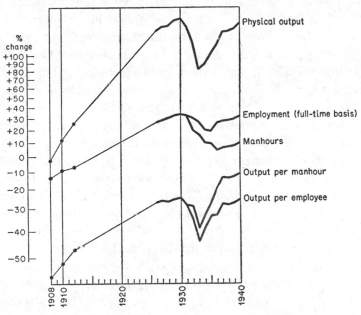

lute level or the relation of that level to the level in private business. Whether government is more or less efficient than nongovernment enterprise is another important question, but one not immediately relevant to the matter under discussion, and in any case not answerable with the data we have considered.

To sum up: Reduction in hours tended to raise employment and the quantity of capital goods used per unit of government product. The other factors we have noted worked, on net balance, in the opposite direction. The net result probably has been a decline in input relative to output. To put it conservatively, not much, if any, of the big increase in government input since 1900 can be attributed to the factors affecting the ratio between input and output. The major factor accounting for the increase in government's use of labor and other resources has been growth in government services.

Increase in Volume of Government Services: Some Indications of the Trend

The volume of government services today is larger than at the opening of the century. The question is, how much larger?

As we already know, there is no direct measure of total government output or even of a substantial sample of its components. We must therefore make shift with what we have learned about government input and productivity to obtain a notion of what has happened to the volume of government services.

Recall that employment in government rose about six-fold between 1900 and 1949. Suppose, as an extreme case, that output per government worker had not changed at all in this interval. Government output would then have risen 500 percent — the same as government employment. It is true that hours fell somewhat, but government capital assets at least kept pace with employment, and purchases grew more rapidly; and the burden of what evidence we have been able to muster is that output increased per unit of all resources, and therefore also per worker. Indeed, the estimate of a 500 percent increase in government output, large as it is, is probably conservative. Yet even a figure of 500 percent would put the rise of government output above that of the output of the private sector of the economy, which was under 300 percent.

Any assumption that productivity in government increased would, of course, widen the difference between the rise in government output and the rise in private output. Suppose, for example, that output per worker in government had risen as much as in private industry — of the order of 75 percent.[42] In that case, gov-

[42] The estimate rests on Simon Kuznets' calculation of real national income (*National Product since 1869*), brought up to 1949 by later unpublished estimates. It is supposed to apply to the whole economy, rather than to private industry alone; but the difference could not be large, and it may therefore be accepted as a rough measure for the latter.

ernment output went up between 1900 and 1949 by the very large amount of 1,000 percent ($1.75 \times 6 = 10.5$).

Readers taking a narrow view of government output may consider a rise of even 500 percent to be unbelievably high. It is necessary to point out, therefore, that the government output discussed here covers services to business and the community at large, as well as services to household and other final consumers. We are viewing the production of a sector of the economy, not the production of a class of final goods. Indeed, we need not concern ourselves with the difficult question: which government services are or are not final goods?[43] Municipal garbage collection is clearly a valuable service, whether we take it to be a final good or only a cost of living and working in cities not to be included in the aggregate net real income of city dwellers; and the same reasoning goes for national defense and similar government services. Further, government output includes all goods and services produced by government, whatever our individual tastes and predilections may lead us to think of their intrinsic value, and whatever some of us may believe their ultimate effect on the economy at large to be. Thus government services include anti-monopoly regulation and administration of tariffs and agricultural price supports, one or the other of which many feel to be detrimental activities. (Similarly, cigars are included in indexes of private output, though this commodity is frowned upon by some.)

Wider Scope and Variety of Government Services

The output of government services expanded through the spread of old services and the addition of new.

The volume of old services grew, first, through a wider diffusion among government units of types of service already rendered here and there in 1900. Every student of American history is familiar with the maps designed to show the states with certain types of legislation at a series of dates, and thus to describe the process of

[43] A brave attempt to set forth the criteria for such a determination will be found in Simon Kuznets' "Government Product and National Income", International Association for Research in Income and Wealth, *Income and Wealth, Series I* (Bowes and Bowes, Cambridge, 1951).

diffusion. In 1900, for example, one state already had legislation providing specifically for aid to the blind. By 1919 the number of states was 10; by 1929, 20; by 1935, 32; and now, under the stimulus of the Social Security Act, the number is 48.[44]

Education provides another example. The fact that standards for the length of school year set by the advanced states in 1900 were later met or approached by other states accounts almost wholly for the rise in public school days per school year from 99 in 1900 to 155 in 1948: there was little change in the length of the school year in the advanced states.[45]

Within areas in which various types of service were already offered, expansion has occurred through wider coverage of the resident population. The national figures on education are suggestive, though they are influenced also by other factors: in 1900, 72 percent of all children 5-17 were enrolled in public elementary and secondary schools, while in 1940 the percentage was 86. And coverage has been expanded also by widening the scope of old activities to absorb peripheral areas, such as extension and adult education courses and nursery classes. Here, of course, the distinction between old and new services becomes hazy.

The continuing trend toward urbanization has been another way in which a larger and larger proportion of the population has been provided various public services. The wide variety of municipal services offered by cities are now enjoyed by a larger percentage of the population than in 1900. The simple movement of people away from the farm and toward the city has thus played a part.

Not only has the percentage of the population enjoying specified public services risen, but there has been a trend also to a higher level of service per capita, such as by improvement in quality. The standard of hospital and institutional care generally has been pushed up: equipment and facilities now frequently include laboratories, X-ray machines, physiotherapy devices, and sun parlors; special dental and dietary services are sometimes provided; there

---

[44] A. E. Geddes, *Research Monograph X*, "Trends in Relief Expenditures, 1910-1935" (Works Progress Administration, 1937), pp. 91-2; *Statistical Abstract of the United States, 1949*, p. 269.

[45] In the next chapter we shall look more closely into the trend of interstate differences in government activity.

is closer segregation of age and disease groups (segregation of tubercular patients, first in wards, then in separate buildings, began early in the twentieth century) ; personnel is better trained and less overworked; hygienic procedures have been improved. Roads are wider, better graded, better paved, sometimes lighted, and more carefully marked; one can now drive from Jones Beach to Hartford over parkways with hardly a stop, little hazard, and some enjoyment. Better trained teachers listen to recitations; equipment in schools is better and more plentiful; pedagogical methods are next to the latest. In 1900 charity was doled out to paupers, usually in almshouses; today, public welfare services and funds are provided clients in their homes.[46]

And, finally, many new services have been added to the production of government units. The examples cited for Detroit, California, and the federal government may create an exaggerated impression of their number since services new to a particular unit of government are often already being rendered elsewhere by similar units or are functions transferred from another type of unit in the same region. But many services new to the United States did appear. Technological advance made possible and sometimes necessary services not possible in 1900. And some services possible, but not provided in 1900, came to be offered by government.[47] Not until the twentieth century, for example, did government really try to conserve our natural resources.

Encroachment on the Private Sphere?

Did government's encroachment on the private sphere play any large role in expanding government activity? The answer hinges on how one defines encroachment. It depends, first, on whether

[46] M. P. Smith, "Trends in Municipal Administration of Public Welfare, 1900-1930", *Social Forces,* March 1932.

[47] Examples of new services and changes in old services are frequently available in the vast number of annual reports of city, county, state, and federal units. Excellent summaries for the federal government appear in the monographs, one for each of 66 federal agencies, published by the Institute of Government Research of the Brookings Institution during the 1920's and 1930's. A recent review of the growth of government's various activities in the field of real estate finance is given by M. L. Colean, *The Impact of Government on Real Estate Finance in the United States* (National Bureau of Economic Research, 1950)

one considers encroachment to be expansion by government in all or only in certain areas of production; and second, on whether one measures encroachment by absolute increase in government's output or only by increase in government's share of output.

The question may be put most narrowly in terms of the area of production in which public enterprises participate. Government in the United States operates many more enterprises than it did in 1900. For the federal government as many as 42 are now listed by the National Income Division of the Department of Commerce.[48] Except for the Post Office, and presumably the armed forces post exchanges and ship stores, none of these existed in 1900.

In 1949 a little over half the state governments operated enterprises, the most important of which were alcoholic beverage monopoly systems, but including also airports, harbors, ferries, and other enterprises. Workmen's compensation funds may also be considered as enterprises for the present purpose. The most important of these were absent in 1900, to judge by their nature (the airports), the factors accounting for them (the alcoholic beverage monopoly systems came into existence after the repeal of the prohibition amendment), or what we know of the time when relevant legislation was passed (the workmen's compensation laws in the country are entirely a fruit of the twentieth century).

[48] The full list follows: Agricultural Marketing Act Revolving Fund, Alaska Railroad Company, Army Post Exchanges, Banks for Cooperatives, Bonneville Power Administration, Boulder Canyon Project, Commodity Credit Corporation, Defense Homes Corporation, Disaster Loan Corporation, Electric Home and Farm Authority, Emergency Crop and Feed Loans, Export-Import Bank, Federal Crop Insurance Corporation, Federal Deposit Insurance Corporation, Federal Farm Mortgage Corporation, Federal Home Loan Bank System, Federal Housing Administration, Federal Intermediate Credit Banks, Federal Land Banks, Federal National Mortgage Association, Federal Prison Industries, Inc., Federal Public Housing Authority, Federal Savings and Loan Insurance Corporation, Home Owners Loan Corporation, Inland Waterways Corporation, Navy Ship Stores and Ship's Service Stores, Panama Canal Zone, Panama Railroad Company, Petroleum Reserves Corporation, Post Office, Production Credit Corporations, Reconstruction Finance Corporation (including Office of Defense Plants, Defense Supplies, Metals Reserve, and Rubber Reserve), Regional Agricultural Credit Corporations, RFC Mortgage Company, Rubber Development Corporation, Rural Electrification Administration, Smaller War Plants Corporation, Tennessee Valley Authority, U. S. Commercial Company, U. S. Maritime Commission (operating activities), War Damage Corporation, War Shipping Administration (commercial operating and war risk insurance activities). *Survey of Current Business,* National Income Supplement, 1947, Table 8, note 17.

One or more utilities and enterprises are currently owned and operated by nine-tenths of our municipalities. Indeed, public enterprises constituted the leading function of cities in 1942 (Table 13).[49] It has also been one of the most rapidly growing (Table 20). Some of this growth may have come about simply through increase in the average population per city, for more of the bigger than of the smaller cities own and operate enterprises.[50] More significant appears to have been increase in the number of cities, which doubled; greater per capita output of water, electricity, and so on, by utilities already held in 1900; and the acquisition of new utilities, e.g., local transportation, taken over from private operators

[49] Ownership and operation of specified public utilities by cities with populations over 5,000 was as follows in 1950:

UTILITY	CITIES REPORTING OWNERSHIP AND OPERATION OF SPECIFIED UTILITY AS A PERCENTAGE OF ALL CITIES	
	Number	Population
Auditorium	19	29
Bus or trolley bus system	2	22
Street railway	0.4	21
Electric distribution only	8	4
Electric generation and distribution	13	11
Gas distribution only	2	1
Gas manufacturing and distribution	2	6
Incinerator	14	52
Port facilities	4	27
Sewage treatment plant	48	63
Slaughter house	2	1
Water distribution only	6	3
Water supply and distribution	68	81
Airport	21	45
One or more of above	89	95
Not reporting	0.4	0.2

Source: *Municipal Year Book, 1950.* Utilities owned but not operated by cities are excluded.

[50] This is suggested by the difference between the two columns in the preceding note's tabulation and the fact that population per city averaged 17,000 in 1900, 22,000 in 1940. However, in 1903 waterworks were operated by cities accounting for 86 percent of the population of all cities over 25,000, as compared with 84 percent of cities over 5,000 in 1950; and the corresponding percentages for electric power were 15 as against 15; and for gas works, 8 as against 8. (Data for 1903 are reported in Census *Bulletin 20,* "Statistics of Cities Having a Population of over 25,000, 1902 and 1903," Table 9.) The 1950 figures are too small because of the inclusion of cities under 25,000. However, for these three utilities — among the largest of municipal enterprises — increase in average size of city seems to have had little effect.

suffering under the handicap of competing transport and rigid fares.

In addition to the increase in federal, state, and municipal utilities, there has developed the type of government unit exemplified by the Port of New York Authority, included in earlier tables among "special districts". Most of these were set up to handle (and finance) new toll bridges and highways and, a product of the twentieth century, public housing projects. The trend, then, has been up here, too.

Data on the output of public enterprises are inadequate, but employment suggests what has happened. Public enterprises employed in 1949 as much as 5.6 times the 1900 number. Relative to other government activities, however, public enterprises merely held their position. They employed no more than 10 percent of all government workers in 1949, 11 percent in 1900 (Table 15). While they contributed to the growth of government activity, they cannot be held accountable for more than a tenth or so of the increase. Measured in this way and in this sense, increased "socialization" of production was a cause of the rise in government production but not a large cause.[51]

Part of the increase in public enterprises came simply because many of the industries in which government operates enterprises (water works, electric power, and the Post Office, for example) have grown relative to most other industries. Even a constant government share of these growing industries would have meant relative expansion of government enterprise. Encroachment, therefore, might be measured only by increase in government's share (which occurred, e.g., in electric power,[52] banking, liquor stores, and local

[51] Perhaps we need to keep in mind that to most Europeans, used to public ownership of the railroads, the telephone, and the telegraph, and even such ventures as mines, the dimensions of public enterprise in this country would seem very modest, and the trend here anything but one towards socialization. In this connection it is interesting to note that if all the railroads and the telephone and telegraph were publicly owned and operated in this country (and — a hazardous assumption — these industries were as large and as efficient in government as in private hands), government employment would be two million larger today, and public employment would account for one out of every six workers.

[52] Publicly owned electric utilities accounted for 8 percent of total utility power produced in 1902, 5 percent in 1922, 10 percent in 1939, and 20 percent in

transit). So measured, encroachment by public enterprises accounted for substantially less than a tenth of the increase in government activity.

Attention need not be confined to public enterprises, which are simply those so financed that their costs are largely or entirely borne by fees or charges levied on the user of their services. Government may be said to encroach on the private sphere also by expanding those of its services for which there is no specific or significant charge to the consumer, but which are also privately produced in relatively substantial quantities. The question now becomes: did absorption by government of functions commonly performed at the opening of the century by private enterprise (as well as by government) play any role in expanding government activity?

The difficulty here (not to mention lack of adequate data) is deciding which functions of government were commonly performed at the opening of the century also by private enterprise. However, we may obtain some rough idea of the possible effect of government encroachment on this area if we suppose that all government functions other than general control, national defense and other public safety, highways, natural resources, and half of the miscellaneous group fall within it. This means including all of sanitation and waste removal, health and hospitals, public welfare, schools, public enterprises, and the other half of the miscellaneous group — surely more than most people would want to.

Growth of these functions accounted for about half of the increase in government expenditures, excluding transfers, between 1903 and the period just before World War II (Tables 7 and 14), less over the full half-century. If we interpret *all* growth in these functions above the level at the opening of the century as encroachment on the private sphere, a very substantial portion indeed of growth in government activity has been the result of encroachment — even after liberal allowance for including rather more functions than we should.

The inquiry may be directed, alternatively, at the change in the

1949: Bureau of the Census, *Historical Statistics of the United States, 1789-1945,* and *Statistical Abstract of the United States, 1951,* Series G184 and G186.

fraction of these functions or industries performed by government, rather than at the absolute change. There is evidence that government's share in a number of them did rise. Voluntary societies have expanded their welfare activities, but government's activities in this field have grown even more rapidly, before as well as after 1929.[53] Housing is an obvious example that does not need documentation. The rise in government's share in finance (from zero in 1900) is indicated by the simple list given in Table 17 of new federal agencies in this field.[54] Enrollments in public institutions of higher learning accounted for 38 percent of total enrollments in 1900, 53 percent in 1940.[55] Government's share in hospitals rose somewhat — from 62 percent of the beds in 1923 to 71 percent in 1949.[56] And it is likely also, though figures are lacking, that government's share in other medical services, and perhaps also construction (including roads), has increased.

On the other hand, private elementary and secondary schools have grown somewhat more rapidly than public: academic personnel, from 7.7 percent of the total in 1900 to 10.5 percent in 1946.[57] And this "industry" is the largest of those mentioned (except construction, about which the trend is more doubtful).

On the whole, however, it is probable that the trend has been up in government's share in this group of activities. There has been decline in the share not only of private enterprise of the profit-making variety, but also of private nonprofit organizations. Just how important a factor this type of encroachment has been, measured in the terms available (employment, real investment, and purchases of goods and services), it is difficult to say, however. Let us suppose that only in education did government fail to grow

[53] Geddes, *loc. cit.*, summarizes the data on outdoor relief expenditures by both private and public agencies for 1910-35.

[54] One would have to go back to the first half of the nineteenth century to find any important amount of direct government activity in the financial field.

[55] President's Commission on Higher Education, cited by George Stigler, *Employment and Compensation in Education* (National Bureau of Economic Research, Occasional Paper 33, 1950), p. 33.

[56] Bureau of the Census, *Historical Statistics of the United States*, Series C105-111; *Statistical Abstract of the United States, 1951*.

[57] Stigler, *op. cit.*, p. 1.

relative to private enterprise; and that *all* government activity in all the other functions had arisen only since 1900, i.e., that the share of government in these functions was zero in 1900. On this rather extreme assumption, about a fourth of the increase in government input (and presumably output) between 1900 and 1940 — less between 1900 and today — would be accounted for by encroachment on the private sphere. This is surely too high a figure. It seems reasonably safe to conclude, therefore, that in the sense considered, encroachment on the private sphere has not been the major factor in swelling government operations, though it has surely played a substantial part.

Encroachment may be defined much more broadly, finally, to include expansion of government services that are also privately produced even in slight degree, or of government services that *could* be produced by private contractors. (In principle, production of these services wholly by government contractors, to be distributed gratis, or even — in some cases — by independent private industry to state-subsidized consumers, is not impossible.) If this be considered encroachment on the private sphere, most of the expansion of government activity since 1900 may be said to have involved encroachment. For there is some private counterpart to most government produced services — witness private watchmen. And there are many services, rendered gratis to the public because government financed, already produced by private contractors — for example, road building and maintenance, and beds for the indigent in private hospitals. But few would wish to put the question in this way.

Encroachment on the private sphere through government subsidies, loans, regulations, tariffs, price supports, and similar means not involving direct ownership and operation is, of course, another matter. It is a matter of great importance. Constriction of the area of the free market, though aimed at obviously beneficial effects, can have serious and less obvious effects on the efficiency of the economy and its rate of advance. Such far-reaching government activities still account for only a small part of the whole job of government, measured by number of workers or other resources used; but these measures are not appropriate.

CHAPTER 6

Interstate Differences in Government Activity

Observation of the time of change, functional pattern of change, and shifts among types of government unit has contributed to our understanding of the trend of government activity and paved the way to further analysis of the factors underlying it. Something should be contributed also by seeing how government activity varies among the states, to which our attention has been drawn by the discussion in the preceding chapter.[1]

To avoid being diverted by differences among states in the division of responsibility among the several layers of government, we shall study state and local government in combination.[2] The government activity of a state will be measured by the aggregate of the expenditures or employment of the state and local governments in it.[3]

---

[1] Readers will discover that the following analysis is rather more technical (and tentative) than that in preceding chapters. It may be skipped without losing the main thread of the discussion.

[2] Expenditure data are available for each of the several types of government unit in each state as well as for each state as a whole. But the states vary among themselves in division of activity among the several types; in some states certain types of unit are entirely absent, or appear only rarely. For example, the percentage of nonschool state and local government employment on *state* government payrolls in April 1945 ranged from 11 in Wisconsin to 58 in West Virginia (*Government Employment, State Distribution of Public Employment in April 1945,* Vol. 6, No. 4, July 1946). The township and town type of government is not used at all in the southern and some western states; in some states there are no special school districts; some states go in for special districts for highways and sewers, others do not; etc.

Some of this variation in intrastate structure of government is associated with the very factors in which we are interested, e.g., urbanization: the percentages mentioned in the preceding paragraph and corresponding percentages of population in urban areas are negatively correlated.

[3] The expenditures analyzed are those on current operation alone, exclusive of outlays on capital assets and enterprises. Employment covers enterprises as well as operation.

Interstate Differences in per Capita Government Expenditure and Employment

Considerable variation among states in the volume of government activity is our first impression from Table 21. Whether we measure activity by per capita expenditure or by per capita employment, the disparity among states is large in both years covered. The extreme ranges are very wide, of course: total expenditures per capita in 1942, for example, ranged from $21 to $100; and employment per 10,000 population, from 167 to 417. But even the less erratic measure of variation given in the next to the last column, the interquartile range, shows wide dispersion in 1942: $21 per capita in the case of expenditures, 80 workers per 10,000 population in the case of employment.

When states vary so widely in level of activity according to these measures, it is proper to ask whether the differences are exaggerated by peculiarities of the measures. The dollar figures on expenditure, in particular, may seem suspect. For they are affected by state differences in price levels, and these price differences are positively correlated with dollar expenditures.[4] But the price differ-

---

[4] On price differences we have three major types of information. One relates to the urban-rural cost of living differential. According to N. Koffsky, "Farm and Urban Purchasing Power", *Studies in Income and Wealth, Volume Eleven* (National Bureau of Economic Research, 1949), p. 170, the cost of living on farms in 1941 was 77 to 88 percent of the corresponding cost of living in cities. The lower percentage relates to the goods and services customarily purchased by farmers; the higher, to goods and services purchased by city families. (Food price differentials contribute a good deal to these differences in price levels.)

The second type of data shows intercity differences in the cost of living. Taking the highest cost city as the reference base (100), the range for 59 cities in March 1935 extended to a low of 80 percent ("maintenance level" budget, 4-person manual worker's family, M. L. Stecker, "Intercity Differences in Costs of Living in March 1935, 59 Cities", WPA, *Research Monograph XII,* 1937, p. 5); for 33 cities on December 15, 1941, to 84 percent (the WPA budget carried forward, "Cost of Living in 1941", *BLS Bulletin 710,* 1942, p. 37); for 34 cities in June 1947 to 88 percent (the city workers "modest but adequate" budget, 4-person family, "Workers' Budget in the United States: City Families and Single Persons, 1946 and 1947", *BLS Bulletin 927,* 1948, p. 23). The interquartile range is much less, of course: 85 to 93 for the March 1935 date — the full range is 80 to 100. It should be noted that the cost of living is correlated with size of city.

Third, to judge from census data on government payrolls and employment, government salary levels rise with the size of city. In cities of 25,000 to 50,000 the average salary seems to be about 80 percent of the average in cities of

(*Footnote concluded on p. 116*)

Table 21

INTERSTATE DIFFERENCES IN STATE AND LOCAL GOVERNMENT
EXPENDITURES PER CAPITA BY FUNCTION (1903, 1942, AND CHANGE
BETWEEN 1903 AND 1942); AND IN STATE AND LOCAL GOVERNMENT
EMPLOYMENT PER CAPITA, SCHOOL AND NONSCHOOL (1942)

(Unit for expenditures is dollars per capita; for employment,
number of workers per 10,000)

	Top State	1st Quartile	2nd Quartile (Median)	3rd Quartile	Bottom State	Difference between 1st and 3rd Quartile	Coefficient of Variation[a]
Expenditures[b]							
General control							
1903	8.4	3.0	2.2	1.4	.51	1.6	36
1942	14.4	6.0	4.7	3.9	2.0	2.1	22
Ratio, 1942 to 1903	5.0	3.0	2.2	1.8	.9	1.2	27
Public safety							
1903	3.4	1.2	.62	.30	.10	.85	69
1942	11.4	6.2	4.2	2.6	1.2	3.6	43
Ratio, 1942 to 1903	57.9	9.0	6.1	4.4	2.6	4.6	38
Highways							
1903	3.3	2.0	1.2	.81	.34	1.2	50
1942	16.4	8.3	6.5	5.1	2.9	3.2	25
Ratio, 1942 to 1903	19.4	7.4	5.6	3.8	1.9	3.6	32
Schools							
1903	10.0	4.7	3.7	2.7	.97	2.0	27
1942	27.5	20.7	19.0	14.3	8.3	6.4	17
Ratio, 1942 to 1903	12.9	6.0	5.0	4.0	2.4	2.0	20
Sanitation							
1903	1.8	.25	.14	.04	.00	.21	75
1942	3.3	1.4	.78	.52	.14	.86	55
Ratio, 1942 to 1903	*	12.0	7.0	4.6	.8	7.4	53
Health, hospitals & public welfare							
1903	3.3	1.4	.92	.66	.21	.72	39
1942	26.2	15.1	12.4	9.7	3.4	5.4	22
Ratio, 1942 to 1903	64.6	15.2	11.7	9.2	6.6	6.0	26
Other							
1903	4.5	.94	.62	.39	.16	.55	44
1942	11.7	6.6	5.3	3.5	1.9	3.1	29
Ratio, 1942 to 1903	17.4	11.5	8.6	6.2	1.8	5.3	31
Total							
1903	24.2	12.8	10.6	6.4	3.0	6.4	30
1942	99.8	65.1	54.3	43.7	21.4	21.4	20
Ratio, 1942 to 1903	9.7	6.4	5.4	4.5	3.1	1.9	18

	Top State	1st Quartile	2nd Quartile (Median)	3rd Quartile	Bottom State	Difference between 1st and 3rd Quartile	Coefficient of Variation[a]
Employment[c]							
Schools							
1942	171	131	107	93	76	38	18
Other							
1942	276	174	156	112	73	62	20
Total							
1942	417	297	260	217	167	80	15

* Denominator is zero.

[a] Semi-interquartile distance as a percentage of the median.

[b] For 1942 further details are available on expenditures, as follows (column headings have been omitted):

Public safety							
Police	6.0	3.1	2.1	1.4	.64	1.7	41
Fire	4.1	1.9	1.0	.68	.28	1.2	60
Other	3.0	1.2	.91	.54	.23	.65	36
Health, hospitals & public welfare							
Health & hospitals	8.9	4.4	3.4	2.3	1.4	2.1	31
Public welfare	21.8	11.0	9.1	4.9	2.0	6.1	34

[c] The employment data include part-time and temporary workers. For non-school functions we have a rough calculation of the full-time equivalent number as well as a calculation limited to permanent full-time employees:

Permanent full-time employees, 1942	175	125	100	76	56	49	24
Full-time equivalent employees, 1942	195	142	126	92	61	50	20

Expenditures include transfers to the public (except interest payments), but not outlays and expenditures of enterprises. Employment includes public enterprises.

ences are small compared with the expenditure differences and therefore could hardly account for much of the variation we find. Nor, it seems, is much trouble caused by the inclusion of transfers to the public (which swell the expenditure figures, especially in 1942), or by the exclusion of capital input. The variation in expenditures appears to be a good indication of the variation in real input. This conclusion is supported, in part at least, by the available data on government employment, for the latter are not questionable in the same way as the expenditure data.

When interest lies in interstate differences in government service per capita — output, rather than input — we need to ask also about the effect of possible differences in productivity. To the extent that there is interchange of information on methods and similarity of conditions and people through the country (even villages use motorized equipment and typewriters) variation in productivity will be kept down. But that interstate differences in productivity exist is certain. However, if the frequently expressed opinion that the rural county and small village are inefficient is grounded in fact, the correlation between productivity and level of per capita input is positive, not negative; for input rises with degree of urbanization and size of county and city. This would mean that interstate differences in input understate rather than exaggerate interstate differences in output or services.

We note, second, that the several functions are characterized by substantially different degrees of variation. For this comparison the

---

(Footnote concluded from p. 113)

1,000,000 or more (with rough allowance for part-time workers; basic data from *Public Employment in the United States: January 1942,* State and Local Government Quarterly Employment Survey, Vol. 3, No. 5, Final General Summary for Jan. 1942, p. 40). (The data for cities under 25,000 are rendered almost useless for the present purpose by the very high proportion of part-time workers, for which a sufficiently precise reduction to a full-time equivalent basis is difficult.) Further allowance for the higher level of skill and training of workers in large cities would probably reduce this range.

It is clear that the price level of a state that is largely rural and whose cities are small will be lower than the price level of an urbanized state containing many big cities. But the difference will not be large compared with the difference between government expenditures. The lower quartile value of government expenditures, 1942, was two-thirds the upper quartile; and the bottom state's expenditures in 1942 was a fifth of the expenditures of the top state (Table 21). Further, while the price level is undoubtedly correlated with dollar expenditure, the correlation is not perfect.

best measure is a coefficient of variation expressing the semi-interquartile range as a percentage of the median. So measured, the largest degree of variation, in both 1903 and 1942, is in expenditures on sanitation and public safety; the least, in school expenditures.

Although our eyes are focused on differences among the states, rather than similarities, we cannot escape taking notice, next, of certain strong points of resemblance. Our third observation, then, relates to changes in the relative importance of the several functions. We have already seen (Chapter 4) what these were: the average change in health, hospitals and public welfare, for example, was large, while that in general control was small. In Table 21 this is indicated by the relative standing of the median ratios of 1942 to 1903.[5] Table 21 tells us further, however, that the relative standing of the average (median) change in a function is representative of the relative standing of the whole distribution of 48 changes it summarizes. In *most* states, expenditures on health and welfare rose very rapidly; in *most* states, expenditures on general control rose modestly:

Ratio of 1942 to 1903, expenditures per capita

	1st Quartile Value	2nd Quartile Value	3rd Quartile Value
Health, hospitals & public welfare	15	12	9.2
Other	12	8.6	6.2
Sanitation	12	7.0	4.6
Public safety	9.0	6.1	4.4
Highways	7.4	5.6	3.8
Schools	6.0	5.0	4.0
General control	3.0	2.2	1.8

The ranking in all three columns is almost identical. We may go further: as is demonstrated in Table 22, in which the individual states are presented, patterns of change are similar from state to state.

Even more striking is the change between 1903 and 1942 in the degree of variation among state levels of per capita expenditure on

[5] Each median ratio is the median of the 48 individual state ratios of 1942 to 1903 per capita expenditure, *not* the ratio of the median expenditure for 1942 to the median expenditure for 1903; and correspondingly for the quartiles and extremes.

Table 22

CHANGE IN THE FUNCTIONAL DISTRIBUTION OF GOVERNMENT EXPENDITURES PER CAPITA, 1903-1942

INDIVIDUAL STATES

STATE AND LOCAL GOVERNMENT EXPENDITURES PER CAPITA, RATIO OF 1942 TO 1903 AND RANK OF RATIO

	General Control	Public Safety	Highways	Schools	Health, Hospitals, & Public Welfare	Sanitation	Other
Alabama	3.1(7)	10.0(3)	8.9(5)	6.7(6)	9.2(4)	14.3(1)	11.0(2)
Arizona	1.5(7)	7.4(3)	6.4(5)	5.7(6)	16.0(2)	*(1)	6.5(4)
Arkansas	2.1(7)	7.2(4)	3.7(6)	4.7(5)	12.4(2)	14.0(1)	11.8(3)
California	1.6(7)	4.0(3)	2.2(6)	2.6(5)	9.3(1)	4.0(4)	6.0(2)
Colorado	1.2(7)	2.6(5)	3.4(4)	2.4(6)	19.0(1)	3.4(3)	4.2(2)
Connecticut	3.8(5)	5.1(4)	3.2(7)	5.6(3)	9.9(1)	3.5(6)	8.1(2)
Delaware	3.0(7)	6.1(3)	4.0(6)	5.8(4)	12.9(2)	5.2(5)	13.8(1)
Florida	4.2(7)	12.1(3)	6.1(6)	7.3(5)	15.0(1)	9.6(4)	13.7(2)
Georgia	3.7(6)	5.3(5)	3.0(7)	7.0(4)	7.4(3)	7.4(2)	9.4(1)
Idaho	1.1(7)	28.0(2)	6.0(5)	3.2(6)	15.3(3)	*(1)	14.6(4)
Illinois	2.2(7)	3.7(5)	3.4(6)	5.2(4)	16.8(1)	7.2(3)	9.7(2)
Indiana	1.6(7)	5.2(4)	4.3(5)	3.8(6)	12.5(1)	6.1(3)	10.1(2)
Iowa	1.7(7)	5.0(6)	5.7(5)	6.4(4)	9.2(2)	6.9(3)	10.1(1)
Kansas	1.7(7)	4.5(6)	6.9(4)	5.1(5)	15.3(1)	8.2(2)	7.1(3)
Kentucky	2.3(7)	4.4(4)	3.9(5)	3.5(6)	7.4(1)	4.6(3)	6.3(2)
Louisiana	3.0(6)	6.6(5)	7.1(3)	10.0(2)	25.7(1)	.8(7)	6.7(4)
Maine	1.8(7)	4.6(5)	7.0(3)	4.8(4)	7.2(2)	3.1(6)	12.9(1)
Maryland	2.2(7)	4.1(6)	4.5(5)	5.0(4)	11.7(1)	6.2(3)	7.5(2)
Massachusetts	2.1(4)	3.2(3)	1.9(5)	3.9(2)	7.0(1)	1.3(7)	1.8(6)
Michigan	2.3(7)	6.1(5)	6.9(4)	4.9(6)	14.7(1)	10.0(3)	10.7(2)
Minnesota	1.8(7)	4.1(6)	4.3(4)	4.2(5)	15.7(1)	7.0(2)	6.2(3)
Mississippi	3.0(7)	6.0(5)	12.5(2)	5.8(6)	9.5(4)	15.5(1)	12.0(3)

Missouri	2.3(6)	3.5(3)	3.4(4)	5.2(2)	15.2(1)	2.8(5)	2.0(7)
Montana	1.1(7)	2.6(6)	4.9(2)	3.4(5)	7.4(1)	3.9(4)	4.6(3)
Nebraska	2.0(7)	6.2(5)	6.5(4)	4.6(6)	16.4(2)	17.2(1)	12.3(3)
Nevada	1.7(7)	57.9(1)	19.1(3)	3.1(6)	6.6(5)	45.5(2)	9.0(4)
New Hampshire	2.0(7)	5.7(4)	5.2(5)	5.9(3)	8.3(2)	5.0(6)	11.2(1)
New Jersey	3.6(7)	5.3(4)	3.8(6)	5.1(5)	10.5(1)	6.4(3)	9.1(2)
New Mexico	1.8(7)	9.4(4)	19.4(2)	12.9(3)	20.4(1)	6.0(6)	6.4(5)
New York	2.1(7)	3.3(5)	2.4(6)	4.1(3)	9.1(1)	3.5(4)	5.7(2)
North Carolina	5.0(7)	16.4(1)	7.3(6)	12.9(2)	9.2(4)	12.4(3)	9.1(5)
North Dakota	.9(7)	9.4(3)	6.0(4)	3.5(5)	12.3(1)	12.3(2)	3.4(6)
Ohio	2.4(7)	4.5(4)	4.4(5)	4.2(6)	9.6(1)	5.7(3)	6.9(2)
Oklahoma	3.0(7)	17.5(2)	9.7(4)	6.1(6)	64.6(1)	14.0(3)	6.4(5)
Oregon	2.0(7)	9.2(2)	4.4(5)	3.3(6)	12.9(1)	4.6(4)	8.1(3)
Pennsylvania	2.7(6)	3.6(4)	2.6(7)	5.0(3)	11.3(1)	3.4(5)	5.1(2)
Rhode Island	3.2(5)	3.4(4)	2.0(7)	4.5(3)	8.9(1)	2.5(6)	5.2(2)
South Carolina	3.2(7)	8.6(6)	8.8(5)	10.3(4)	11.6(2)	10.5(3)	17.4(1)
South Dakota	1.9(7)	14.3(2)	12.3(3)	3.7(6)	11.7(4)	340.0(1)	10.2(5)
Tennessee	2.9(7)	7.4(5)	8.5(3)	8.5(2)	13.3(1)	7.8(4)	6.9(6)
Texas	2.7(7)	9.1(3)	7.4(4)	4.7(6)	10.7(1)	9.6(2)	5.4(5)
Utah	1.9(7)	6.5(3)	4.5(6)	7.1(2)	29.0(1)	4.8(5)	6.2(4)
Vermont	3.9(7)	11.3(3)	5.6(5)	4.6(6)	11.7(2)	7.0(4)	14.9(1)
Virginia	4.2(7)	8.8(3)	7.9(4)	6.7(5)	9.1(2)	5.6(6)	12.1(1)
Washington	1.5(7)	7.6(3)	2.4(6)	3.2(5)	21.0(1)	11.7(2)	5.2(4)
West Virginia	2.9(7)	7.6(5)	9.8(4)	5.2(6)	13.3(2)	11.0(3)	13.3(1)
Wisconsin	2.0(7)	5.2(5)	5.8(4)	5.2(6)	12.7(2)	15.7(1)	9.0(3)
Wyoming	1.7(7)	6.1(5)	8.1(3)	5.4(6)	7.1(4)	11.8(2)	14.1(1)
Average Rank	6.8	4.0	4.7	4.6	1.7	3.4	2.9

* Denominator is 0.

Figure in parentheses is the rank of each ratio.

each function. The coefficients of variation were reduced for every function listed in Table 21 as well as for the total. Indeed, the average cut was about a third. For the total, moreover, the coefficient of variation that can be calculated for 1932 lies between the coefficients for 1903 and 1942, and the coefficient for 1890 is above the one for 1903. The figures for 1903 and 1942 lie on a downward sloping trend line.[6] There appears to have been appreciable leveling-out of government services provided by the 48 states.

We know that every state expanded practically every one of its services.[7] The leveling-out process therefore meant faster than average increases by states that were backward in 1903. It is apparent in Chart 16 that a state with a per capita expenditure of $4 in 1903 had, on the average, multiplied its expenditures about 6.5-fold by 1942; one with an expenditure of $10 in 1903, about 5.5-fold; and a state in the upper ranks of 1903, say with an expenditure of $20, less than 4-fold. Corresponding pictures for the several individual functions would be similar. The vanguard states of 1903 moved ahead and kept their relatively advanced positions. The rearguard states also moved ahead but remained in the rear. The relative distance between the front and rear was reduced in

---

[6] The coefficients of variation in total per capita expenditures are as follows: 1890, 37 percent; 1903, 30 percent; 1932, 27 percent; 1942, 20 percent. The 1890 coefficient is derived from data given in *Wealth, Debt, and Taxation, 1890;* that for 1932, from data in *Historical Review of State and Local Government Finances,* pp. 31-2 (both, Census Bureau). The 1890 data exclude Oklahoma and otherwise are not quite comparable with those for later years. However, the coefficient for 1903 based on data comparable with those for 1890 is barely different from the coefficient above.

These changes too could have been influenced by the price and productivity factors mentioned earlier. It is quite likely, e.g., that reduced difference in degree of urbanization (over a half, measured by the interquartile coefficient of variation, between 1900 and 1940) helped lessen price disparities; but it could also have lessened productivity disparities, which may be inversely correlated with price disparities. The net effect is likely to have been small compared with the changes in Table 21.

[7] Table 21 shows that the *lowest* 1942/1903 ratio for some functions was under 2. Prices rose by a ratio of 2 or more, which would suggest a decline in per capita real input (of labor and purchased goods and services) by some states. On the other hand, productivity probably rose. There seems to be hardly any exception to the statement in the text, and any exception that appears might well result from deficiencies in the statistics, especially with respect to classification of expenditures by functions.

Chart 16

States Classified by Total Expenditures on Current Operations Per Capita in 1903 and 1942

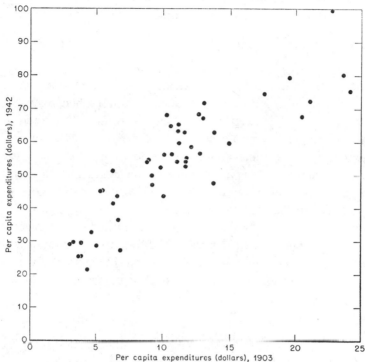

every function listed.[8]

This might easily be interpreted in terms of a diffusion of standards: at given levels of ability to pay or need for government service (e.g., urbanization) there may have developed more uni-

---

[8] Decline in degree of difference as measured by the coefficient of variation does not, of course, mean decline in absolute difference. If we measure the latter by the difference between the first and third quartiles the absolute difference rose, from 1903 to 1942, in every function except general control and schools. (The comparison has to be in constant prices; for this purpose we used price indexes of 206.5 for nonschool expenditures, 350.8 for school expenditures, and 245.4 for total expenditures, 1942 relative to 1903; see App. D.) The interquartile difference for total expenditures rose from $6.4 to $8.7 (measured in 1903 prices), or 36 percent. It is sensible, however, to compare this with the rise in the median — which of course is what our coefficients of variation do.

formity in levels of service provided. But there could also be another factor: ability to pay or need for service might have become more uniform too. This poses the question of the factors affecting government activity, which is the problem of the next section.

Factors Affecting Interstate Differences in Government Expenditure in 1942

Tracing relationships between government activity and the factors affecting it involves a good deal of speculation. To help keep our feet on the ground, let us start by taking advantage of the quantitative information made possible by our system of government. For each of the 48 more or less independent jurisdictions there are, as we have seen, separate statistics on aggregate state and local government activity in 1942 — only a part of total government activity in this country, it is true, but a substantial part.

These data reveal considerable interstate differences in government activity. How are these interstate differences in amount and kind of activity associated with three measurable factors to which previous work in the field points: income, urbanization, and density of population?[9]

[9] Arnold Brecht, "Three Topics in Comparative Administration — Organization of Government Departments, Government Corporations, Expenditures in Relation to Population", *Public Policy* (Harvard University Press, 1941); an article by members of Gerhard Colm's seminar at the New School for Social Research, "Public Expenditures and Economic Structure in the United States", *Social Research,* February 1936; and J. Berolzheimer, "Influences Shaping Expenditure for Operation of State and Local Governments", *Bulletin of the National Tax Association,* March, April, May, 1947. We have benefited also from reading a draft of Carol P. Brainerd's doctoral dissertation, "Non-federal Governments and their Growth, 1909-1948" (University of Pennsylvania).

Other measurable factors might be listed, e.g., industrialization and size of government unit. But there is a limit to what our data can stand — there are only 48 observations — and to what we can do. On the other hand, these factors are usually correlated with the three we have selected for analysis and are therefore more or less represented by them. Indeed, as we shall see, there is a question whether anything is gained by including urbanization.

To avoid the influence of short-run fluctuations in income, we take the average of income in 1938-42 to be the measure of this factor. Government activity in a given year is influenced more by the average income of the preceding five years than by the current level of income.

Note that the measure of urbanization, the percentage of the population in communities of over 2,500, tells us nothing of the distribution by community size above this limit; and that the measure of density reflects only average density per square mile, not irregularities of population distribution associated with barren mountain areas, etc.

These three factors together account for a little over 70 percent
of the variance among states in per capita total expenditures
(Table 23).[10] In the variables selected we have the major factors,
or representatives of them, involved in interstate differences in
government activity.

Of the three variables, income is the most important. This is
indicated most simply by the elasticity coefficient which may be
derived from the equations (Table 24). Thus a 1 percent increase
in income (urbanization and density unchanged) was associated
in 1942 with a slightly smaller percentage increase in expenditures,
about .9. The corresponding changes in expenditures when urbanization or density is raised 1 percent (the other two variables held
constant) are much smaller: about .1 percent in the case of urbanization; only —.07 percent in the case of density. Indeed, the figure
for urbanization is not significantly different from zero, as is indicated by the standard error of the urbanization coefficient in the
equation. On the other hand, the standard error for the density
term is small.[11]

The actual effect on a dependent variable of variation in an
independent variable will depend not only on the magnitude of the
elasticity but also on the range of variation of the independent
variable. Thus the coefficients of variation (semi-interquartile
range as a percentage of the median) of the three independent
variables are: income, 24; urbanization, 26; density, 67. If we
take these measures to indicate the relative ranges of variation of
the three independent variables, income is still most important.
This may be illustrated by asking how expenditures would change

[10] The fraction of variance accounted for equals the square of the multiple
correlation coefficient ($.85^2 = .72$).

[11] When the urbanization term is dropped, the multiple correlation coefficient
is not appreciably lowered. The equation for total expenditures excluding the
urbanization variable is:

Per capita expenditures = 4.5 + .089 Income — .033 Density.
                                    (.008)   (.010)

For some of the individual functions, however, the urbanization factor is significant. On the other hand, the density and income factors are not significant
for others. We could, of course, have dropped terms from every equation to
which they did not contribute anything, but it did not seem worth while to
go through the additional computations.

Table 23

STATISTICAL RELATIONS BETWEEN GOVERNMENT EXPENDITURES PER
CAPITA OF THE 48 STATES IN 1942 AND THEIR RESPECTIVE LEVELS
OF INCOME PER CAPITA, URBANIZATION, AND DENSITY

DEPENDENT VARIABLE *Expenditure per Capita (1942)*	CON- STANT TERM	REGRESSION COEFFICIENT OF INDEPENDENT VARIABLE			COEFFICIENT OF MULTIPLE CORRELA- TION
		Per Capita Income (1938-42)	*Urbani- zation (1940)*	*Density (1940)*	
General control	.31	.0119 (.0017)	−.0456 (.0216)	−.0010 (.0019)	.77
Public safety					
Police	−1.02	.0042 (.0008)	.0173 (.0097)	.0015 (.0008)	.90
Fire	−.80	.0012 (.0005)	.0284 (.0064)	.0015 (.0006)	.92
Other	−.55	.0020 (.0005)	.0085 (.0068)	−.0006 (.0006)	.75
Highways	3.14	.0123 (.0031)	−.0554 (.0402)	−.0070 (.0035)	.54
Schools	5.58	.0240 (.0040)	−.0155 (.0512)	−.0102 (.0045)	.77
Sanitation	−.58	.0008 (.0006)	.0236 (.0078)	.0006 (.0007)	.79
Health, hospitals & public welfare					
Health & hospitals	−.89	.0078 (.0013)	−.0002 (.0167)	.0015 (.0015)	.85
Public welfare	−1.99	.0072 (.0045)	.1835 (.0582)	−.0212 (.0051)	.67
Other	.12	.0110 (.0022)	−.0176 (.0284)	−.0048 (.0025)	.68
Total	3.32	.0822 (.0178)	.1271 (.1516)	−.0396 (.0132)	.85

An equation for all the nonschool functions combined may be derived from the sum of the equations for the separate nonschool functions above:

Expenditure on nonschool operations = −2.26 + .0583 Income + .1427 Urbanization − .0294 Density.

Expenditure is in dollars per capita; income is personal income in dollars per capita; urbanization is percentage of population in cities of 2,500 or more; density is population per square mile.

Figures in parentheses are standard errors of the coefficients.

Table 24

ELASTICITY OF STATE AND LOCAL GOVERNMENT EXPENDITURES PER
CAPITA WITH RESPECT TO INCOME PER CAPITA, URBANIZATION
AND DENSITY

Derived from Data for the 48 States, 1942

	Elasticity with Respect to			
	Income per Capita	Urbanization	Density	Three Independent Variables Combined
General control	1.39	—.43	—.02	.94
Public safety				
Police	1.02	.34	.06	1.42
Fire	.50	.97	.10	1.57
Other	1.21	.42	—.06	1.57
Highways	1.02	—.37	—.10	.55
Schools	.78	—.04	—.06	.68
Health, hospitals, & public welfare				
Health & hospitals	1.20	—.002	.04	1.24
Public welfare	.48	.99	—.24	1.23
Sanitation	.43	1.08	.06	1.57
Other	1.23	—.16	—.09	.98
Total	.90	.11	—.07	.94
Total, excl. school	.96	.19	—.08	1.07

The elasticity measure is the percentage change in per capita expenditures
associated with a 1 percent change in the independent variable specified. The
change in the independent variable is calculated with its arithmetic mean value
as the point of departure, the two other independent variables being held constant at their mean values. Elasticities calculated from change between first
and second quartile values of the independent variables, and between their
second and third quartile values, are substantially the same as those above,
with the following exceptions:

	Independent Variable	Elasticity between	
		1st & 2nd Quartile	2nd & 3rd Quartile
General control	Urbanization	—.46	—.32
	Three combined	.87	1.14
Highways	Urbanization	—.40	—.28
	Three combined	.56	.72
Public welfare	Density	—.15	—.07
Other	Three combined	.97	1.11

were each variable independently altered from its third to its first quartile value in 1942 (Table 25). The results show how much more influence would be exerted by income than by urbanization or density. Similar proportions appear when we inquire into the

Table 25

CHANGE IN STATE AND LOCAL GOVERNMENT EXPENDITURES PER CAPITA ASSOCIATED WITH CERTAIN CHANGES IN INCOME PER CAPITA URBANIZATION, OR DENSITY

Derived from Data for the 48 States, 1942

Independent Variable	Change in Independent Variable from 3rd to 1st Quartile Value	Associated Change in per Capita Government Expenditure	Change in Independent Variable from 1903 to 1942 Mean	Associated Change in per Capita Government Expenditure
Income	276	22.7	246	20.3
Urbanization	22.2	2.8	15	1.9
Density	66.0	−2.6	40	−1.6
Total		22.9		20.6

Units are as defined in Table 23. Dollar figures are in 1942 prices. The calculation for any independent variable holds the other two variables constant at their mean values.

effects of changes from the 1903 to the 1942 mean values of the independent variables.

The relations expressed by the equations in Table 23 may be read also in absolute terms. Thus the relation between expenditures and each independent variable (the other two variables being held constant at their mean levels) may be put as follows. An additional $10 of per capita income, at given levels of urbanization and density, was accompanied in 1942 by about $.82 of additional state and local government expenditure per capita. Every shift of 1 percent of the population from rural areas to cities of 2,500 or more was accompanied by additional per capita government expenditures of $.13. And every addition to population of one person per square mile was accompanied by a fall in per capita government expenditure of $.04.[12]

The main conclusion to be drawn from these implications of our statistics is that urbanization is by itself a minor factor, much less important than income and not more important than density. The major factor accounting for interstate differences in government expenditures is income. Urbanization, in the simple correlations that have been made in the past, is apparently a strong influence on expenditures only because it is itself highly associated with income.[13] At a given level of income (and density), even fairly

[12] These results are based on the linear equation in Table 23. We also calculated the relation on the assumption that it was curvilinear:

Per capita expenditures $= 7.2 + 0.135$ Income $- 0.00004$ Income^2
$\qquad\qquad\qquad\quad$ (0.05) $\qquad\qquad$ (0.00004)
$\qquad\qquad\qquad - 0.59$ Urbanization $+ 0.008$ Urbanization^2
$\qquad\qquad\qquad\quad$ (0.49) $\qquad\qquad$ (0.005)
$\qquad\qquad\qquad - 0.165$ Density $+ 0.0002$ Density^2
$\qquad\qquad\qquad\quad$ (0.03) $\qquad\qquad$ (0.00005)

The coefficient of multiple correlation is .91.

This equation may be read as follows: As income rises, per capita expenditures rise also, at an almost constant rate. Every $10 of additional income, at given levels of urbanization and density, is accompanied by about $1 of additional government expenditures. Because of the curvature in the relation, the amount added to government expenditures is a little more at low incomes, a little less at high incomes, but the difference is slight and probably not significant.

Curvature is somewhat more pronounced in the case of urbanization. There is a slight tendency for expenditures to fall as urbanization rises from the lowest to the medium levels, then a tendency to rise. But the curve is very flat through most of the relevant range. Only at the highest levels of urbanization, above the upper quartile, is the slope of the curve appreciably different from zero; and we know from the standard error that even this may be insignificant.

Density has a clear negative relation with expenditures through almost the whole range. However, as density rises, a given increase is accompanied by a smaller and smaller decline in expenditures. At the lower quartile point of density, a rise of 1 person per square mile is associated with a fall of about $.15 in expenditures per capita. At the upper quartile point, the corresponding fall in expenditures is only $.10. Only when extremely high levels of density are reached, 413 or more per square mile, is increase in density associated with rise. The rate of rise is low, however.

These results are not much different from those derived from the linear equation. The only interesting and statistically significant difference bears on the curvature of the expenditure-density relation. This is something that we might expect a priori. The curvature in the expenditure-urbanization relation also conforms with expectation, but it is not statistically significant.

[13] This association between income and urbanization is well known to students of income statistics; see, e.g., the table in Simon Kuznets' *National Income: A Summary of Findings* (National Bureau of Economic Research, 1946), p. 27.

pronounced differences in degree of urbanization are associated with only slight differences in per capita expenditures.[14]

These relationships make sense. At given levels of urbanization and density, our measure of income indicates differences in real per capita income plus price differences mainly associated with community size (and not held constant by our measure of urbanization). Higher levels in either would tend to make for higher levels in government expenditure: the price factor, for the obvious reason that salary rates, rents, and other "local" commodities — which make up some half of the expenditures — would be high in generally high price areas, low in generally low price areas; the real income factor, because it will increase both the demand for public services and the tax capacity basic to their supply.

At a given level of income and density, urbanization would have little, but positive, effect on expenditures: little, because community-size differentials in expenditures would largely be eliminated

[14] Perhaps we need to emphasize that we are considering only the direct effects of urbanization on government expenditures, apart from its effects via income. If urbanization — because of the production advantages it brings — is a significant factor determining income, through income it may exercise an important influence on government expenditures. Its direct influence, however, appears small.

The following example may assist some readers to follow the discussion in the text. Suppose I (income) is a simple linear function — the sum — of U (urbanization) and X, X being independent of U; and that E (expenditures) equals 10 percent of I. Let us assume, further, that there are three states with zero U, three with U of 1, three with U of 2, and so on; and that one of each group of three is characterized by a value of X equal to 1, another by a value equal to 2, and the third by a value equal to 3. The following distribution would result:

E at Specified State Levels of U and I

		0	1	2	3	4	5	6	. . .
	0	—	.1	.2	.3	—	—	—	
	1	—	—	.2	.3	.4	—	—	
	2	—	—	—	.3	.4	.5	—	
U	3	—	—	—	—	.4	.5	.6	
	.								
	.								
	.								

It is quite clear that when I is held constant, as in each column, the correlation between U and E is zero. When U is held constant, as in each row, the correlation between I and E is perfect. That is, U has no effect whatever on E apart from its effect through I.

through the income factor; positive, because not all would be.[15] What was left would mean more expenditures, again partly because of the rural-urban price differential, partly because of the rural-urban service differential.[16]

Finally, increased density, at given levels of income and urbanization, acts to reduce expenditures — presumably because when public facilities can be used more intensively the cost of meeting specified levels of public service per head is lessened.

What would the combined effect of these factors be if all three changed? Since the relation we have derived is, by assumption, a simple additive one, the answer also is simple: it is the sum of the separate effects.[17] In terms of the elasticities mentioned earlier, a 1 percent increase in each of the three independent variables would be associated with an increase of a little less than 1 percent in expenditures per capita. This is, in fact, close to the amount associated with a 1 percent increase in income alone. The effects of urbanization and density work in opposite directions and almost offset one another. When changes of a relative order of magnitude proportional to the coefficients of variation of the three variables are assumed (Table 25), the influence of density becomes slightly more important, but not enough to modify seriously the preceding results.

We have been asking how expenditures compare with the average when all three independent variables are above or below average. The Mountain States are above average in income, but below

[15] The larger a city (measured by population) the larger its government expenditure per capita tends to be. But so also does its per capita income.

[16] It is money income, not real income, that is being held constant. At a given level of *money* income, a high level of urbanization might really mean a low level of *real* income, and a low level of urbanization, a high level of *real* income. The real income factor thus associated with urbanization might help — because of its negative effect — to offset, in part, some of the other factors — with positive effects — associated with urbanization. This may help to explain the slight importance ascribed to urbanization at given levels of income and density.

[17] We could, of course, have tested the existence of two- (or three-) factor product terms in the regression equation. If such terms had significant (and substantial) coefficients, the answer to the above (and to our earlier) questions would not be as simple. But the strength of the correlation could not have been raised much above the present level by adding such terms.

average in density. In these states, therefore, income and density work in the same direction: per capita expenditures are exceptionally high.[18]

The elasticities that express the relation between total expenditures and each independent variable are weighted averages of the elasticities for the several functional groups making up the total. The latter are interesting in their own right, and the average elasticities in fact summarize figures for them that are rather widely different (Table 24).

Income is still the most important influence on all functions except fire, sanitation, and welfare. For these three, urbanization is outstanding. This is reasonable; what is surprising is that police is not also an exception. Density is of tertiary importance, measured by its elasticity, in all functions except schools and health and hospitals. In these two, it is secondary. It is curious that density is not more important in the case of highways and less important in the case of welfare. Urbanization appears to be a negligible influence only in the case of schools and health and hospitals, though statistically insignificant also in the case of "other". The school figure suggests that educational standards were so widely diffused as to eliminate urban-rural differences (at given income and density levels). Income is never negligible, but it is statistically insignificant in the case of sanitation and public welfare.

All functional expenditures are positively correlated with income. In the case of urbanization and density, however, there are some interesting differences in sign. Urbanization, which has positive influence on total expenditures and half the individual functional groups, works in the opposite direction in the case of general control, highways, health and hospitals, schools and "other". However, the results for general control and "other" may merely reflect the tendency toward more specialization of function and better

---

[18] In technical language, we have been moving along only one direction on the surface that describes the relation between expenditures and the three independent variables under consideration: the direction in which all the independent variables rise. If we move from the mean of the surface in a direction in which income increases substantially and density decreases substantially, we get other results. The movement, in this case, would be toward the portion of the surface where the Mountain States are congregated: these had high levels of expenditure per capita.

records in the more urbanized states. The result for highways and schools must surely mean intensive use of facilities. Density's influence is negative in the case of total expenditures and most of the individual functions; the exceptions are police, fire, sanitation, and health and hospitals.

The aggregate effect of a 1 percent change in each variable is substantially more on the three public safety functions, health and hospitals, public welfare, and sanitation than on total expenditures. It is about the same on general control and "other" expenditures. It is less in the case of schools and highways. If instead of a uniform 1 percent change in each independent variable we take the change from the 1903 mean levels of income, urbanization, and density to their 1942 mean levels, we get somewhat different results. Now, only highways and schools would increase less than total expenditures, but these make up a good part of the total. All the other functions would increase more than total expenditures.

Factors Affecting Interstate Differences in Government Employment in 1942

We have suggested that the strong association between expenditures and income, urbanization and density reflects interstate price differentials in some degree. But how important are these price differences? In particular, does income have an outstanding influence because both it and expenditures are influenced by the common factor, interstate price differences?

In our review of interstate differences in expenditures we concluded that price differences could not account for the entire differences in expenditures. The range of variation in expenditures is very wide compared with that in prices, and any deflation would cut it only a fraction. The same, of course, goes for income. Nevertheless, the price factor affects our results.

Perhaps the simplest way to get rid of a good deal of its influence is to substitute government employment, in terms of number of workers, for government expenditures and see how the relationship turns out (Table 26).[19] The coefficient of correlation is sub-

---

[19] The substitution is somewhat deficient, however, because of the differences between expenditures and employment mentioned in footnote 3, above.

Table 26

STATISTICAL RELATIONS BETWEEN GOVERNMENT EMPLOYMENT PER
CAPITA IN THE 48 STATES IN 1942 AND THEIR RESPECTIVE LEVELS OF
INCOME PER CAPITA, URBANIZATION, AND DENSITY

DEPENDENT VARIABLE *Employment per Capita (1942)*	CON- STANT TERM	REGRESSION COEFFICIENT OF INDEPENDENT VARIABLE			COEFFICIENT OF MULTIPLE CORRELA- TION
		Per Capita Income (1938-42)	*Urbani- zation (1940)*	*Density (1940)*	
Schools	125.6	.0540 (.0270)	−.8543 (.3473)	−.0486 (.0303)	.58
Other	41.4	.1710 (.0493)	.4123 (.6348)	−.1190 (.0554)	.62
Total	166.9	.2250 (.0638)	−.4420 (.8218)	−.1677 (.0718)	.54

The employment data, in terms of government workers per 10,000 population, include part-time and temporary workers. For nonschool functions a rough calculation of the full-time equivalent number yields an alternative equation (see below; column headings have been omitted). This is combined with the above equation for schools to yield another equation for total employment.

Other than school	20.3	.1448 (.0255)	.4568 (.3282)	−.0782 (.0287)	.83
Total	145.8	.1988 (.0413)	−.3975 (.5322)	−.1268 (.0465)	.66

Figures in parentheses are standard errors of the coefficients.

stantially reduced: the three independent variables account for a much smaller percentage of the variance in employment than they did of the variance in expenditures. Nevertheless, the general outlines of the relations remain substantially the same. Income, though less important, still exerts the major influence, as indicated by the elasticity coefficient (Table 27). Urbanization now exerts a negative influence but is still statistically insignificant. Density continues to exercise a negative influence and is now more important.

For individual functions the question about the influence of interstate price differentials is less easily answered. We have information on only two separate categories of government employment by states: school and nonschool. When we relate interstate differences in nonschool employment to corresponding differences in

Table 27

ELASTICITY OF STATE AND LOCAL GOVERNMENT EMPLOYMENT PER
CAPITA WITH RESPECT TO INCOME PER CAPITA, URBANIZATION
AND DENSITY

Derived from Data for the 48 States, 1942

Elasticity with Respect to

	Income per Capita	*Urbanization*	*Density*	*Three Independent Variables Combined*
Schools	.28	—.36	—.04	—.12
Other				
Full & part-time	.67	.13	—.08	.72
Full-time equivalent	.72	.18	—.07	.83
Total				
Full & part-time	.50	—.08	—.06	.36
Full-time equivalent	.50	—.08	—.05	.37

The elasticity measure is the percentage change in per capita employment
associated with a 1 percent change in the independent variable specified. The
change in the independent variable is calculated with its arithmetic mean as
the point of departure, the two other independent variables being held constant at their mean values. Elasticities calculated from change between the
quartile values of the independent variables are substantially the same as
those above.

income, urbanization, and density, we again have confirmation of
the results for expenditures, as we would expect from the comparison of the totals.

In the case of the school functions, however, the change is considerable. School expenditures are correlated positively with income, negatively with density and urbanization. This is also true
of school employment. But the three independent variables differ
greatly in relative importance. The major factor is now urbanization. In schools, then, the price factor is of outstanding importance.
School salary levels are highly correlated with income; the regression coefficient has a very substantial value; and salaries constitute
the preponderant part of school expenditures (Table 11). It appears that school expenditures are high in high income states
mainly, but not entirely, because salaries are high. As income, urbanization, and density increase, school employment per capita
tends to fall. The decline in school employment per capita resulting
from greater urbanization and density (because of fewer public

school children per capita and more pupils per teacher) is more
than enough to offset the increase due to higher income. But since
salaries rise with higher income and urbanization, school expenditures per capita tend to rise. The price differential probably reflects
some quality difference,[20] but it is hardly possible to argue that
quality accounts for the entire price differential. Among states, the
levels of school service rendered per capita of the total population,
taking into account both quantity and quality, seem surprisingly
similar.

It is doubtful if the price factor is as important in any of the
individual nonschool functions. The range of school salaries seems
to be exceptionally wide.

Bearing of the 1942 Analysis on Changes between 1903 and 1942

May we use our results for 1942 in interpreting *change* in government expenditure between 1903 and 1942? The declining interstate differences in urbanization already noted, and other data,
suggest that at the opening of the century interstate differences in
income were greater than before World War II. But as we do not
have any data on income by states before World War I, we cannot
determine either the "cross-sectional" relationship for 1903, for
which data on state and local government expenditures as well as
measures of urbanization and density by states are available, or
the relationship between changes since then in income, urbanization, and density, and changes in government expenditures.[21] The
question initially posed is therefore important; and experience
with the application of cross-sectional savings functions to changes
in time suggests that the answer is not obvious.

Statistically, about all we can do is to return with another question: how well does our 1942 relationship conform to the 1903
relationship? While we lack the latter, we do know one thing about

[20] Cf., George Stigler, "Employment and Compensation in Education", *Occasional Paper 33* (National Bureau of Economic Research, 1950), p. 17.

[21] Wealth, available for both the early and recent periods, would seem to be a
likely substitute for income, but it could not be used because seriously affected
by the high values which the wealth estimates include for public lands in the
West and by other deficiencies.

it: it must exactly fit the means of expenditures, income, etc., for 1903; that is, the surface describing it must pass through the point defined by the mean of the system. (We do not have state data on incomes in 1898-1902, it is true, but Simon Kuznets has provided a rough national estimate and therefore the basis for a first approximation to the mean state income per capita. Both income and expenditures in the earlier period need, of course, to be put into the prices of the later period.) If the 1942 relationship conforms to the 1903 relationship, it too will pass through the mean of the 1903 system, although this is not a guarantee that it conforms in all respects to the latter.

Table 28

STATE AND LOCAL GOVERNMENT EXPENDITURES PER CAPITA, ACTUAL 1942 AND 1903 LEVELS AND ESTIMATED 1903 LEVELS, IN 1942 PRICES

	Actual 1942 (1)	Actual 1903 (2)	Estimated 1903 (3)	Difference 1903 (2)-(3) (4)
Total expenditures	$53.51	$27.93	$32.87	−$4.94
General control	5.01	5.10	2.81	2.29
Public safety	4.76	1.90	2.01	−.11
Highways	7.04	2.97	5.12	−2.15
Schools	17.86	13.65	12.59	1.06
Health, hospitals, & public welfare	12.58	2.27	6.89	−4.62
Sanitation	1.04	.47	.47	.00
Other	5.23	1.57	2.98	−1.41

Column 3 is estimated from the 1903 average levels of income, urbanization, and density, and the equations derived from the 1942 data (Table 23). The per capita expenditures shown are the unweighted averages of the 48 individual state per capita expenditures.

Substitution of the 1942 mean income (584), urbanization (47.3), and density (97.7), in our 1942 equation (Table 23) of course yields the 1942 mean total expenditure per capita, $53.51. Substitution of the corresponding 1903 values (338, 32.1 and 58.2) in the 1942 equation yields an estimate of mean expenditures in 1903 of $32.87 (in 1942 prices). The actual 1903 mean expenditure was $27.93, about $5 less (Table 28).

To answer the question, then, it seems that the two relationships differ by a modest amount, and this difference (if significant) is reasonable because it shows a secular rise in expenditures (at given levels of income, urbanization, and density) during the four decades.[22] In other words, the data are not inconsistent with the hypothesis that the 1942 relationship is applicable to the 1903 data and to the 1903-42 changes, subject only to the addition of a time or trend factor.[23] The trend factor is positive, taking 1903 as the point of reference. This means that the chief cause of rising per capita expenditures would be rising income. Greater urbanization and the "passage of time" would add a little. Increased density would subtract a little.

The results of parallel explorations of the data for the separate functions may be noted briefly (Table 28). On the assumptions listed, the effect of the passage of time would be to increase the expenditures on highways, health, hospitals, and public welfare, and "other" functions, and to reduce the expenditures on general control. Its effects on the expenditures on schools, public safety, and sanitation would seem negligible, well within the margins of error.

These implications also seem reasonable, on the whole, for the period and environment to which they relate. For example, we expect expenditures on general control to decline (relative to total government expenditures) as government activity, and with it specialization, increases: incidental functions performed by the general control group of offices or bureaus would be split off when

[22] In technical language, the one point that we know lies on the earlier surface does not lie also on the recent surface; but the difference between the two surfaces, in the vicinity of that point, is of reasonable sign and magnitude. There is some question whether the difference is large enough to be significant. In this connection we may note that the more elaborate equation given in footnote 12, above, yields an estimate for 1903 that is only about a dollar above the actual 1903 figure — i.e., differs from it by only three percent. On the other hand, the equation in footnote 11, which excludes the urbanization variable, gives about the same result as the equation in Table 23; and the employment equation in Table 26 also yields an estimate for 1903 higher than the actual 1903 (the "actual" in this case is itself a rather rough estimate derived by interpolating between the 1900 and 1910 figures in Table B13).

[23] More exactly, the constant term in the original 1942 equation, 3.32, is now assumed to consist of two components: a different constant term, -1.64, and a trend term, $+.127t$, where t is the number of years since 1903.

they grew large enough to be administered by special bureaus or offices devoted entirely to them, and these would usually be classified outside the general control function. To explain a positive trend factor for highways we may appeal to the advent of the motor car, among other things. And in connection with health, hospitals, and public welfare, and "other functions", a trend toward higher standards of service might be mentioned. (In the case of schools, raised standards could have been offset by reduction in the relative importance of school children in the population.)

While there seems to be some merit in the assumptions from which these implications are drawn, it is necessary to note that other and quite different assumptions are also consistent with the existing statistical data; and these also can be made to appear reasonable. Thus the differences we have accounted for by a time trend could be accounted for instead by changes in the regression coefficients. There is, indeed, some indication that this is so for one functional category. To judge from hints supplied by equations for 1903 and 1942 in which the independent variables are urbanization and density, increase between 1903 and 1942 in the income regression coefficient did play the significant role in raising expenditures on health, hospitals, and public welfare.[24] Such a change could reflect, for example, the assumption after 1903 of welfare activities on which the "marginal propensity to spend", as urbanization rises, is above the corresponding propensity to spend on the 1903 type of welfare and health activities.[25] For all other functions, and for the total as well, however, the same evidence seems to support the (competing) hypothesis first considered, namely, that

[24] The equations appear in the appendix, Table E3.

[25] This possibility may be illustrated with the figures in Table E3. Suppose that the "health, hospitals, and public welfare" group in 1903 consisted entirely of health and hospital activities, and was therefore related to urbanization and density in 1942 in accord with the 1942 equation for "health and hospitals" alone. Then, as we can see in the table, the urbanization coefficient in 1903 would not be much different from the 1942 urbanization coefficient. The addition of welfare activities, related to urbanization and density in accord with the 1942 equation for "public welfare", would cause the urbanization coefficient of the two subgroups combined to rise between 1903 and 1942 to the extent indicated in the table.

the 1942 relationships are reasonably applicable to 1903 and to the changes between 1903 and 1942 (with the addition of a time factor in the cases noted above).[26]

[26] Note, first, that the regression coefficients of the urbanization variable in 1903 are not significantly different from those in 1942, with the one exception of expenditures on health, hospitals, and public welfare. Now, urbanization and income are strongly correlated. If in both 1903 and 1942 they are related in a simple linear fashion,

Urbanization $= a + b$ (Income) $+ c$ (Years since 1903),

which is probably not too far fetched an assumption, then the urbanization coefficients in the equations in Table E3 will be proportionate to the income coefficients in which we are interested. Therefore, the ratio of the 1942 to the 1903 regression coefficients of urbanization will be identical with the corresponding ratio for income. That is, change in the urbanization coefficient will indicate change in the income coefficient: when the former is negligible, so is the latter.

Second, according to Table E3, the constant term is substantially altered between 1903 and 1942 in the directions and cases postulated earlier in the text. However, on the assumption made in the preceding paragraph, change in the constant terms in the Table E3 equations overstates degree of change in the constant terms in the equations in which income rather than urbanization is the independent variable.

While it is the urbanization, rather than the density, variable which is more important in all cases, we may note the substantial declines (ignoring signs) that occurred in the density regression coefficients for schools and general control. These may reflect the influence of improved transportation and some of the other developments we have noticed.

All this is merely suggestive, for it is difficult to connect the equations in Table E3 with those in Table 23, and the correlation coefficients of the former are usually rather low. It would seem worthwhile, however, to study further the equations in Table E3, adding corresponding equations for 1890, 1913 (though some difficulties would be encountered), 1932, and — when the data become available — 1952. (The 1952 Census of Governments will make it possible also to determine equations for 1952 corresponding to those in Table 23 and thus check, to some extent, the validity of the hypotheses discussed above.)

When interest lies in change in the average level of per capita state and local government expenditures for the United States as a whole, another factor enters the scene, to join those discussed above. This is the correlation between expenditures and population size. For the level of per capita state and local government expenditures in the United States as a whole is the mean of the individual state levels, each state level being weighted by the population of the state. Change in the correlation between expenditure and population may therefore help to explain changes in the United States level.

Shifts in this correlation, in fact, had an appreciable effect on the United States level of per capita expenditures devoted to some of the individual functions for which we have separate data. This may be seen if we compare changes in the weighted averages, which reflect shifts in population, with changes in the unweighted averages, which do not (Table E4). The United States weighted mean level of per capita state and local government expenditures on general control rose from $2.15 in 1903 to $5.07 in 1942, or 136 percent. The unweighted mean of the 48 state levels rose from $2.47 to $5.01, or 103 percent. (Both percentages relate to expenditures in current, not constant, prices.) The difference is in the opposite direction and largest in the case of highways, the weighted mean having risen 299 percent, the unweighted mean, 389 percent. For the other functions the differences are smaller, and indeed negligible in the case of the composite "health, hospitals, and public welfare", and perhaps also schools and sanitation.

For expenditures as a whole the differences cancel out almost completely.

CHAPTER 7

Factors Affecting the Trend of Government Activity

The causes of the trend of government activity since 1900 must be sought in the tendencies present in the economy of 1900, modified or strengthened by the forces that entered the scene in later years. To get at these, let us take brief stock of the situation in which the twentieth century opened and note the changes after 1900 that seem most significant. We can then ask some pertinent questions. Are the causes suggested by our review themselves reflections of a more basic cause underlying them all? What is needed to confirm the significance of the factors thrown up by analysis of the American experience of a half-century? And what does the future appear to hold in store in the light of this analysis?

Tendencies in 1900

Government's role was a modest one when the twentieth century opened. Yet modest as it was by present standards, government seems to have been more important in 1900 than it had been in earlier decades. In our detailed discussion we could touch only briefly on changes before 1900. The figures on the labor force, it will be recalled, show a rise between 1870 and 1900 in government employment relative to total employment, though perhaps not as rapid as after 1900; and the figures on tax-exempt property trace a rising trend between 1880 and 1900 in the proportion of the nation's capital assets held by government. Information on the ratio of government expenditures (including interest, transfers, etc.) to national income is conflicting but seems also to indicate an increase, though rather slight, between 1890 and 1903. These suggestions are consistent with the general evidence on government activity before 1900 noted briefly in Chapter 1, and with details on activities added by Detroit and California in the nineteenth century, reported in the studies cited in Chapter 4.

There already existed, then, a record of expansion in government activity.

The forces that had brought that expansion were still alive as the century opened. And other forces were already in motion and soon to add their impetus to the trend of government activity. Many of these, as we saw in Chapter 1, were already apparent in 1900. Recall, for example, that the Industrial Commission was uncovering problems and offering solutions to them; that experience was revealing what was needed to amend the monopoly and railroad acts; that the United States had recently entered the international arena; and that Secretary Gage was not yet satisfied with our banking system. Groups were already in the habit of addressing appeals or demands to government for aid and protection.

Tendencies toward further increase in government activity, it therefore seems fair to say, were already present at the turn of the century. But we need not consider the situation of 1900 in detail. The underlying forces are sufficiently well illustrated in our review of changes after 1900, on which we concentrate. For many of the same factors were at work.

Changes after 1900

Population change, always a striking aspect of our national growth, comes first to our attention.

On the one hand, the doubled density of population tended to diminish the relative importance of government activity, with resulting economies in the use of government facilities, such as we have found in our analysis of interstate differences in 1942. And decline in rate of population increase (from 2 percent per annum at the opening of the century to $1\frac{1}{4}$ percent in the 1940's) also may have operated in this direction by tending to cut per capita government outlays on many items of construction and equipment, just as it tends to reduce per capita outlays on residential construction, except for replacement needs.

On the other hand, however, accompanying changes in population composition worked to step up the relative importance of government activity. Decline in number of children per family meant a higher value placed on each child, and a larger amount of money available for each child. Parents wanted longer schooling for their children, and more and better health, sanitation, hospital, and recreational services. Thus the number of school teachers rose more rapidly than the population, despite the decline in the percentage of children in the population. And increase in the percentage of older people in the population, together with urbanization, made the problem of the older worker more serious. Old age and survivors insurance is a recent step by government to meet the problem.

The increase in population and the ceaseless movement westward accompanying it brought also the end of the frontier in 1890.[1] This caught the attention of Frederick Jackson Turner in 1893 and provided a clue to the meaning of American history that fired the imagination of the next generation of historians. Whatever the merits of Turner's theory, the safety valve theory that was its corollary — or even more, the wider spread and less sophisticated reasoning from the simple fact of the frontier's disappearance — influenced opinions and provided ammunition for proponents of a "positive program" by government. Later, along with decline in the rate of population growth, the end of the frontier came to be a major factor in policies based on the theory of economic maturity and stagnation. But the impression that opportunity had diminished with the end of the frontier did its work long before the 1930's.

More directly, the end of the frontier led to a reassessment of the value of conserving and developing the nation's natural resources. The nineteenth century's "slaughter" of the great eastern forest and its "mining" of the soil seemed to create no problems as long as virgin land lay farther west. The twentieth century came to think otherwise. Federal control, regulation, and development of natural resources, reflected in extensive and increasing expenditures on reclamation and river development, for example, appeared early. Timber reservations and national parks expanded

---

[1] Customarily, and rather crudely, defined as the band of land with a population of 2 to 6 persons per square mile.

to cover substantial areas. More recently, soil conservation took hold and the Tennessee Valley Authority began its activities. The development was cumulative. "By 1947 Stimson was prepared to admit — perhaps even to claim — what he had denied in 1935, that the principle of TVA, as an adventure in the effective use of national resources, was a direct outgrowth of the position he and other conservationists had taken back in 1912."[2] The three volume report of the President's Water Resources Policy Commission, published in 1950, is the latest in the series of discussions of conservation held in the last half-century. And the work of the Departments of the Interior and Agriculture has grown in correlated ways; for example, the former has studied shale and coal as possible sources of oil supply.

Ever advancing science and technology also had their impact on government activity. The automobile, for example, stimulated road building and betterment, a task of government already taking on a new lease on life in the early years of the century, even before the auto had become important. (More and better roads, in turn, helped swell the number of automobiles, and thus the need for still more and still better roads.) The automobile created a demand for state and national parks and state police. It led to a reorganization and expansion of rural and suburban schools. Advance in economic science and statistics improved our knowledge of interstate and intrastate differences in needs and capacities and may have helped stimulate the system of state and federal grants-in-aid. It strengthened belief in the possibilities of dealing with social problems by collective action. It made for increase in the statistical and other fact-finding activities of government. Advance in chemical and biological science made possible and stimulated the growth of government work on sanitation, garbage disposal, health, and the control of pests, and plant and animal disease: witness, for example, the growth of state and municipal laboratories for testing water, food, and blood.

Indirectly, the advance and diffusion of science and technology had even more important effects. The main channel was through

[2] Henry L. Stimson and McGeorge Bundy, *On Active Service in Peace and War* (Harper, 1948), pp. 43-4.

industrial change, in which increased population density, rise of national income, and other factors already mentioned or to which we refer below, also played a role. Two major developments may be selected for emphasis: changes in agriculture and in size of business operations.

Decline in agriculture relative to other industries, already on the way well before 1900, turned into an absolute decline, in terms of employment, about 1910. Commercialization of agriculture was a parallel process of lessening self-sufficiency and increasing specialization. These trends, stimulated by important changes in technology in and out of farming, illustrate a major theme and contribute to a minor theme of our history.

The major theme is growing economic interdependence. No farm is truly self-sufficient; it is dependent in some degree on supplies from the nonagricultural sphere. Yet the impact of change in the prices of farm products and farm supplies, if not also in tax and interest rates, is small when the farmer produces little for the market and much for himself. Independence diminishes as farms become commercialized. Correspondingly, interdependence increases as urban industries grow in relative importance and as limits on specialization widen with expanded markets. Not only are people more dependent on one another, they come to feel so. Thus was altered the climate of opinion in and out of farming on the need for positive government programs to deal with problems as diverse as public welfare, health, conservation, resource development, and business regulation.

The minor theme is increase in the share of government activity devoted to agriculture. Many industries have risen and declined in our history. Declining industries are as characteristic of an expanding economy as are rapidly growing industries, as Arthur F. Burns has demonstrated.[8] But none has ever had the political influence of agriculture. It is a very large industry; furthermore, in this country it directly controls a disproportionately large number of legislative votes. It benefits also from the fact that so many people's grandfathers were or are farmers. Viewed as the "seed

[8] *Production Trends in the United States since 1870* (National Bureau of Economic Research, 1934), Ch. 3-4.

bed" of population, the chief refuge of the independent spirit, and a major segment of the "sound middle class" sustaining democracy, it enjoys a unique position. Many of the increases we have noted in government activity thus were, in one way or another, to aid the farmer far beyond the degree prevailing in 1900: by mortgage and other credit (recall the provisions of the Federal Reserve Act favoring agricultural credit, the revival of the War Finance Corporation in 1921 to assist in financing and rehabilitating agriculture, the Agricultural Credits Act of 1923, and so on), the wheat and cotton purchase programs of 1929, and the stream of measures instituted in the 1930's.

Increase in the size of business establishment and enterprise, another trend apparent before 1900, gave rise to the Interstate Commerce Commission Act in 1887 and the Sherman Act in 1890. These led the way for a host of other government measures to prevent, combat, or regulate industrial monopolies and public utilities. The Elkins and Hepburn Acts which strengthened the ICC, the antitrust prosecutions, the life insurance investigations, the Federal Trade Commission and Clayton Acts came before World War I. The Cellar Anti-merger Act marks the latest episode. Increasing size of enterprise was important also in supporting the case for government encouragement of trade unions and "small business", for example through provisions of the Clayton Act and antichain store and resale price maintenance legislation.

The drift of people to the cities, so closely associated with the decline in agriculture and its other side, industrialization, deserves a separate word. Indirectly, of course, this truly secular trend influenced government activity in many ways; the insecurity of old age has been mentioned. Here we emphasize its direct influence: the need to provide services which rural life finds unnecessary or takes care of among family chores. Included are many of the great host of expanding municipal services: sanitation, waste removal, water supply, recreation and parks, local transportation.

While these services are mainly to final consumers, they are in fact largely costs to be charged against the attraction of urban incomes. For urbanization, and the industrialization accompanying it, meant higher real income per capita. This trend toward higher income also affected government activity, both by raising demand for government services and by making it possible to meet the costs of providing more such services.

Higher incomes influenced all levels of government. It would be impossible to explain much of the rise in educational expenditures in this country without referring to increased demand for more and better educational services per capita. The percentage of population enrolled in schools, mostly public, rose between 1900 and 1940 from 80 to about 95 for the 10-14 age group, and from 42 to over 75 for the 15-17 group.[4] And the kind of changes in the quality of educational service is obvious to anyone who compares the facilities and equipment of the modern school building and the training of the modern teacher with those of 1900, of which exhibits are still available. Municipal services also grew in quantity, quality, and variety. One simple illustration will suffice: inspection of restaurants and other eating and drinking places rose in relative importance along with higher incomes. State and federal activities also responded to higher incomes. Increase in state hospitals, for example, and in federal social security have been justified in terms both of long-term investment in productive human resources and of decent standards of responsibility for the immediate well-being of those who cannot help themselves. Both ability to invest and standards of responsibility rose with higher income levels.

The recurrence of business depression played its part. We are too close to the great depression of the 1930's, and to its influence on social security, labor, banking, agricultural, and other legislation, to need to emphasize its role. But we need to recall that the government developments associated with the New Deal constituted only the latest, if also greatest, of a series of step-wise movements along an upward trend. In some degree the Populist movement of the 1890's bore its fruit after 1900. The panic of 1907 underscored Secretary Gage's complaint of 1900 and led to the formation of a National Monetary Commission and eventually to the Federal Reserve System. The collapse of 1920-21 started a number of schemes in later years: agricultural legislation has

[4] Such factors as compulsory school-attendance laws are largely results rather than causes of high enrollments (see George Stigler, *op. cit.*, App. B). The more basic factor is undoubtedly income together with urbanization.

already been mentioned. And the depression of the 1930's made its mark even before 1933: recall the Reconstruction Finance Corporation. Not only depression but also prosperity contributed: by stimulating labor and other movements agitating for the expansion of government activity, and by expanding local government outlays and commitments whose effects persist, in terms of government employment, purchases, and services rendered, even after the boom has passed.[5]

Developments in other parts of the world also contributed to the expansion of government activity in the United States. A number of innovations in social legislation and standards in their application came from Europe. The opening and development of new farming areas abroad played a part in the decline of American farming, and thus in its influence on the rise of government.

Also important, of course, was change in the international situation which brought war and the increased possibility of war. Even before World War II — and certainly for the entire period under review — the trend in the number directly engaged in national defense, including civilians in the nation's military establishment as well as uniformed men, was steeper than the trend of population. By 1925, at the middle of the period under review, persons engaged in national defense had more than doubled since 1900; before Korea they numbered seven times the 1925 figure. Expenditures (apart from payrolls) grew even more rapidly, as equipment, vehicles, and ships used by the forces became more elaborate and "mechanization" proceeded. To this must be added expansion in the State Department and, in recent years, membership in international organizations and international relief, rehabilitation, and development. The residues of war and of preparation for or against war also must be counted: Veterans Administration activities, a subsidized Merchant Marine, higher tariffs to protect war-born infant industries, a heritage of war plants (Muscle Shoals which culminated, after some hesitation, in the Tennessee Valley Authority; and the Atomic Energy Commission), the Canal Zone, and expansion of the statistical activities of government. In the condi-

[5] D. W. Gilbert, "Cycles in Municipal Finance", *Review of Economic Statistics* (November 1940).

tions and policies determining the magnitude of the peacetime defense effort — that is, the changing international scene and our reactions to it — we have, then, another factor contributing substantially to the growth in government activity.

The century opened with the people largely though not wholly against government "interference" and "paternalism". But then came stimulated growth of the elements in the climate of opinion that look to government to deal with social and economic problems, and lowered resistance to such a program. Socialist ideology gained ground — although more in Europe than here; and in opposition to it there emerged a "positive program for democracy" to ward off radicalism by training the strong forces of government on the great problems of the day. And the problems themselves multiplied.

In addition, confidence swelled in the ability of government to do a job, partly because of changes in the organization and efficiency of government itself. The corruption so much raked over around 1900 lessened with the spread of the merit system and the formation of a professional attitude and skill among government workers. The state government executive was strengthened and its responsibility established. New methods of control and audit were devised, and a budgetary system introduced and expanded. Finally, the waging of a great war persuaded many people that government can do a big job well, and some jobs even better than private enterprise.

With this shift of attitude the ground was paved for the other factors we have noted to work their effects. The change in attitude helped to push farther the role of government in economic life by establishing a condition essential for that advance.

Government's Expansion as a Concomitant of Economic Growth

The various factors in our list have had pervasive influence on government activity. There is hardly any function or activity of government untouched by most of them. In this obvious sense, they are inter-related, operating as joint causes. But they are inter-related in other ways that deserve emphasis.

The factors have operated not only on government activity but also on one another, and through one another on government activity. We have noted some of these connections; only lack of space prevents illustrations in every section and paragraph.

Most important, the various factors we have paraded — with the important exception of the international situation — may be viewed as largely different aspects of one central cause or group of causes. That is the cause or causes of the economic growth — in population, per capita income, and aggregate income — that has characterized the United States during the last half-century. Change in population composition of the kind we have experienced, the end of the frontier, advance and diffusion of science and technology, industrialization, urbanization, increase in size of enterprise, and business cycles were concomitants of that growth and suggest themselves as distinctive characteristics of a growing economy. If this view is sound, the rising trend of government activity also is a concomitant of economic growth.

The developments underlying our economic growth disturbed the security of individuals and groups — the farmer, the older wage-earner, the smaller shopkeeper are examples — and posed serious social and economic problems of adjustment and protection. Economic development multiplied problems of monopoly and industrial relations and finance; created new, and enlarged old costs — of transport, communication, sanitation — involved in the operation of urbanized society; unearthed some resources but depleted others; spurred demand for the services — educational, recreational, health — that expand with increasing income. At the same time, it raised the nation's standards of responsibility for the economic welfare of the groups composing it, thus stimulating government production in general as a channel for the distribution of income as well as government production of the services meeting the particular needs of the groups requiring assistance. Economic development, further, swelled the number of activities in which the private return, but not the social return, compares unfavorably with its cost — examples are conservation and protection. Economic development may have improved government's efficiency in production relative to the efficiency of the private sector in certain areas — or led people to think this true. Finally, economic development may also have created, in Professor Schumpeter's phrase,[6] "growing hostility" to the system of private enterprise and a predisposition towards "interventionism" involving increased government regulation, protection, subsidy, and participation in the production process.

This explanation of the trend of government activity in the United States since 1900 forms a persuasive hypothesis. Like all hypotheses, however, it raises questions that need to be explored before we may accept it confidently.

If increasing government activity was the result of our economic development and a concomitant of economic growth since 1900, there should have been increasing government activity before 1900, when economic growth was rapid. And the evidence does suggest that immediately before the turn of the century government activity was rising in relative importance. However, we do not know how far back the trend goes; nor is it clear whether the trend before 1900 was as steep as it was afterward. It is not unlikely, of course, that developments associated with the very rapid economic growth after the Civil War led to an increase in government activity but with a long lag, that is, not until after 1900; and we have noted this possibility in our discussion: that is one reason why we started with the situation in 1900 and spoke of its "tendencies". But how long the lag may have been we do not know. Nor can we do more than mention the possibility that the lag itself may have been shortened in this century, in part because of the very development and elaboration of the scope, organization, and apparatus of government and the accompanying changes in the habits and attitudes of people.[7]

[6] Joseph Schumpeter, *Capitalism, Socialism, and Democracy* (Harper, 1942), Ch. 13.

[7] Relaxation of government's grip on economic life has been pointed to as a cause of the Industrial Revolution. If true, economic growth at that time was accompanied by decline in the relative importance of government regulation and supervision in economic life. However, there are a number of reasons why this explanation of what happened then is not necessarily inconsistent with the hypothesis discussed above. Other causes than government action or lack of action may have been important in the eighteenth century. Also, government activity and government regulation are not identical, nor are all types of gov-

Again, if increasing government activity in the United States was the result of its economic development, did not other countries, which also grew economically, expand the activities of their governments? Population, income per capita, and aggregate income rose also in most other nations in the western world. And their history, too, shows changed population composition, increased density, technological advance, industrialization, urbanization, increase in the size of enterprise, and the cycle of prosperity and depression. We know that government activity did grow in many other countries. Some of the social legislation we established came from them. And the recent movement toward socialization in England has attracted considerable attention.[8] In 1938 expenditures by government (not including public service enterprises) on goods and services, as a percentage of gross national product, were about 15 percent in the United Kingdom, Sweden, and Canada, as well as in the United States. But no systematic survey has been made of the course of events that established these levels. The inductions of Adolph Wagner and Henry C. Adams, which led them to formulate their "laws" of "increasing State activities among progressive peoples" and of "public expenditures for progressive peoples" may be said to find support in the history of the United States during the twentieth century; but these "laws" were based on very fragmentary nineteenth century data on government expenditures and taxes in a few countries without the advantage of adequate information on national income, not on the kind of information we have been able to collect for the United States

---

ernment regulation similar in their effects. And lags are involved: decline in government regulation can be a cause of economic growth; in turn, the changes associated with economic growth can — later — cause a return to government regulation and increase in government activity generally. (Eventually, to proceed another step, increased government activity may affect the rate of economic growth: some of these activities are designed to do so, as has been mentioned earlier; others may have unintended "side" effects on growth. The net outcome would depend on the kinds of government activity and their relative weights.)

[8] The percentage of workers on government payrolls in Britain has been estimated to be 6 in 1911, 9 in 1921, 10 in 1930, and 25 in 1950 (A. L. Bowley, *London and Cambridge Economic Service, Special Memo. 17A,* Dec. 1926; D. Dewey, *Journal of Political Economy,* June 1950; and T. M. Ridley, *Journal of the Royal Statistical Society,* Series A [General], Part II, 1951).

since 1900.[9] The impressions one obtains of vast changes in the role of government abroad need to be systematically checked. What are the similarities and differences between the current level in other countries and ours? What are the similarities and differences between their trends and ours? Have the factors that seem to underlie trends here played a similar role abroad, and how important have they been? With such a comparative study completed, we can be surer of the causes of developments in this country.[10]

Not all the factors affecting the trend of government activity can be said to be aspects of economic development. We noted the important exception of the international situation, which contributed so much to expansion in our government activity. Some would argue, of course, that international rivalry, and the war, preparations for war, and problems of postwar adjustment created by it, are consequences of economic growth. But important noneconomic factors are involved also. Given international rivalry as an independent factor, however, economic growth and the developments associated with it may have contributed to swelling its effect. Here we can only ask what are the relative weights of these economic and noneconomic factors and how have they influenced one another and worked their effects on the trend of government activity?

Chance, too, has a part, large or small, in all events; and the trend of government activity must therefore in some degree be interpreted as a series of historical accidents. But chance denotes only causes lying outside the system of variables constructed for an analysis. Their importance can be determined, if at all, only by the comparative historical and international analyses suggested above.

[9] Adolph Wagner, *Grundlegung der Politischen Oekonomie* (Leipzig, 1893), Erster Theil, Zweiter Halbband, p. 894; Henry C. Adams, *The Science of Finance: An Investigation of Public Expenditures and Public Revenues* (Henry Holt, 1898), Part I, Book I. Adams did not go beyond stating that total public expenditures would tend to increase with economic progress; Wagner explicitly stated his belief that economic progress brings a *relative* increase in the importance of government activities.

[10] A study of government activity in Western Europe was recently started at the National Bureau of Economic Research by Moses Abramovitz.

Shape of the Future

What may be said about the future trend of government activity must be surrounded with a number of reservations, in view of the work that still remains to be done on the factors affecting that trend. "Economic forecasting," Wesley C. Mitchell has pointed out, "is a notoriously hazardous enterprise, and political forecasting is perhaps even more risky." But enough is known for us to meet the challenge with more confidence than usual. "The chances of forming approximately correct anticipations are best when we are dealing with a secular trend: when we can ascertain the more potent forces that have shaped this trend in the recent past, and when we have reason to believe that these forces will retain their character and their potency during the limited future of which we are thinking." And having quoted Mr. Mitchell's preamble, we can do no better than follow it with his own vision of the future growth of government, written though it was in 1936:

"We expect technological progress to continue, for it rests upon scientific discovery, which does not seem to be approaching a limit, and upon man's desire to get larger returns for his economic efforts, which shows no signs of failing. Presumably, technological progress will continue to throw men out of work, to depreciate old investments, to shift sources of supply, to introduce novel products. The growth of very large business enterprises has not been checked; the economic, political, and social problems to which their operations give rise have not been solved. In nations that retain a capitalistic organization these changes will bear heavily upon numerous individuals, while they benefit others largely. Economic life will continue to be full of uncertainties, and those who suffer mischances will follow the precedents our generation is setting and make even larger demands for government aid. Social security legislation is more likely to expand than to contract in the great democracies, and dictatorial governments will practice paternalism. Business enterprises will increase their efforts to limit or suppress competition, for the more we mechanize industry and specialize machinery, the heavier will be overhead costs and the more dangerous competition will become to vested interests. The problems that the courts and the legislatures face in devising and enforcing rules of fair competition will grow more subtle and difficult. It will not be surprising if investors in great industries that are threat-

ened with loss by technological progress organize campaigns for government purchase and operation. The draft upon exhaustible natural
resources will grow greater and the movement for conservation
through government regulation will wax stronger. Communities will
become increasingly interdependent and the task of planning water
supplies, sewage disposal, protection of streams against pollution,
highway systems, power lines, and the like will be one in which the
central governments will be forced to take a larger share. Nor can we
leave out of account the probability of future wars and the practical
certainty that, if they occur between great nations, each belligerent
government will seek to effect a more drastic economic mobilization
than was effected in the latest world war. It is most unlikely that this
trend toward national economic planning will rise steadily. Its course
will be diversified by accelerations and retardations, perhaps by some
vigorous reactions toward *laissez faire*. But the indications seem to me
fairly clear that in the long run men will try increasingly to use the
power and resources of their governments to solve their economic
problems even in those nations that escape social revolutions."[11]

To this we need add only two things. First, with technological
advance, and the rising national income it brings, government as
well as private enterprise will be called upon to produce an increasing volume of the educational, recreational, health, and other
services that people demand when they are richer. Second, World
War II has already added impetus to the tendencies summed up
by Mr. Mitchell.

And a final question must be mentioned. Even before the New
Deal had made much headway, Gerhard Colm pointed out how
important government had become in the markets for labor, goods,
and money.[12] Its importance has grown considerably since, and
poses many questions about basic changes in the nature of the
economy. Government has become the biggest banker (and bor-
rower) of the country, and in this way and through its influence
on Federal Reserve policies has come to determine the rate of
interest basic to all loans; through its employment of an eighth of

[11] "Intelligence and the Guidance of Economic Evolution", in *The Backward
Art of Spending Money* (McGraw-Hill, 1937), pp. 124-6.
[12] "Theory of Public Expenditures", *Annals of the American Academy of
Political and Social Science*, January 1936, p. 11.

the labor force, its administration of the public contract and minimum wage laws, and its participation in key wage negotiations, it exerts great influence on the general level of wage and salary rates and hours of work and on many particular levels; it has become the country's biggest single buyer of commodities in general and the buyer of most of the output of some commodities, and thus directly, and in many ways indirectly, influences individual commodity prices; it now operates the country's largest insurance company. All this means that the role of government in our life has grown so large that its "collateral" effects, as well as its direct aims, range wide and deep. What unforeseen effects increasing recourse to government as "an agency of national progress and social betterment" may have, therefore, on the efficiency with which resources are allocated to alternative uses, on the rate of economic progress and, most important, on the character of the people and the limits of their personal freedom, is the very real question which is being put to us.

Appendices

SOURCES OF DATA IN TEXT TABLES AND CHARTS

Table

1   Census data are from Table B1. Payroll data for government employees are from Table B13. Total full-time equivalent employment is from the Department of Commerce, *Survey of Current Business*, National Income Supplement, 1951, for 1930-1949, and from Simon Kuznets, *National Income and its Composition* (National Bureau of Economic Research, 1941), for 1920.

2   Tables C1 and C2 and Solomon Fabricant, "Government-Owned Nonmilitary Capital Assets since 1900", *Studies in Income and Wealth, Volume Twelve* (National Bureau of Economic Research, 1950), with some corrections to take account of new data on education assets.

3   Same as Table 2.

4   Table 3.

5   Tables D1-4, D6.

6   For employment, Table B13; for purchases, Table D5 and *Survey of Current Business*, National Income Supplement, 1951; and for capital assets, Table C2.

7   Same as Table 5.

8   Table B13.

9   Same as Table 2.

10   Same as Table 5.

11   Same as Table 5.

12   Tables B15 (with some rough guesses as to further details for "all other local" employment), C3, and D12.

13   Table D12.

14   Tables D8-12, with the addition of rough estimates for missing items.

15   Figures on the total, national defense, schools, total regular employees, and public emergency workers are from Table B13. The public enterprise figures for 1940 and 1949 are from the *Survey of Current Business*, National Income Supplement, 1951. The 1900 public enterprise figure consists mostly of workers in the Post Office (Table B4) with a very rough estimate for the small number of employees of state and local public enterprises.

16   Table D8.

17   Employment data are from "Federal Personnel by Types of Work Performed", *Monthly Labor Review*, June 1941. Dates of establishment of the different agencies are from various issues of the *U. S. Government Manual*, especially 1948 (see Appendix A of this Manual for dead agencies). We revised the functional classification to follow that in Table B15.

18   Table D9.

19   Table D11.

20   Table D10.

21-23 Computed from data in Table E2.
24 Computed from equations in Table 23 and data in Table E2.
25 The equations used are from Table 23. The 1903 values of urbanization and density are from Table E2; the 1898-1902 real per capita income is from unpublished estimates by Simon Kuznets.
26 Computed from data in Table E2.
27 Computed from equations in Table 26 and data in Table E2.
28 Computed from equations in Table 26 and data in Table E2. 1903 data were converted to 1942 prices by using implicit indexes derived from Tables D2-5. Separate indexes were used for school and non-school data.

Chart
1 Tables B1-2 and B13. There are some slight discontinuities in the census data, but they have virtually no effect on the trend.
2 Government employment is from Table B13. Total employment is from the *Survey of Current Business,* National Income Supplement, 1951, and Simon Kuznets, *National Income and its Composition* (National Bureau of Economic Research, 1941), extrapolated by line (6) of Table B1.
3 Table B13 for employment data; Table C2 for data on government capital assets.
4 Tables D1-4, D6.
5 Tables B6, B9-11, and B13.
6 Same as Table 2.
7 Same as Chart 4. The large differences between the DC and N.B.E.R. estimates for federal payrolls and other purchases occur because the DC estimates exclude Post Office expenditures.
8 Table B3.
9 Tables D12 and B15 (with some adjustments as for Table 12).
10 Table D7.
11 Table B7.
12 Table C1 and Solomon Fabricant, "Government-Owned Nonmilitary Capital Assets Since 1900", *Studies in Income and Wealth, Volume Twelve,* Table 2.
13 Table D9. Total expenditures shown do not include enterprises.
14 Table D10. Total expenditures include enterprises.
15 Table E1.
16 Table E2.

DATA ON GOVERNMENT EMPLOYMENT

The Two Sources of Information

Government employment can be measured in two ways. One is to ask people what kind of work they do or for whom they work, as in the Census of Population and the Census Bureau's *Monthly Report on the Labor Force* (census data). The other is to ask employers, in this case government units, how many people are on their payrolls on a certain date, or on the average for a period, as in the questionnaires sent out by the Governments Division of the Census Bureau (payroll data).

Aside from errors in reporting, conceptual differences will cause these two methods to yield different estimates. For example, census data cover only persons devoting all or most of their time to government work: a person with two or more attachments is requested to report only the one taking the major portion of his time. Payroll data, on the other hand, include everyone — with some minor exceptions — who does any work at all for the government during the period covered.[1] Further, payroll data count a person twice when he is on two government payrolls during the period covered; for exam-

---

[1] According to unpublished data of the Bureau of the Census relating to January 3-9, 1943, 2.6 percent of all employed workers (including self-employed persons) held more than one "continued" job. Of these, the secondary job of 7.0 percent was in "government", and of 10.4 percent, in "professional service". Assuming half the professional service workers to be government employees (see Table B3) and the number of government workers in industries other than the two mentioned to be negligible, there were 160,000 secondary workers in government. These would appear in the payroll but not in the census data.

Of those reporting themselves as government workers few, except some teachers, worked under 30 hours a week. It does not seem likely, therefore, that many persons were led by prestige considerations to report their government affiliation as primary when in fact it was secondary. (Hours of government workers as a whole were not tabulated separately in the 1940 Census, but less than 3 percent of those in "government" and less than 11 percent in "education", including private schools, worked fewer than 30 hours during the survey week.)

ple, when he regularly works (full- or part-time) for two government units, or transfers from one to another during a single payroll period.

Census Data

The only attempt by the Bureau of the Census to make a complete count of government workers was in the 1940 Population Census. All employees, except those on emergency work, were asked whether they were working for the government. The total, plus an estimate for United States troops and other government employees stationed outside the continental United States who were not covered by the census, yields an estimate of regular government employment. To this may be added the number of public emergency workers, if they are considered to be employed by government. Figures after 1944, based on a sample of households, appear in the *Monthly Report on the Labor Force*.[2]

Censuses prior to 1940 did not report separately the number of employed government workers. It was necessary for us to estimate first, the number of workers (employed and unemployed) attached to government, and second, the number of these actually employed. The methods and data are described in the notes to Table B1. Only two points need comment.

First, until 1940 the Census asked workers only what their occupation and industry were, not whether they worked for government. Daniel Carson estimated, mainly from census data, the number of persons, employed and unemployed, attached to three major categories of government service — the Post Office, public schools, and "government, not elsewhere classified" — during 1870-1940. The third category omits government workers in industries such as medical and health services, public utilities, construction, and shipbuilding, which accounted for 1.3 million of the workers attached to government in 1940. For this reason Carson's series is only a crude index of change in the total number attached to government, and is possibly biased downward.[3]

[2] The 1950 Census of Population, when finally tabulated, will provide another figure based on a complete count.

[3] Except for 1940 no separate data are given for public, as distinct from private, education, and Carson based the separation on Office of Education and National Education Association data, both "payroll data". For this reason, the payroll and the census data are not truly independent and comparison provides only an inadequate check on their accuracy. However, one could avoid using the payroll data on education in preparing the census estimate, treating

Second, with respect to the number "attached" to government, but actually unemployed, the 1930 Census supplied such information only for the three government "industries" Carson distinguished, and even these required some manipulation before they could be put on something like the 1940 basis. The 1920 Census gave no information whatever on unemployment. Gladys L. Palmer and Ann Ratner have published census data on the percentage employed in 1910 for industries sufficiently comparable with Carson's groups.[4] The 1900 Census provided employment data only by occupation and on a basis different from that of later censuses.[5]

Payroll Data

Payroll data have several advantages over census data: they are available at more frequent intervals; they relate directly to employment

---

the census figures on total educational employees as relating to a "characteristic" occupation of the kind mentioned in the next paragraph. The resulting census estimate would be substantially the same as Carson's.

"Government, not elsewhere classified", an assortment of such activities as general government administration and regulation, national defense, police and fire protection, and the courts, not covered by the usual industrial classification, is given by the census as an industry only in 1910, 1930, and 1940. For all the other years it must be estimated from data on characteristic occupations such as policemen and firemen, soldiers and sailors, and officials (government).

In Table B1, line 2, we used Carson's estimates as they stand only back to 1910. As Carson's 1900 figures depend to a considerable extent on payroll data, we replaced them with our own estimates, based on census data. Extrapolating Carson's 1910 figures for the three divisions of government back to 1900 by the census data for characteristic occupations, such as teachers and professors, mail carriers, soldiers, sailors, and marines, policemen and detectives, we got a 1900 estimate almost entirely independent of payroll data, which we can use as a check on the estimates based on payroll data. For years before 1900 we extrapolated our 1900 estimate by Carson's figures. The characteristic occupations for government covered about 84 percent of the number Carson reported for "government" in 1910. The percentages were 64, 104, and 70 for postal service, education, and government n.e.c., respectively. The important clerical occupations could not be used directly in estimating government employees because they consist largely of nongovernment workers. Carson's methods, however, do permit the relative increase in clerical occupations in total gainful workers to influence his estimate before 1910.

[4] *Industrial and Occupational Trends in National Employment*, Research Report No. 11, Industrial Research Department, Wharton School of Finance and Commerce, 1949.

[5] The 1900 question asked the number of months employed between June 1, 1899 and May 31, 1900, rather than whether unemployed at the time of the census. By using the ratios of manmonths employed to available manmonths, for occupations wholly or largely associated with government, employment was estimated for Carson's three industries in 1900.

and exclude unemployed workers; they cover all types of government activity, rather than only the selected industries or occupations covered in the censuses before 1940; and, coming from the records of employing agencies, they are probably more reliable than the reports of workers or their relatives. On the other hand, there are many individual government units, and even some whole types, for which there is no payroll information at all. Data for counties and minor civil divisions are lacking before 1929, and the samples for state and city governments rapidly shrink as we go back of 1929, almost disappearing by 1900.

A few points about the payroll data need to be brought to the attention of the reader of the tables that follow.

The data for the Post Office Department in Table B4 are the figures for several types of Post Office employees distinguished in the annual reports of the Postmaster General. We use their sum instead of the totals in the annual reports of the Civil Service Commission because the latter vary considerably from year to year in their treatment of such employees as third and fourth class clerks and those whose relation to the Post Office Department is more that of contractor than of employee. We eliminated contractors, such as star route contractors, from our figures, but we included certain employees, such as third and fourth class clerks, who were actually employees of the postmasters, paid out of their salaries and allowances, not government employees. Since these clerks were numerous in the earlier years, omitting them would cause the Post Office series to rise more rapidly than we show. The third class clerks became government employees only in 1946. Because of irregular reporting, we excluded temporary and substitute employees whenever possible, but they could not always be separated from regular employees. The number of fourth class postmasters and clerks in third and fourth class offices, who are almost entirely part-time workers, has been decreasing steadily; the other categories of postal workers, all full-time, have been almost continuously increasing. For this reason our rough estimate of the full-time equivalent number of postal workers, made by reducing the number of postmasters in fourth class offices and clerks in third and fourth class offices 75 percent, rises much more rapidly than total postal workers.[6]

[6] The Census reports a much larger number of mail carriers in every year than the number of carriers shown in Table B4. The difference seems too large to be accounted for by the number of unemployed or substitute carriers;

The armed forces series shows the number in the Army, Navy, and Marine Corps, usually as of June 30. However, during the Spanish-American War, World War I, and the period from 1939 on, when the number was changing rapidly, we present annual averages and add, whenever possible, active members of the Reserve, the National Guard, U.S. Volunteers, etc.

The rest of the data for the executive branch of the federal government are almost entirely from compilations of the Civil Service Commission. For the most part, we used the unrevised figures from the original *Annual Reports* instead of the revised series in recent *Statistical Abstracts* and Civil Service Commission reports because most of the revisions appeared to be in the Post Office Department, which we had treated separately, and it was usually not possible to decide the extent or the nature of the revisions applying to the rest of the data.[7]

The sources for nonschool state and local government employment from 1929 to 1949 are Census Bureau periodic reports on *Government Employment,* and the WPA-BLS State, County, and Municipal Survey. *Government Employment,* which supplied the 1940-49 figures, reports the results of a survey made each quarter by a direct mail canvass of a carefully selected sample of local governments and all state governments. The figures for the missing units are estimated from employment per capita in reporting units, except for any states or cities over 100,000 which may not report. In such cases the figures are estimated individually on the basis of previous reports.

Government Employment shows figures for permanent full-time employment and total employment. We derive our estimate for full-time equivalent employment by adding to permanent full-time em-

---

the census may have put other types of postal employees and postal contractors into this category. Its figures for postmasters are lower than ours in every year, though the difference was small in 1940. This was to be expected, for some fourth class postmasters report themselves to the Census as engaged mainly in some other kind of work; and fourth class postmasters, who accounted for almost the entire number of postmasters in 1896, have declined until they were only about 50 percent of the total by 1949.

[7] The figures before 1921 are dubbed "approximate" in *Historical Statistics of the United States.* Most were probably derived from benchmark years by adding and subtracting hirings and separations. The main benchmarks were counts of government employees in 1896 and 1903. For several years when the Civil Service Commission did not report any figures, or did not show the Post Office separately, we estimated the totals by interpolation, as described in the notes to Table B6.

ployees a third of the number of temporary and part-time employees, the fraction used for the same purpose by the Department of Commerce.

The data for 1929 to 1939 are from the State, County, and Municipal Survey. Monthly data were collected by field agents from payroll records of all state governments, all cities with populations of 50,000 or more in 1930, and a stratified sample of smaller cities, counties, townships, and special purpose government units such as school districts and housing authorities.

Since the two series do not overlap, we linked them by using the Department of Commerce figures for state and local nonschool employment, excluding work relief. According to the Department of Commerce (*Technical Notes on Sources and Methods Used in the Derivation of National Income Statistics*), figures on payrolls from the two sources seemed comparable, but the figures on employment did not. The Department attributes the discrepancy to the inclusion of more nominal employees in the later figures. In the earlier survey, part-time employees were included, but nominal employees (persons with brief or intermittent employment) were, when possible, either scaled down in terms of time worked or excluded. The *Government Employment* figures apparently specifically exclude only members of school boards as nominal employees.

The state government nonschool employment figures (Table B8) were extrapolated back from 1929 to 1920, 1910 and 1900 by per capita employment in a varying sample of states ranging in number from three to six. A similar procedure was used to derive the earlier figures on municipal employment (Table B9). For counties and minor civil divisions (Table B10) we could estimate employment in only one year before 1929 and even that, 1902, only roughly via nonschool expenditures.[8]

School employment (Table B11) rests on a more substantial foundation for the period as a whole, the primary sources for all the data being the annual reports of the Commissioner of Education, the *Biennial Survey of Education,* and the State, County, and Municipal Survey. The original figures for the earlier years had to be stepped up to take account of noninstructional staff, but this group was small compared with teachers, for whom figures are available for the entire period.

[8] It will be seen (App. D) that the expenditure data underlying the 1902 calendar year employment estimate are based on reports for fiscal years ending between July 1, 1902 and June 30, 1903, inclusive.

Table B12 shows, by program, the number of emergency workers, none of whom is included in any of the preceding tables based on payroll data.

Functional classifications of government workers, in the maximum detail available, appear in Tables B15-18.

Comparison with Other Estimates

A word may be desirable on why our estimates differ from (a) earlier estimates published by the National Bureau,[9] (b) current estimates of the Department of Commerce, National Income Division. Kuznets' estimates differ from ours mainly because we could use more recent data, notably the WPA-BLS survey and the compilations of the Governments Division of the Bureau of the Census. We also adjusted the postal service workers to a full-time basis, increased somewhat the sample of state and local governments for which employment data were obtained, and applied somewhat different methods in passing from the sample to our final estimate.

The Department of Commerce estimates for 1929-49 differ from ours mainly because we include all federal employees abroad. The main effect is to put the peak of government employment in 1945 instead of 1944.

[9] Simon Kuznets, *National Income and Its Composition, 1919-1938* (National Bureau of Economic Research, 1941), Table G-7.

Table B1

GOVERNMENT LABOR FORCE AND TOTAL LABOR FORCE

Census Data, 1870-1950

(Unit: 1,000 persons or 1 percent)

	June 1 1870	June 1 1880	June 1 1890	June 1 1900	April 15 1910	Jan. 1 1920	April 1 1930 Comparable with earlier years	April 1 1930 Comparable with later years	March 24-30 1940	March 5-11 1950
Government Labor Force										
Employed and unemployed workers										
(1) In all industries									4,480	7,245
(2) In industries operated wholly by governments	265	419	631	940	1,360	1,988	2,504	2,586	3,211	
Employed workers only (excluding public emergency workers)										
(3) In all industries				1,110	1,736	2,529	3,206	3,310	3,762	
(4) In industries operated wholly by governments				847-883	1,331		2,455	2,534	2,892	
Total Labor Force										
(5) Employed and unemployed workers	12,925	17,392	23,739	29,164	36,786	41,731	48,919	47,493	53,449	63,021
(6) Employed workers only (excluding public emergency workers)				26,257-27,710	35,649	40,212	44,990	45,042	45,488	58,898
Government in Relation to the Total										
(7) Employed government workers as % of all employed workers				4.1	4.9	6.3	7.1	7.3	8.3	12.3
(8) Labor force in industries operated wholly by government as % of total labor force	2.1	2.4	2.7	3.2	3.7	4.8	5.1	5.4	6.0	

NOTES TO TABLE B1

Line

1   The total labor force attached to government in 1940 is estimated as
     follows (figures are in thousands):

     Reported total, government workers employed (excluding
     those in emergency work)   3,845
     Reported total, government workers, experienced, seeking
     work   363
     Less:
        NYA student workers erroneously reported as employed   −14
        Public emergency workers erroneously reported as employed   −257
        NYA and public emergency workers "usually" government
        workers, erroneously reported as seeking work   −20
     Plus:
        U. S. armed forces overseas   150
        Public emergency workers "usually" government workers   371
        Omitted entries "usually" government workers   42
     Total   4,480

     The reported totals are from 16th Census: 1940, *Population, Vol.
     III, The Labor Force,* Table 78. The estimates of the number of per-
     sons erroneously reported as employed are from 16th Census: 1940,
     *Population, Estimates of Labor Force, Employment, and Unemploy-
     ment in The United States, 1940 and 1930* (1944), by John D.
     Durand and Edwin D. Goldfield. The same source estimated the total
     number erroneously reported as seeking work and we assumed that
     the proportion of those who were "usually" government workers was
     the same as the proportion of government workers to all employed
     workers: 8.5 percent (see Table B3). U. S. armed forces overseas are
     from *Census Release, P-44, No. 12.* We estimated the number of pub-
     lic emergency workers who had "usually" been government workers
     from an industrial classification of the last jobs of public emergency
     workers (*Census Release, P-14, No. 13*), assuming that the ratio of
     government to total in each industry was the same as in Table B3. We
     estimated the number of omitted entries (persons for whom employ-
     ment status was not reported) usually attached to government by
     taking 8.5 percent of the estimated number who were actually em-
     ployed or seeking work (see Durand and Goldfield, *op. cit.*).
        A different figure for troops overseas, 119,000, is given in the 1940
     Census, *Population, Vol. I,* p. 6, but this seems low because even the
     higher figure is based on an estimated total military strength of
     417,000, compared with a BLS estimate of 433,000 as of April 1,
     1940.

2   Data for 1910-40 from Table I of Daniel Carson, "Changes in the
     Industrial Composition of Manpower Since the Civil War," *Studies
     in Income and Wealth, Vol. XI,* to which we added U. S. armed
     forces overseas. The 1900 estimate was derived from Carson's 1910
     figures for the three government "industries", public education, the
     Postal Service, and government n.e.c., by extrapolating them back by
     data on occupations characteristic of government (16th Census: 1940,
     Comparative Occupation Statistics for the U. S., 1870-1940 by Alba
     M. Edwards), and then adding armed forces overseas. For 1870-90

Line

the figures are extrapolated back from 1900 by Carson's totals. The figure for armed forces overseas in 1940, 150,000, is from *Census Release P-44, No. 12*. The earlier figures are as follows (see *Historical Statistics of the U. S.*, p. 25): 1930, 89,453; 1920, 117,238; 1910, 55,608; 1900, 91,219. Since the data for 1870-90 do not include troops overseas, the figure for 1900 comparable with earlier years would be 849,000.

3   1940 Census, *The Labor Force*, Table 78. We added U. S. troops and other employees outside the continental U. S. (see note to line 2) and 8.5 percent of the estimated number of employed persons for whom no employment status was shown, and subtracted NYA student workers and public emergency workers erroneously reported as employed, assuming that all were reported as government workers (see Durand and Goldfield, *op. cit.* and Table B3). Figures for 1930 and earlier years except 1920 were estimated by extrapolation via line 4, and 1920 was interpolated via line 2. The figure for 1950 is from the *Monthly Report on the Labor Force*, March 1950, with U. S. armed forces overseas included.

4   1940: for employees other than education, 1940 Census, *The Labor Force*, Table 74, "government". For education employees, Carson's total labor force in public education multiplied by the ratio of employed to total labor force in all education, from *Census Release P-14, No. 13*. We added armed forces overseas (see note to line 2).

1930: for employees other than education, 1930 Census, *Unemployment*, Table 3, ratio (for public service, n.e.c.) of gainful workers other than Class A unemployed to total gainful workers, multiplied by Carson's government employees other than public school. To these we added U. S. troops and some others stationed outside the continental U. S. For school employees the same method, using Carson's public school employment. Class A unemployment in 1930 was assumed to be approximately equivalent to the 1940 concept of experienced workers seeking work, and the government occupations for which data are presented for 1930 are assumed to be representative of the industries Carson included. For support of the assumption about unemployment, see Durand and Goldfield, *op. cit.*

1910: Carson's figure for government workers, multiplied by the ratio of employed to gainfully occupied in the part of government employment shown in Gladys L. Palmer and Ann Ratner, *Industrial and Occupational Trends in National Employment*, Research Report No. 11, Industrial Research Department, Wharton School of Finance and Commerce, 1949, App. Table 1C. To this figure we added the armed forces overseas (see note to line 2).

1900: for education employees, the number attached multiplied by minimum and maximum ratios of manmonths worked to available manmonths. The ratios are based on the figures for "teachers and professors" in the 1900 Census, *Special Report on Occupations*, Tables 1 and 25. Since school teachers not at work during the summer were reported as unemployed, teachers "unemployed" 1 to 3 months were counted as working 12 months. For other employees, except troops

NOTES TO TABLE B1 (concluded)

Line

serving overseas, employment was estimated using the ratios in Solomon Fabricant, "The Changing Industrial Distribution of Gainful Workers", *Studies in Income and Wealth, Vol. XI,* derived similarly to school employment, above, using occupations attached wholly or largely to government. For armed forces outside the continental U. S., see note to line 2.

5   Figures for 1870-1930 (comparable with earlier years) except 1910, are from Carson, *op. cit.,* Table 1. The 1910 figure is from Fabricant, *op. cit.,* Table 2. The figures for 1940 and 1930 (comparable with 1940) are from Durand and Goldfield, *op. cit.* The 1940 total is not exactly comparable with that for 1950 because of changes in the schedule in July 1945. The 1940 figure comparable with 1950 would be 54,890,000 (*Census Release P-50, No. 2*). The 1950 figure is from the *Monthly Report on the Labor Force* for March 1950. We adjusted all these totals, beginning with 1900, to include U. S. armed forces overseas (see note to line 2) ; the 1900 figure excluding these is 29,073,000.

6   The 1950 figure, which includes armed forces overseas, is from the *Monthly Report on the Labor Force,* March 1950. Those for 1940 and 1930 are from Durand and Goldfield, *op. cit.,* plus armed forces overseas. The 1940 figure comparable with 1950, adjusted for the schedule change in July 1945, would be 46,530,000 (*Census Release P-50, No. 2,* p. 4). The 1920 total is full-time equivalent employment from Simon Kuznets, *National Income and Its Composition,* pp. 334 and 340. The figures for 1900 and 1910 are line 5 less armed forces overseas, multiplied by the ratio of employed workers to total gainful workers, plus armed forces overseas. The 1910 ratio is from Palmer and Ratner, *op. cit.,* and the 1900 ratio is from Fabricant, *op. cit.,* Table 1. The 1900 estimate excluding armed forces overseas is 26,166,000-27,619,000.

7   Line 3 as a percentage of line 6. The 1940 ratio comparable with 1950 would be 8.1 percent (see note to line 6).

8   Line 2 as a percentage of line 5. The 1900 ratio comparable with earlier years is 2.8 percent (see note to lines 2 and 5).

Table B2

GOVERNMENT AND TOTAL EMPLOYMENT, EXCLUDING EMERGENCY WORKERS

Census Data, 1940-1950

(Unit: 1,000 persons or 1 percent)

	March 24-30 1940	March 3-9 1946	March 2-8 1947	March 7-13 1948	March 6-12 1949	March 5-11 1950	Annual Average 1946	Annual Average 1947	Annual Average 1948	Annual Average 1949	Annual Average 1950
Workers employed by government	3,762	10,150	6,810	6,706	6,916	7,245	8,759	6,481	6,594	6,906	7,317
Civilian	3,332	5,530	5,240	5,470	5,425	5,899	5,309	5,041	5,288	5,440	5,817
Armed forces	430	4,620	1,570	1,236	1,491	1,346	3,450	1,440	1,306	1,466	1,500
All employed workers	46,530	57,080	57,630	58,565	59,138	58,897	58,700	59,467	60,684	60,175	61,457
Civilian	46,100	52,460	56,060	57,329	57,647	57,551	55,250	58,027	59,378	58,709	59,957
Armed forces	430	4,620	1,570	1,236	1,491	1,346	3,450	1,440	1,306	1,466	1,500
Employed government workers as % of all employed workers	8.1	17.8	11.8	11.5	11.7	12.3	14.9	10.9	10.9	11.5	11.9
Employed civilian government workers as % of all employed civilian workers	7.2	10.5	9.3	9.5	9.4	10.3	9.6	8.7	8.9	9.3	9.7

The 1940 data are from the 1940 Census, *The Labor Force,* Table 78, revised for omitted entries and for public emergency and NYA student workers on the basis of data in Durand and Goldfield, *op. cit.* (see notes to Table B1). The armed forces figure is from *Census Release P-50, No. 2,* p. 2 and Table II. The 1946 figures are from *Labor Force Bulletin 7,* April 1947, and *Census Release P-50, No. 2.* The figures for 1947-50 are from *Census Release P-50, No. 13, No. 19, No. 31.*

Table B3

INDUSTRIAL DISTRIBUTION OF GOVERNMENT AND TOTAL
EMPLOYMENT, 1940 (CENSUS DATA)

(Unit: 1,000 persons or 1 percent)

	Government Workers		All Workers		Government Workers as % of Total Workers
	NUMBER	%	NUMBER	%	
Agriculture	23	0.5	8,750	17.7	0.3
Forestry, except logging, & fishery	26	0.6	120	0.2	22.0
Mining	4	0.1	1,044	2.1	0.4
Construction	462	11.0	2,765	5.6	16.7
Manufacturing	*123*	*2.9*	*11,470*	*23.2*	*1.1*
Printing, publishing, & allied industries	7	0.2	673	1.4	1.0
Iron & steel products other than blast furnaces, steel works, & rolling mills	25	0.6	776	1.6	3.2
Ship & boat building & repairing	59	1.4	163	0.3	36.2
Apparel & accessories	20	0.5	824	1.7	2.4
Other manufacturing	13	0.4	9,034	18.3	0.1
Transportation, comm., & public utilities	*174*	*4.1*	*3,337*	*6.7*	*5.2*
Street railways & bus lines	16	0.4	210	0.4	7.6
Water transportation	12	0.3	213	0.4	5.6
Utilities	135	3.2	565	1.1	23.9
Other	11	0.3	2,348	4.7	0.5
Wholesale trade	....	....	1,284	2.6	....
Retail trade	11	0.3	6,839	13.8	0.2

Table B3 (continued)

	Government Workers		All Workers		Government Workers as % of Total Workers
	NUMBER	%	NUMBER	%	
Banking & other finance	15	0.4	494	1.0	3.0
Insurance & real estate	3	0.1	1,041	2.1	0.3
Business & repair services	1	*	948	1.9	0.1
Personal services	5	0.1	4,379	8.8	0.1
Amusement, recreation, & related services	11	0.3	460	0.9	2.4
Professional & related services	1,497	35.6	3,422	6.9	43.7
Educational services	1,256	29.8	1,606	3.2	78.2
Medical & other health services	225	5.3	1,052	2.1	21.4
Charitable, religious & membership organizations	16	0.4	395	0.8	4.1
Other professional services	1	*	369	0.7	0.3
Government	1,811	43.0	1,811	3.7	100.0
Postal service	310	7.4	310	0.6	100.0
National defense	310	7.4	310	0.6	100.0
Federal government (n.e.c.)	307	7.3	307	0.6	100.0
State & local government (n.e.c.)	884	21.0	884	1.8	100.0
Industry not reported	41	1.0	1,329	2.7	3.1
Total	4,208	100.0	49,493	100.0	8.5

* Less than .05 percent.

Data are from the 1940 Census, *Population, Vol. III; The Labor Force*, Part 1, Tables 74 and 78. Figures include employed workers (except emergency) and experienced workers seeking work, and are the original census figures, not revised as in Table B1.

Table B4

POST OFFICE DEPARTMENT EMPLOYEES, 1896-1949

(Unit: 1,000 persons)

Year	Postmasters 1st, 2nd and 3rd class (1)	Postmasters 4th class (2)	Assistant Postmasters (3)	Clerks and Supervisory Force 1st and 2nd class (Regular Employees) (4)	3rd and 4th class (5)	Carriers (Regular Employees) City (6)	Rural (7)	Village (8)	Railway Mail Service Employees (Regular) (9)	Watchmen, Messengers and Mail Handlers (Regular Employees) 1st and 2nd Class (10)	Motor Vehicle Service (Govt. Owned) (11)	Departmental Employees, P.O. Inspectors and Clerks (12)	Operating Force, Public Buildings (13)	Misc. (14)	Total Number (15)	Total Full-Time Equivalent Number (16)
1896	3.6	66.7	.7	13.1	87.5	12.8	...	...	7.4	.5	...	.8	...	.3	193.4	77.8
1897	3.8	67.3	.8	13.3	88.2	12.9	.1	...	7.6	.5	...	.8	...	.3	195.6	78.9
1898	3.8	69.8	.9	13.5	91.4	13.7	.1	...	8.0	.5	...	.9	...	.3	202.9	82.0
1899	4.0	71.0	1.1	13.7	93.2	14.3	.4	...	8.4	.5	...	1.0	...	.3	207.9	84.8
1900	4.2	72.5	1.1	14.8	95.2	15.3	1.3	...	8.7	.6	...	1.1	...	.4	215.2	89.4
1901	4.5	72.5	1.3	16.8	95.4	16.4	4.3	...	9.1	.6	...	1.2	...	.4	222.5	96.6
1902	4.7	71.2	1.4	19.9	94.0	17.8	8.5	...	9.6	.8	...	1.3	...	.4	229.6	105.7
1903	5.0	69.1	1.5	22.2	91.7	19.5	15.1	...	10.4	.9	...	1.3	...	.4	237.1	116.5
1904	5.4	65.8	1.7	24.3	87.7	20.8	24.6	...	11.4	.9	...	1.4	...	.5	244.5	129.4
1905	5.7	62.5	1.7	25.4	83.8	21.8	32.1	...	12.3	1.0	...	1.5	...	.5	248.3	138.6
1906	5.9	59.7	1.7	24.0	80.6	23.0	35.7	...	13.4	.9	...	1.6	...	.5	247.0	141.8
1907	6.3	56.3	1.7	26.4	77.2	24.6	37.6	...	14.2	1.0	...	1.7	...	.5	247.5	147.4
1908	6.8	53.9	1.9	28.2	75.0	26.4	39.1	...	15.2	1.1	...	1.7	...	.6	249.9	153.2
1909	7.2	52.9	2.0	29.9	74.5	27.6	40.5	...	15.9	1.1	...	1.7	...	.6	253.9	158.3
1910	7.6	52.0	2.1	31.8	74.0	28.7	41.0	...	16.6	1.2	...	1.7	...	.6	257.3	162.8
1911	8.0	51.3	2.2	32.3	73.8	29.2	41.6	...	16.8	1.3	...	1.7	...	.6	258.8	165.0
1912	8.3	50.5	2.3	33.7	73.5	30.0	42.1	...	16.7	1.3	...	1.7	...	.7	260.8	167.8
1913	8.4	49.6	2.4	35.5	72.8	30.9	42.7	.1	17.5	1.4	...	1.8	...	.7	263.8	172.0
1914	8.6	48.2	2.4	38.0	73.0	32.3	43.5	.2	19.7	1.6	...	1.8	...	.7	270.0	179.1

Year																
1915	180.3	269.9	.7	…	1.8	…	1.6	19.3	.2	43.7	32.9	72.0	38.8	2.5	47.5	8.9
1916	181.5	270.5	.8	…	1.8	…	1.7	18.8	.2	42.8	34.1	72.0	40.1	2.3	46.7	9.2
1917	184.2	271.2	.8	…	1.8	…	1.8	17.6	.5	43.3	34.5	71.0	41.8	2.6	45.0	10.4
1918	185.6	268.5	.8	…	1.8	1.2	1.8	17.8	.8	43.3	34.5	66.8	42.7	2.6	43.7	10.6
1919	188.0	266.5	.8	…	1.9	1.9	1.9	18.1	.9	43.2	35.1	62.4	44.7	2.6	42.3	10.8
1920	195.1	270.3	.9	…	1.9	3.9	2.1	19.0	.9	43.3	36.1	59.2	47.6	2.8	41.1	11.5
1921	206.2	276.7	.9	…	1.9	4.2	2.5	19.4	1.1	43.6	38.1	55.9	53.7	2.8	38.1	14.1
1922	210.6	278.6	.9	…	1.9	4.4	3.1	19.8	1.1	44.1	39.1	53.2	56.0	2.7	37.5	14.4
1923	212.1	277.8	.9	…	1.9	4.5	3.3	19.8	1.1	44.3	40.1	50.4	57.2	2.7	37.2	14.4
1924	222.9	287.5	1.0	…	1.9	3.7	3.9	20.5	1.2	44.6	43.8	49.7	63.2	2.7	36.5	14.8
1925	228.0	291.7	1.0	…	2.0	3.8	4.1	20.3	1.2	45.1	46.1	49.2	65.1	2.7	35.8	15.1
1926	231.3	294.3	1.0	…	2.1	3.8	4.1	19.8	1.1	45.2	48.1	48.6	67.1	2.7	35.4	15.5
1927	234.4	296.6	1.1	…	2.1	3.8	4.3	20.0	.9	44.6	50.1	48.0	68.7	2.7	34.8	15.5
1928	236.8	298.2	1.2	…	2.1	3.8	4.5	20.2	.9	44.2	51.1	47.5	69.8	2.8	34.3	15.6
1929	239.6	300.2	1.4	…	2.1	3.8	4.7	20.5	.9	43.7	52.1	47.1	71.0	2.8	33.8	15.7
1930	241.1	301.2	1.4	…	2.1	3.8	4.9	20.6	.9	43.2	53.8	46.7	72.0	2.8	33.4	15.6
1931	240.4	299.9	1.4	…	2.2	3.9	4.9	21.0	1.0	42.3	53.4	46.3	71.6	2.8	33.1	15.7
1932	237.0	295.9	1.4	…	2.2	3.8	4.8	21.0	1.0	41.5	52.8	45.9	70.5	2.7	32.7	15.5
1933	229.3	287.9	1.3	…	2.1	3.7	4.6	19.8	1.0	39.9	51.2	45.5	68.5	2.7	32.6	15.0
1934	224.4	282.2	1.0	8.0	2.0	3.6	4.5	18.8	1.0	37.0	48.3	44.8	64.2	2.5	32.4	14.1
1935	223.9	281.2	1.2	9.3	2.0	3.5	4.7	18.5	1.0	34.8	49.1	44.1	64.7	2.6	32.3	13.4
1936	237.1	293.3	1.2	11.4	2.0	3.5	4.9	19.7	1.0	34.0	53.9	43.4	70.5	2.6	31.5	13.7
1937	241.5	296.6	1.2	12.8	2.1	3.6	5.0	20.0	.9	33.5	54.9	42.8	72.3	2.6	30.7	14.2
1938	246.2	300.5	1.2	15.5	2.1	3.6	5.2	19.8	.9	33.1	55.7	42.3	73.8	2.7	30.1	14.5
1939	249.0	302.5	1.2	16.2	2.1	3.6	5.2	19.9	.9	32.8	56.6	41.8	75.2	2.7	29.5	14.8
1940	254.6	307.5	1.1	17.3	2.2	3.7	5.5	20.1	.9	32.6	58.5	41.4	77.4	2.8	29.2	14.9
1941	262.2	314.6	1.2	18.6	2.3	3.8	5.5	20.4	.9	32.4	61.1	41.0	80.6	2.8	28.8	15.0
1942	267.5	319.0	1.1	18.8	2.3	3.8	5.7	20.6	.8	32.2	62.9	40.5	84.1	2.8	28.2	15.2
1943	257.9	307.6	1.1	16.1	2.4	3.6	5.5	20.1	.6	32.1	58.6	39.5	82.3	3.2	26.9	15.7
1944	263.0	310.8	1.1	18.4	2.6	3.6	4.9	20.6	.3	32.0	58.0	38.5	85.2	3.4	25.3	16.9
1945	270.0	313.6	3.6	18.6	2.7	3.6	4.8	20.5	.2	32.0	58.0	35.3	89.1	3.4	22.9	18.9
1946	288.2	329.6	1.2	15.1	2.9	4.1	5.2	22.5	.1	32.1	65.8	35.7	99.8	3.4	19.6	22.1
1947	293.8	335.0	1.2	15.5	2.9	4.2	5.2	24.2	.1	32.2	67.7	35.5	101.1	3.4	19.4	22.4
1948	321.7	363.9	1.4	15.5	2.9	4.3	8.1	24.5	.1	32.3	78.1	35.7	116.0	3.4	20.5	21.1
1949	342.4	384.6	1.5	15.7	2.9	4.6	9.9	26.2	.1	32.5	86.4	35.5	124.3	3.4	20.7	20.9

NOTES TO TABLE B4

These figures exclude most temporary employees and certain classes of part-time employees, contractors, and contractors' employees, such as star route contractors, screen wagon drivers, and mail messengers. Part-time employees are of some importance, but temporary employees seem unimportant, at least before 1940 (see BLS *Bulletin 574* and notes below). A series for the number of part-time employees, 1926-49, is given in the *Annual Report of the Post-master General, 1949.*

Not all the persons we included have been direct employees of the federal government during the entire period covered. Clerks in fourth class post offices, for example, are employees of the postmaster rather than of the government. Clerks in third class offices became government employees only in 1946.

Figures are as of June 30, except when otherwise noted.

Notes to each column, when necessary, follow:

Column

1 & 2   The number of postmasters of each class is measured by the number of post offices. Figures for 1896-1912, 1921-34, and 1937-49 are given in the *Annual Report of the Postmaster General* for 1905, 1912, 1921-34, 1944, and 1949. For 1913-20, we used the figures as of July 1 in the reports for 1919 and 1921. For 1935 and 1936 we calculated the number of post offices in each class on June 30 by adding the increases and decreases during the year to the July 1 figures for the preceding years.

3   Figures for 1913-49 from the *Annual Report of the Postmaster General, 1949;* those for 1899-1904 and 1907-12 from reports for the individual years. The 1896 figure is from the U. S. Civil Service Commission report, *Tables Showing the Number of Positions in the Executive Civil Service of the U. S., 1896.* Those for 1897, 1898, 1905, and 1906 were derived by straight-line interpolation. Until 1901 assistant postmasters were paid out of appropriations for clerks; there may, therefore, be some duplication between columns 3 and 4.

4   1915-49: *Annual Report of the Postmaster General, 1949;* 1906-15: *1915 Annual Report.* 1899-1905: annual reports for each year; 1896: Civil Service Commission *Tables* for 1896; 1897-98: straight-line interpolations between 1896 and 1899. Temporary clerks, not included, ranged from 3.1 thousand in 1906 to 1.2 thousand in 1910.

5   1906: *Annual Report of the Postmaster General;* 1913-17 and 1923-32: various issues of the *Annual Report of the Civil Service Commission.* All other figures are interpolated and extrapolated by the number of third and fourth class post offices.

6, 7   Figures for 1913-49 for city and village delivery carriers, and for
& 8   1926-49 for rural delivery carriers are from the *Annual Report of the Postmaster General, 1949;* other figures for 1896-1925 are from *Postal Statistics of the United States, 1789-1940.* Delivery by rural carriers was inaugurated in October, 1896, delivery by village carriers in 1913. Temporary rural carriers are not included.

9   1926-49: *Annual Report of the Postmaster General, 1949,* including only regular full-time employees. All the other figures, except 1906, 1907, 1917, and 1920, are from the annual reports for the individual

NOTES TO TABLE B4 (concluded)

Column

years, and exclude acting employees but include all regular employees. The figures for the four missing years are interpolations based on total Railway Mail Service employment.

10   1913-49: *Annual Report of the Postmaster General, 1949;* 1908, 1910, and 1912: BLS *Bulletin 574.* The 1909 and 1911 figures are straight-line interpolations. Those for 1897-1907 are interpolated between 1908 and 1896 by number of clerks and supervisory employees in first and second class offices. The 1896 source is the Civil Service Commission *Tables* for 1896. Until 1909, watchmen, messengers and mail handlers were paid from the appropriation for clerks; there may therefore be some duplication between columns 10 and 4.

11   Government-owned motor vehicle service was inaugurated in October 1914, but no data on employment are given for years before 1918. The figures for 1926-49 are from the *Annual Report of the Postmaster General, 1949;* those for 1918-25, from the annual reports for the individual years. Substitutes are included in the figures for 1918-23.

12   1926-49: *Annual Report of the Postmaster General, 1949;* 1925: the annual report for that year; 1908, 1910, and 1912: BLS *Bulletin 574;* 1896: Civil Service Commission *Tables* for 1896. Figures for all other years are straight-line interpolations.

13   Until October 1933, when they were transferred to the Post Office payroll, the operating force for public buildings housing post offices and other government agencies was on the rolls of the Treasury Department. The decrease in 1946 was due to the fact that a number of employees were transferred from the full-time category to part-time. Figures are from the *Annual Report of the Postmaster General, 1949.*

14   Includes foreign mail transportation, domestic air mail, manufacture and distribution of stamps, equipment shop employees, etc. Figures for 1926-49 are from the *Annual Report of the Postmaster General, 1949;* the 1896 figure is from the Civil Service Commission *Tables* for 1896. Other figures are interpolations.

15   Sum of the preceding 14 columns.

16   Column 15, with the number of 4th class postmasters and 3rd and 4th class clerks reduced by 3/4. This ratio is arbitrary; in part, however, it is supported by the evidence supplied by earnings.

Table B5
ARMED FORCES, 1896-1949
(Unit: 1,000 persons)

Year	Army (1)	Navy (2)	Marine Corps (3)	Coast Guard (4)	Total (5)
1896	27.0	10.5	2.5		40.0
1897	27.5	11.9	2.7		42.1
1898	155.4	25.4	3.7		184.5
1899	102.4	16.4	3.7		122.5
1900	101.2	19.0	5.7		125.9
1901	84.9	21.1	5.9		111.9
1902	80.5	24.3	6.0		110.8
1903	69.0	30.4	6.1		105.5
1904	69.8	32.7	7.3		109.8
1905	67.0	34.3	7.0		108.3
1906	68.4	35.7	8.2		112.3
1907	63.6	36.8	8.2		108.6
1908	76.4	43.4	9.0		128.8
1909	84.5	48.3	9.7		142.5
1910	80.7	49.3	9.6		139.6
1911	83.3	52.1	9.8		145.2
1912	91.5	52.0	9.9		153.4
1913	92.0	53.0	10.1		155.1
1914	97.8	58.0	10.2		166.0
1915	106.0	58.0	10.3	2.5	176.8
1916	107.6	60.4	10.6	4.3	182.9
1917	527.3	159.9	23.1	4.6	714.9
1918	2,399.9	419.0	53.4	5.9	2,878.2
1919	836.9	272.3	48.8	5.1	1,163.1
1920	200.4	121.8	17.2	4.3	343.7
1921	227.4	132.8	23.0	4.5	387.7
1922	146.1	100.2	21.2	4.7	272.2
1923	131.0	94.1	19.7	4.7	249.5
1924	140.6	98.3	20.3	6.0	265.2
1925	134.6	95.3	19.5	9.4	258.8
1926	133.0	93.4	19.2	9.9	255.5
1927	133.1	95.0	19.2	11.2	258.5
1928	134.3	96.0	19.0	11.8	261.1
1929	137.4	97.3	18.8	12.4	265.9
1930	137.5	97.1	19.4	12.4	266.4
1931	138.6	93.4	18.8	12.3	263.1
1932	133.0	93.4	16.6	12.8	255.8
1933	135.0	91.4	16.1	11.3	253.8
1934	137.0	92.5	16.4	10.4	256.3
1935	138.0	95.5	17.3	10.7	261.5
1936	166.1	106.2	17.2	10.0	299.5
1937	178.1	113.4	18.2	10.5	320.2
1938	183.4	118.6	18.4	10.4	330.8

Table B5 (continued)

Year	Army (1)	Navy (2)	Marine Corps (3)	Coast Guard (4)	Total (5)
1939	192.0	124.0	19.0	10.0	345.0
1940	324.0	163.0	31.0	14.0	532.0
1941	1,291.0	278.0	55.0	20.0	1,644.0
1942	3,071.0	684.0	146.0	67.0	3,968.0
1943	6,733.0	1,744.0	311.0	156.0	8,944.0
1944	7,889.0	2,860.0	453.0	170.0	11,372.0
1945	7,734.0	3,248.0	464.0	162.0	11,608.0
1946	2,291.0	1,226.0	186.0	48.0	3,751.0
1947	1,059.0	494.0	98.0	20.0	1,671.0
1948	964.0	424.0	84.0	20.0	1,492.0
1949	1,090.0	443.0	86.0	23.0	1,642.0

Data for years prior to 1939 are from annual reports of the War Department, for the Army; of the Navy Department, for the Navy and Marine Corps; and of the Treasury Department, for the Coast Guard; or from compilations from these reports by the Bureau of the Census published in the *Statistical Abstract of the U. S.* Data for 1939 and following years are from BLS compilations.

It is not always clear to what extent reserves, militia, and volunteers are included, especially during the Spanish War and the Philippine Islands insurrection. We tried to include such auxiliary personnel, if active, whenever possible.

Figures are as of June 30, except those for 1939-49 and occasional years noted below, which are annual averages.

Column

1   All figures for 1900-38 except 1917 and 1918 are from the 1924 and 1949 *Statistical Abstract*. The figures for 1898 and 1899 are annual averages from the reports of the War Department for 1898, 1899, and 1900. U. S. volunteers are included from May 1898 to 1902. The 1917 and 1918 figures are annual averages and include the National Guard, federalized in May 1917, and members of reserve forces on active duty. The 1919 figure seems close to the average for the year, judging from reported data on discharges; it excludes reserve forces and national guardsmen not serving in the U. S. Army.

2   Figures from the 1948 and 1949 *Statistical Abstract* are interpolated and extrapolated by earlier series on the number of Navy personnel. Figures for 1917 and 1918 are annual averages. The Coast Guard is not included in the 1917 and 1918 figures, though it was part of the Navy. The 1919 figure includes members of the naval reserve on active duty.

3   Figures from the 1948 and 1949 *Statistical Abstract* are interpolated and extrapolated by earlier series on the number of Marine personnel. The 1917 and 1918 figures are annual averages.

4   The Coast Guard was formed in 1915 from the Revenue Cutter Service and the Life Saving Service of the Treasury Department. Until 1915 these employees were included among civilian personnel. Our 1915 figure is the number on July 1, 1914 as reported in the *Annual Report of the U. S. Civil Service Commission, 1915*. Civilians are included, except in 1920 and 1921, but the number is very small.

Table B6

FEDERAL GOVERNMENT

TOTAL EMPLOYEES AND THEIR DISTRIBUTION BY MAJOR BRANCHES, 1896-1949

(Unit: 1,000 persons)

Year	Executive Branch, Civilian		Judicial Branch	Legislative Branch	Government Corporations	Civilian Total		Armed Forces	Grand Total	
	TOTAL NUMBER	FULL-TIME EQUIVALENT NUMBER				TOTAL NUMBER	FULL-TIME EQUIVALENT NUMBER		TOTAL NUMBER	FULL-TIME EQUIVALENT NUMBER
	(1)	(2)	(3)	(4)	(5)	(6)	(7)	(8)	(9)	(10)
1896	259.5	143.9	3.3	.8		263.6	148.0	40.0	303.6	188.0
1897	261.5	144.8	3.3	.8		265.6	148.9	42.1	307.7	191.0
1898	276.7	155.8	3.3	.8		280.8	159.9	184.5	465.3	344.4
1899	295.5	172.4	3.3	.8		299.6	176.5	122.5	422.1	299.0
1900	307.9	182.1	3.3	.8		312.0	186.2	125.9	437.9	312.1
1901	322.1	196.2	3.3	.8		326.2	200.3	111.9	438.1	312.2
1902	330.8	206.9	3.2	1.1		335.1	211.2	110.8	445.9	322.0
1903	334.5	213.9	3.0	1.4		338.9	218.3	105.5	444.4	323.8
1904	348.5	233.4	2.9	1.8		353.2	238.1	109.8	463.0	347.9
1905	370.5	260.8	2.9	1.9		375.3	265.6	108.3	483.6	373.9
1906	382.6	277.4	2.9	2.0		387.5	282.3	112.3	499.8	394.6
1907	394.9	294.8	2.9	2.2		400.0	299.9	108.6	508.6	408.5
1908	403.3	306.6	2.9	2.3		408.5	311.8	128.8	537.3	440.6
1909	417.6	322.0	3.0	2.5		423.1	327.5	142.5	565.6	470.0
1910	433.6	339.1	3.0	2.6		439.2	344.7	139.6	578.8	484.3
1911	439.8	346.0	3.0	2.7		445.5	351.7	145.2	590.7	496.9
1912	442.7	349.7	3.0	2.9		448.6	355.6	153.4	602.0	509.0
1913	442.6	350.8	2.9	2.9		448.4	356.6	155.1	603.5	511.7
1914	455.3	364.4	2.8	3.0		461.1	370.2	166.0	627.1	536.2
1915	448.7	359.1	2.8	3.1		454.6	365.0	176.8	631.4	541.8
1916	457.7	368.7	2.7	3.2		463.6	374.6	182.9	646.5	557.5

Year										
1917	491.8	404.8	2.6	3.2		497.6	410.6	714.9	1,212.5	1,125.5
1918	883.2	800.3	2.5	3.3		889.0	806.1	2,878.2	3,767.2	3,684.3
1919	821.0	742.5	2.4	3.4		826.8	748.3	1,163.1	1,989.9	1,911.4
1920	682.3	607.1	2.3	3.4		688.0	612.8	343.7	1,031.7	956.5
1921	585.6	515.1	2.3	3.5		591.4	520.9	387.7	979.1	908.6
1922	556.8	488.8	2.2	3.6		562.6	494.6	272.2	834.8	766.8
1923	540.5	474.8	2.1	3.7		546.3	480.6	249.5	795.8	730.1
1924	546.0	481.4	2.0	3.7		551.7	487.1	265.2	816.9	752.3
1925	554.8	491.1	1.9	3.8		560.5	496.8	258.8	819.3	755.6
1926	549.0	486.0	1.8	3.9		554.7	491.7	255.5	810.2	747.2
1927	547.0	484.8	1.8	3.9		552.7	490.5	258.5	811.2	749.0
1928	556.0	494.6	1.7	4.0		561.7	500.3	261.1	822.8	761.4
1929	573.0	512.4	1.6	4.1	15.2	593.9	533.3	265.9	859.8	799.2
1930	593.1	533.0	1.8	4.2	14.9	614.0	553.9	266.4	880.4	820.3
1931	600.4	540.9	1.8	4.3	14.7	621.2	561.7	263.1	884.3	824.8
1932	594.7	535.8	1.8	4.4	15.9	616.8	557.9	255.8	872.6	813.7
1933	592.3	533.7	1.8	4.4	19.5	618.0	559.4	253.8	871.8	813.2
1934	690.3	632.5	1.8	4.7	21.3	718.1	660.3	256.3	974.4	916.6
1935	741.9	684.6	1.9	4.9	22.8	771.5	714.2	261.5	1,033.0	975.7
1936	852.9	796.7	2.0	5.1	23.5	883.5	827.3	299.5	1,183.0	1,126.8
1937	880.8	825.7	2.1	5.2	24.4	912.5	857.4	320.2	1,232.7	1,177.6
1938	863.6	809.3	2.1	5.2	25.0	895.9	841.6	330.8	1,226.7	1,172.4
1939	934.3	880.8	2.3	5.4	25.5	967.5	914.0	345.0	1,312.5	1,259.0
1940	1,017.9	965.0	2.4	5.9	26.5	1,052.7	999.8	532.0	1,584.7	1,531.8
1941	1,369.6	1,317.2	2.5	6.1	29.6	1,407.8	1,355.4	1,644.0	3,051.8	2,999.4
1942	2,206.2	2,154.7	2.6	6.4	32.1	2,247.3	2,195.8	3,968.0	6,215.3	6,163.8
1943	3,137.4	3,087.7	2.6	6.2	35.6	3,181.8	3,132.1	8,944.0	12,125.8	12,076.1
1944	3,262.3	3,214.5	2.7	6.2	35.9	3,307.1	3,259.3	11,372.0	14,679.1	14,631.3
1945	3,696.4	3,652.8	2.8	6.4	34.3	3,739.9	3,696.3	11,608.0	15,347.9	15,304.3
1946	2,555.0	2,513.6	3.1	6.6	33.2	2,597.9	2,556.5	3,751.0	6,348.9	6,307.5
1947	1,983.7	1,942.5	3.2	7.1	30.9	2,024.9	1,983.7	1,671.0	3,695.9	3,654.7
1948	1,943.7	1,901.5	3.5	7.3	28.7	1,983.2	1,941.0	1,492.0	3,475.2	3,433.0
1949	1,969.6	1,927.4	3.6	7.7	27.6	2,008.5	1,966.3	1,642.0	3,650.5	3,608.3

Notes to Table B6

Column

1   Most of the data are from tables published in U. S. Civil Service Com-
     mission annual reports and in the *Statistical Abstract of the U. S.*
     Other data are from *Tables Showing the Number of Positions in the
     Executive Civil Service of the U. S., 1896; The Classified Executive
     Civil Service of the U. S. Government, 1933,* and annual reports of
     the Post Office Department. Our estimates of Post Office employment
     (Table B4) were substituted for the postal figures in the Civil Service
     Commission tables. All paid employees within the continental U. S.
     and abroad are included. The numbers are as of June 30 except in
     1903 (July 1), 1918 (Nov. 11), 1920 and 1921 (July 31).

     There are no Civil Service Commission totals for 1897-1900 or
     separate Post Office figures for 1897-1900 or 1918-19. The earlier fig-
     ures are estimated by interpolation between 1896 and 1901 via salary
     expenditures from various issues of the *Annual Report of the Secre-
     tary of the Treasury.* For 1918-19, employment other than postal is
     interpolated by total employment.

     For 1933 we added to the reported total 9.2 thousand employees
     of certain new agencies not reporting to the Civil Service Commission
     until a later date (see *Statistical Abstract, 1936,* p. 156) ; and for
     1943, we subtracted from the reported total 3 thousand unpaid em-
     ployees (see *Statistical Abstract, 1946,* p. 208). Because the reported
     figures for 1896, 1901-12, 1914, and 1917 apparently do not include
     State Department employees abroad, we added estimates for them (in
     thousands: 1896, 1901, 1902, .8; 1903, 1.1; 1904-12, 1.2; 1914, 1.0;
     1917, 2.4).

2   Column 1, with the full-time equivalent number of post office em-
     ployees (Table B4) substituted for the total number of such employees.

3 & 4 Data for 1929-49 are from the Bureau of Labor Statistics, and for
     1901, 1904, and 1912, from annual reports of the Civil Service Com-
     mission. Figures for other years are straight-line interpolations or ex-
     trapolations; those for 1929-49 are annual averages.

5   Covers corporations not already included in the Executive Branch,
     among which are the Panama Railroad Company, the Federal Reserve
     Banks (which employed 10,000 in 1929), and banks of the Farm
     Credit Administration. Data are annual averages (except for 1949,
     which is as of July 1), and are from the Bureau of Labor Statistics.
     Figures for earlier years are not available.

6   Sum of columns 1, 3, 4, and 5.

7   Sum of columns 2, 3, 4, and 5.

8   See Table B5.

9   Sum of columns 6 and 8.

10   Sum of columns 7 and 8.

Table B7

Federal Government
Main Functional Distribution of Employees, 1896-1949
(Unit: 1,000 persons)

Year	National Defense (1)	Post Office Full-time Equivalent Number (2)	Other (3)	Total, Full-time Equivalent Number (4)
1896	61.3	77.8	48.9	188.0
1897	63.5	78.9	48.6	191.0
1898	210.6	82.0	51.8	344.4
1899	159.9	84.8	54.3	299.0
1900	165.9	89.4	56.8	312.1
1901	156.4	96.6	59.2	312.2
1902	155.3	105.7	61.0	322.0
1903	150.7	116.5	56.6	323.8
1904	157.0	129.4	61.5	347.9
1905	156.1	138.6	79.2	373.9
1906	162.6	141.8	90.2	394.6
1907	159.2	147.4	101.9	408.5
1908	179.5	153.2	107.9	440.6
1909	196.9	158.3	114.8	470.0
1910	197.9	162.8	123.6	484.3
1911	205.5	165.0	126.4	496.9
1912	213.4	167.8	127.8	509.0
1913	210.6	172.0	129.1	511.7
1914	224.0	179.1	133.1	536.2
1915	235.1	180.3	126.4	541.8
1916	256.3	181.5	119.7	557.5
1917	806.9	184.2	134.4	1,125.5
1918		185.6		3,684.3
1919		188.0		1,911.4
1920	580.9	195.1	180.5	956.5
1921	526.0	206.2	176.4	908.6
1922	379.3	210.6	176.9	766.8
1923	343.5	212.1	174.5	730.1
1924	357.5	222.9	171.9	752.3
1925	353.5	228.0	174.1	755.6
1926	347.7	231.3	168.2	747.2
1927	344.2	234.4	170.4	749.0
1928	350.7	236.8	173.9	761.4
1929	363.7	239.6	195.9	799.2

Table B7 (continued)

Year	National Defense	Post Office Full-time Equivalent Number	Other	Total, Full-time Equivalent Number
	(1)	(2)	(3)	(4)
1930	364.4	241.1	214.8	820.3
1931	365.2	240.4	219.2	824.8
1932	351.3	237.0	225.4	813.7
1933	348.5	229.3	235.4	813.2
1934	386.0	224.4	306.2	916.6
1935	398.7	223.9	353.1	975.7
1936	449.1	237.1	440.6	1,126.8
1937	480.9	241.5	455.2	1,177.6
1938	493.6	246.2	432.6	1,172.4
1939	540.6	249.0	469.4	1,259.0
1940	787.5	254.6	489.7	1,531.8
1941	2,207.4	262.2	529.8	2,999.4
1942	5,326.7	267.5	569.6	6,163.8
1943	11,223.2	257.9	595.0	12,076.1
1944	13,811.0	263.0	557.3	14,631.3
1945	14,415.5	270.0	618.8	15,304.3
1946	5,262.2	288.2	757.1	6,307.5
1947	2,572.2	293.8	788.7	3,654.7
1948	2,380.3	321.7	731.0	3,433.0
1949	2,524.5	342.4	741.4	3,608.3

Column

1 Sum of armed forces (Table B5) and employees in the War Department, Navy Department, and World War II agencies (annual reports of the U. S. Civil Service Commission). Including the Veterans Administration, the Maritime Commission, Panama Canal, etc., the figures would, of course, be larger.

The 1900 figure is interpolated between 1896 and 1901 by the number in the armed forces.

Figures are as of June 30 with some exceptions (see Tables B5 and B6).

2 From Table B4. Figures are as of June 30.

3 Column 4 minus columns 1 and 2.

4 From Table B6.

Table B8

STATE GOVERNMENTS, NONSCHOOL EMPLOYEES
TOTAL AND FULL-TIME EQUIVALENT NUMBER, 1900-1949

Annual Averages

(Unit: 1,000 persons)

Year	Total Number	Full-time Equivalent Number		Year	Total Number	Full-time Equivalent Number
1900	80	68		1935	412	350
1902	89	76		1936	454	386
1910	127	108		1937	480	408
1920	215	183		1938	533	453
1921	220	187		1939	535	454
1922	226	192		1940	538	457
1923	235	200		1941	538	469
1924	242	206		1942	509	439
1925	253	215		1943	466	413
1926	258	219		1944	457	404
1927	292	248		1945	465	410
1928	291	247		1946	547	486
1929	311	264		1947	622	555
1930	328	279		1948	666	597
1931	352	299		1949	708	642
1932	360	306				
1933	361	307				
1934	390	331				

1940-49: Bureau of the Census, Governments Division, *Government Employment,* January, April, July, and October 1950. We computed annual averages for each year from the figures for January, April, July, October, and January of the following year, weighting each January by $\frac{1}{2}$.

Full-time equivalent employment is estimated as the sum of permanent full-time employees and $\frac{1}{3}$ of the number of temporary and part-time employees.

These estimates were extrapolated back to 1900 by the following series:

1939-40: Department of Commerce, *Survey of Current Business,* National Income Supplement, 1951, total state and local government employees (other than work relief and public education).

1929-39: WPA-BLS, State, County, and Municipal Survey, *Employment and Payrolls of State and Local Governments, 1929-1939,* nonschool state government employment.

1900-29: Population-weighted average state government employment per capita in a sample of states, multiplied by population in all states: 1929-20, Massachusetts, Illinois, New Jersey, New York, and Vermont; 1910-1900, Alabama, New York, and Vermont.

Between 1920 and 1929, the figures were interpolated by employment in a somewhat different sample of states: 1929-28, Maryland, Massachusetts, Illinois, Michigan, New Jersey, New York, and North Carolina; 1928-26: Mary-

NOTES TO TABLE B8 (concluded)

land, Massachusetts, Illinois, Michigan, New Jersey, and New York; 1926-24: Maryland, Massachusetts, New Jersey, and New York; 1924-23: Maryland, Massachusetts, Illinois, New Jersey, and New York; 1923-22: Maryland, Massachusetts, and New York; 1922-21: Maryland, Massachusetts, and New York; 1921-20: Illinois and New York.

The employment figures exclude education with the exception of those for Colorado and Maryland, which are classified employment only, including education. Most of the data are from annual reports of state civil service commissions or letters from them. The figures for Ohio, 1921-26, are derived from total wages as given in auditors' reports, and estimates of average wages prepared by Simon Kuznets. The figures for Massachusetts, 1921-24, are derived from total wages as given in the Massachusetts Commission on Administration and Finance, *Payroll Statistics,* and Kuznets' estimates of average wages.

The 1902 figures are rough estimates derived by straight-line interpolation between 1900 and 1910.

State government employment per 1,000 population in the states included in our decennial sample is as follows:

	1929	1920	1910	1900
Massachusetts	3.13	2.70		
Illinois	1.64	1.18	.45	
New Jersey	2.26	1.42	.99	
Colorado		1.33	.38	
Alabama		.59	.48	.34
New York	2.19	1.82		
		1.61	1.38	1.06
Vermont	5.06	3.78	1.03	.83
Total sample	2.23	1.76		
		1.39	.94	
			1.20	.91

Table B9

MUNICIPAL GOVERNMENTS, NONSCHOOL EMPLOYEES
TOTAL AND FULL-TIME EQUIVALENT NUMBER, 1900-1949

Annual Averages

(Unit: 1,000 persons)

Year	Total Number	Full-time Equivalent Number		Total Number	Full-time Equivalent Number
1900	230	194	1935	785	663
1902	256	216	1936	837	707
1905	296	250	1937	852	719
1910	398	336	1938	877	740
1915	497	420	1939	887	749
1920	508	429	1940	893	754
1921	541	457	1941	901	764
1922	578	488	1942	890	754
1923	612	517	1943	871	736
1924	667	563	1944	861	736
1925	713	602	1945	874	745
1926	745	629	1946	944	805
1927	779	658	1947	1,004	855
1928	808	682	1948	1,046	894
1929	805	680	1949	1,082	933
1930	832	702			
1931	864	730			
1932	817	690			
1933	783	661			
1934	778	657			

1940-49: Bureau of the Census, Governments Division, *Government Employment,* January, April, July, and October 1950. We computed annual averages from figures for these months of each year and January of the following year, weighting each January ½.

Full-time equivalent employment is the sum of permanent full-time employees and ⅓ of the number of temporary and part-time employees.

These estimates were extrapolated back to 1900 by the following series: 1939-40: Department of Commerce, *Survey of Current Business,* National Income Supplement, 1951, total state and local government employees (other than work relief and public education).

1929-39: WPA-BLS, State, County, and Municipal Survey, *Employment and Pay Rolls of State and Local Governments, 1929-1939.* Data are for cities with populations of 50,000 and over.

1900-29: Population-weighted average city nonschool employment per capita in a sample of cities, multiplied by population in all cities; 1929-20: St. Paul, Los Angeles, Milwaukee, Trenton, Jersey City, Paterson, Newark, Chicago, Minneapolis, Detroit, and cities in New York State including New York City;

NOTES TO TABLE B9 (concluded)

1920-15: St. Paul, Los Angeles, Milwaukee, Chicago, Minneapolis, Detroit, and cities in New York State; 1915-10: Los Angeles, Milwaukee, Chicago, Detroit, and cities in New York State; 1910-05: Los Angeles, Milwaukee, and cities in New York State; 1905-1900: Milwaukee and New York City.

Most of the city employment figures are from the annual reports of the Civil Service Commissions of the cities, or as derived from these annual reports by C. H. Wooddy in "The Growth of Governmental Functions," *Recent Social Trends in the United States* (McGraw-Hill, 1933). The exceptions are New York State cities other than New York City, which are from the annual reports of the State Civil Service Commission; and the Philadelphia figures for 1920-22, from Bureau of Municipal Research, *The Turnover Among City Employees, Citizens' Business, No. 880*. The 1920 figures for Trenton, Jersey City, Paterson, and Newark are estimated by interpolation between figures for 1918 and 1921.

The figures are for total nonschool city employees, except for Milwaukee and Chicago, which include schools; New York State cities other than New York City, which include only the classified service; and Philadelphia, 1920-22, which include only competitive positions.

The 1902 figure is a rough estimate derived by straight-line interpolation between 1900 and 1905.

Cities used to interpolate between 1920 and 1929 include St. Paul, Cincinnati, Baltimore, San Diego, Philadelphia, Detroit, Minneapolis, Los Angeles, New York State cities, for 1929-27; St. Paul, Cincinnati, Baltimore, San Diego, Philadelphia, Minneapolis, Los Angeles, New York State cities, for 1927-25; St. Paul, San Diego, Philadelphia, Minneapolis, Los Angeles, New York State cities, for 1925-21; and St. Paul, Philadelphia, Minneapolis, Los Angeles, New York State cities, for 1921-20.

Municipal employment per 100 population in the cities included in our quinquennial sample is as follows:

	1929	1920	1915	1910	1905	1900
St. Paul	1.05	1.14	.81			
Los Angeles	1.48	1.16	1.03	.96	1.02	
Milwaukee	1.94	1.29	1.60	1.37	1.15	1.12
Trenton	1.08	.76				
Jersey City	1.26	.83				
Paterson	.74	.60				
Newark	1.41	1.06				
Chicago	1.40	1.17	1.31	1.03		
Minneapolis	1.16	1.14	1.20			
Detroit	1.26	.95	1.19	.90		
N. Y. C.	1.27	.97	1.05	1.11	.98	.90
N. Y. State cities						
(excl. N. Y. C.)	1.01	.86				
		.84	.98			
			.97	.80		
				.79	.63	
Total sample	1.28	1.01				
		1.02	1.12	1.03		
				1.04	.90	
					.99	.92

Table B10

LOCAL GOVERNMENTS OTHER THAN MUNICIPALITIES
NONSCHOOL EMPLOYEES
TOTAL AND FULL-TIME EQUIVALENT NUMBER, 1900-1949

Annual Averages

(Unit: 1,000 persons)

	COUNTIES		OTHER LOCAL GOVERNMENTS		TOTAL	
Year	Total Number	Full-time Equivalent Number	Total Number	Full-time Equivalent Number	Total Number	Full-time Equivalent Number
1900					170	123
1902					189	137
1929					451	326
1930					477	345
1931					500	362
1932					521	377
1933					511	370
1934					544	394
1935					580	420
1936					573	415
1937					586	424
1938					615	445
1939					609	441
1940	339	286	274	158	613	444
1941	331	284	260	152	591	436
1942	337	283	226	138	563	421
1943	318	273	228	139	546	412
1944	322	275	222	135	544	410
1945	315	271	242	140	557	411
1946	352	296	223	130	575	426
1947	368	319	247	150	615	469
1948	402	343	270	176	672	519
1949	408	355	278	180	686	535

Notes to Table B10

1940-49: Bureau of the Census, Governments Division, *Government Employment,* January, April, July, and October 1950. We computed annual averages from the figures for January, April, July, October, and January of the following year, weighting each January by ½.

Full-time equivalent employment is the sum of permanent full-time employees and ⅓ of the number of temporary and part-time employees.

These estimates were extrapolated back to 1900 by the following series:
1939-40: Department of Commerce, *Survey of Current Business,* National Income Supplement, 1951, total state and local government employees (other than work relief and public education) minus our estimates of the number of state and municipal government employees.
1929-39: WPA-BLS, State, County and Municipal Survey, *Employment and Pay Rolls of State and Local Governments, 1929-1939,* total nonschool local employees minus our estimates for municipal nonschool employees.
1902-32: Nonschool expenditures data for minor civil divisions (*Wealth, Debt and Taxation,* 1902 and 1932) divided by expenditures per employee for states and cities, 1932 and 1902.
1900-02: State and municipal government employment, 1900-02.

Table B11

Schools

Total and Full-time Equivalent Number of Persons Employed by State and Local Governments, 1900-1949

Annual Averages

(Unit: 1,000 persons)

Year	Total Number	Full-time Equivalent Number		Total Number	Full-time Equivalent Number
1900	483	467	1925	1,010	976
1901	493	476	1926	1,047	1,011
1902	505	488	1927	1,071	1,035
1903	514	497	1928	1,090	1,053
1904	520	502	1929	1,120	1,082
1905	525	507	1930	1,150	1,110
1906	532	514	1931	1,160	1,120
1907	549	530	1932	1,148	1,109
1908	565	546	1933	1,122	1,084
1909	578	558	1934	1,122	1,083
1910	596	576	1935	1,152	1,112
1911	612	591	1936	1,174	1,134
1912	631	610	1937	1,206	1,165
1913	650	628	1938	1,239	1,196
1914	675	652	1939	1,267	1,224
1915	700	676	1940	1,273	1,228
1916	723	698	1941	1,281	1,234
1917	755	729	1942	1,270	1,223
1918	786	759	1943	1,244	1,198
1919	807	780	1944	1,226	1,181
1920	835	807	1945	1,224	1,181
1921	880	850	1946	1,277	1,224
1922	917	886	1947	1,334	1,277
1923	942	910	1948	1,369	1,312
1924	971	938	1949	1,433	1,368

1929-49: U. S. Department of Commerce, *Survey of Current Business,* National Income Supplement, 1951.

These estimates were extrapolated back to 1900 by the following series:

1919-29: Simon Kuznets, *National Income and Its Composition, 1919-1938* (National Bureau of Economic Research, 1941), p. 814.

1909-19: W. I. King, *The National Income and Its Purchasing Power* (National Bureau of Economic Research, 1930), p. 361.

1900-09: Bureau of Education, as given in the *Statistical Abstract, 1922,* p. 103; figures include teachers in public elementary and secondary schools.

Table B12

PUBLIC EMERGENCY EMPLOYMENT UNDER WORK RELIEF PROGRAMS
EXCLUDING ADMINISTRATIVE EMPLOYEES, 1933-1943

Annual Averages
(Unit: 1,000 persons)

	1933	1934	1935	1936	1937	1938	1939	1940	1941	1942	1943
Federal											
Civilian Conservation Corps	168	311	396	348	293	274	281	272	195	42	0
National Youth Administration											
Student work program	0	0	61	277	272	246	288	325	305	136	39
Out-of-school work program	0	0	0	151	159	195	235	281	364	105	0
Works Projects Administration	0	0	482	2,544	1,792	2,761	2,407	1,912	1,328	625	46
Civil Works Program	427	992	0	0	0	0	0	0	0	0	0
Other federal agency projects financed from emergency funds	57	394	351	592	343	194	199	64	8	0.4	0
Total of above	652	1,697	1,290	3,912	2,859	3,670	3,410	2,854	2,200	908	85
Full-time equivalent	373	787	728	2,334	1,627	2,130	1,996	1,789	1,364	601	47
State and Local											
Total	1,724	1,834	2,097	91	56	19	39	38	17	5	0
Full-time equivalent	299	603	765	55	33	6	11	11	6	2	0

U. S. Federal Security Agency, Social Security Administration, *Social Security Bulletin*, Feb. 1943, pp. 25-6, and Feb. 1944, p. 27, for federal data. Full-time equivalent federal series and both series of state and local government figures are estimates of the National Income Division of the Department of Commerce (*Survey of Current Business*, National Income Supplement, 1951, Tables 24 and 25), and *Technical Notes on Sources and Methods Used in the Derivation of National Income Statistics*, Section on

Wages, Salaries and Employment; they are on a 40-hour week basis.

Department of Commerce estimates for earlier years for state and local government full-time equivalent workers are: 1929, 0; 1930, 4; 1931, 44; 1932, 87; and for state and local total number including part-time: 1929, 0; 1930, 20; 1931, 299; 1932, 592. Before 1933 the federal figures, and after 1943 all the figures, are zero.

Table B13

Total Government Employment, 1900-1949
Full-time Equivalent Number
(Unit: 1,000 persons)

	1900	1910	1920	1921	1922	1923
Federal Government	312	484	956	909	767	730
Civilian	186	345	613	521	495	481
Armed forces	126	140	344	388	272	250
State & Local Government	852	1,209	1,654	1,738	1,821	1,893
Nonschool	385	633*	847*	888*	935*	983*
States	68	108	183	187	192	200
Cities, towns, & villages	194	336	429	457	488	517
Counties ⎱	123					
Townships, spec. dist. ⎰						
School	467	576	807	850	886	910
Total Regular Employees	1,164	1,693	2,610	2,647	2,588	2,623
Public Emergency Workers	0	0	0	0	0	0
Grand Total	1,164	1,693	2,610	2,647	2,588	2,623
National defense	166	198	581	526	379	344
Other, incl. public emergency	998	1,495	2,029	2,121	2,209	2,279
Other, excl. public emergency	998	1,495	2,029	2,121	2,209	2,279

	1934	1935	1936	1937	1938	1939
Federal Government	917	976	1,127	1,178	1,172	1,259
Civilian	660	714	827	857	842	914
Armed forces	256	262	300	320	331	345
State & Local Government	2,465	2,545	2,642	2,716	2,834	2,868
Nonschool	1,382	1,433	1,508	1,551	1,638	1,644
States	331	350	386	408	453	454
Cities, towns, & villages	657	663	707	719	740	749
Counties ⎱	394	420	415	424	445	441
Townships, spec. dist. ⎰						
School	1,083	1,112	1,134	1,165	1,196	1,224
Total Regular Employees	3,382	3,521	3,769	3,894	4,006	4,127
Public Emergency Workers	1,390	1,493	2,389	1,660	2,136	2,007
Grand Total	4,772	5,014	6,158	5,554	6,142	6,134
National defense	386	399	449	481	494	541
Other, incl. public emergency	4,386	4,615	5,709	5,073	5,648	5,593
Other, excl. public emergency	2,996	3,122	3,320	3,413	3,512	3,586

* Interpolated between 1900 and 1929 by data for states and cities.
Based on Tables B6-12.

1924	1925	1926	1927	1928	1929	1930	1931	1932	1933
752	756	747	749	761	799	820	825	814	813
487	497	492	490	500	533	554	562	558	559
265	259	256	258	261	266	266	263	256	254
1,989	2,089	2,163	2,262	2,307	2,352	2,436	2,511	2,482	2,422
1,051*	1,113*	1,152*	1,227*	1,254*	1,270	1,326	1,391	1,373	1,338
206	215	219	248	247	264	279	299	306	307
563	602	629	658	682	680	702	730	690	661
					326	345	362	377	370
938	976	1,011	1,035	1,053	1,082	1,110	1,120	1,109	1,084
2,741	2,845	2,910	3,011	3,068	3,151	3,256	3,336	3,296	3,235
0	0	0	0	0	0	4	44	87	672
2,741	2,845	2,910	3,011	3,068	3,151	3,260	3,380	3,383	3,907
358	354	348	344	351	364	364	365	351	348
2,383	2,491	2,562	2,667	2,717	2,787	2,896	3,015	3,032	3,559
2,383	2,491	2,562	2,667	2,717	2,787	2,892	2,971	2,945	2,887

1940	1941	1942	1943	1944	1945	1946	1947	1948	1949
1,532	2,999	6,164	12,076	14,631	15,304	6,308	3,655	3,433	3,608
1,000	1,355	2,196	3,132	3,259	3,696	2,556	1,984	1,941	1,966
532	1,644	3,968	8,944	11,372	11,608	3,751	1,671	1,492	1,642
2,883	2,903	2,837	2,759	2,731	2,747	2,941	3,156	3,322	3,478
1,655	1,669	1,614	1,561	1,550	1,566	1,717	1,879	2,010	2,110
457	469	439	413	404	410	486	555	597	642
754	764	754	736	736	745	805	855	894	933
{ 286	284	283	273	275	271	296	319	343	355
{ 158	152	138	139	135	140	130	150	176	180
1,228	1,234	1,223	1,198	1,181	1,181	1,224	1,277	1,312	1,368
4,415	5,902	9,001	14,835	17,362	18,051	9,249	6,811	6,755	7,086
1,800	1,370	603	47	0	0	0	0	0	0
6,215	7,272	9,604	14,882	17,362	18,051	9,249	6,811	6,755	7,086
788	2,207	5,327	11,223	13,811	14,416	5,262	2,572	2,380	2,524
5,427	5,065	4,277	3,659	3,552	3,635	3,987	4,239	4,375	4,562
3,627	3,695	3,674	3,612	3,552	3,635	3,987	4,239	4,375	4,562

Table B14

TOTAL GOVERNMENT EMPLOYMENT, 1900-1949

FULL-TIME AND PART-TIME NUMBER

(Unit: 1,000 persons)

	1900	1910	1920	1930	1940	1949
Federal Government	438	579	1,032	880	1,585	3,650
Civilian	312	439	688	614	1,053	2,008
Armed Forces	126	140	344	266	532	1,642
State & Local Government	963	1,385	1,888	2,787	3,317	3,909
Nonschool	480	789*	1,053*	1,637	2,044	2,476
States	80	127	215	328	538	708
Cities, towns, & villages	230	398	508	832	893	1,082
Counties					339	408
Townships, special districts	170			477	274	278
School	483	596	835	1,150	1,273	1,433
Total Regular Employees	1,401	1,964	2,920	3,667	4,902	7,559
Public Emergency Workers	0	0	0	20	2,892	0
Grand Total	1,401	1,964	2,920	3,687	7,794	7,559
National Defense	166	198	581	364	788	2,524
Other, incl. public emergency	1,235	1,766	2,339	3,323	7,006	5,035
Other, excl. public emergency	1,235	1,766	2,339	3,303	4,114	5,035

* Interpolated between 1900 and 1930 by data for states and cities.
Based on Tables B6-12.

Table B15

FUNCTIONAL CLASSIFICATION OF GOVERNMENT WORKERS, BY TYPE OF GOVERNMENT UNIT, 1940

(Unit: 1,000 persons)

	Federal	State	City	County	Sub-Total	All Other Local	Total
General control							
General administrative & financial	89	45	63	97	294	44	424
Legislative	4	2	42		48		
Judicial	2	5	11	20	38		
National defense	669				669		669
Public safety, other							
Law enforcement	14	34	132	15	195	6	319
Fire			118		118		
Highways & waterways	25	178	125	103	431	86	588
Sanitation & waste removal			71		71		
Health	8	19	24	9	60	19	613
Hospitals	2	112	55	45	214		
Public welfare							
Veterans' services & benefits	40	67	27	26	279		
Public welfare, other*	119	28		9	41		
Correction							
Development & conservation of natural resources	66	30		4	100		100
Recreation & parks	4	3	47		54		54
Agricultural, industrial & commercial development	41				41		41
Regulation	45				45		45
General information & research	17				17		17
Schools	1	211	181	50	442	878	1,320
Libraries & museums	2	1	17	3	23		23
Other general functions		19	45	17	81	6	87
Postal service	255				255		255
Water supply			76		76		76
Gas & electric systems	6		19		25		25
Other public enterprises	36	15	59	1	111		111
Total	1,447	768	1,113	400	3,728	1,039	4,767

* Includes direct relief, social security, work programs, and Indian affairs.

NOTES TO TABLE B15

Blank spaces indicate either zero or small amounts not shown separately but included in the figures for other functional categories. The federal government figures are for June 1940; the school figures (other than federal) for the school year 1939-40; the other figures, for Oct. 1940. Employment is measured by the total number of full- and part-time workers, with no adjustment to a full-time equivalent basis except in the case of the Post Office. Public emergency workers are excluded.

Federal government data (except for the Postal Service figure, which is from Table B4) are from "Federal Personnel by Types of Work Performed, June 1940 and 1941," *Monthly Labor Review*, Dec. 1941. State and local government data are from the Census Bureau's *Public Employment and the War* (State and Local Government Quarterly Employment Survey, Vol. 1: No. 31A, Feb. 1942), except that the breakdown of school employment by type of government and some details of the functional distribution of "all other local" employment were roughly estimated by us. We altered the classification of federal employees by distributing public works among the other functional categories, splitting Engineer Corps employment between highways and waterways and conservation and development, shifting soil conservation and development to conservation and development, and marketing and crop control to regulation, by placing the Veterans Administration and Indian affairs under welfare, and by making several other less important changes.

Table B16

FUNCTIONAL CLASSIFICATION OF FEDERAL WORKERS, 1896 and 1939

	Number (1,000)		% of Total Incl. Postal Service & National Defense		% of Total Excl. Postal Service & National Defense		1939 Relative to 1896
	1896	1939	1896	1939	1896	1939	
General control	29.9	97.4	15.4	7.4	52.6	19.6	3.3
Law enforcement	1.6	14.1	.8	1.1	2.8	2.8	8.8
Highways & waterways	10.1	30.2	5.2	2.3	17.8	6.1	3.0
Development & conservation of natural resources	1.9	66.9	1.0	5.1	3.3	13.5	35.2
Agricultural, industrial, & commercial development	5.2	36.6	2.7	2.8	9.2	7.4	7.0
Regulation	1.1	42.2	.6	3.2	1.9	8.5	38.4
Health	1.1	9.7	.6	.7	1.9	2.0	8.8
Public welfare	4.3	154.5	2.2	11.7	7.6	31.1	35.9
Public enterprises other than postal service	0.0	35.5	0.0	2.7	0.0	7.2	*
General information & research	1.2	6.6	.6	.5	2.1	1.3	5.5
Education & reference	.4	2.5	.2	.2	.7	.5	6.2
Subtotal	56.8	496.1	29.3	37.6	100.0	100.0	8.7
Postal service	77.8	249.0	40.1	18.8			3.2
National defense	59.2	575.9	30.5	43.6			9.7
Total	193.8	1,321.0	100.0	100.0			6.8

* Denominator is zero.

The figures for 1896 are as of June 30; those for 1939 are as of Dec. 31, except for the postal service which are as of June 30. Postal workers are on a full-time equivalent basis. Public emergency workers are excluded.

The 1896 figures (except for the postal service) are from U. S. Civil Service Commission, *Tables Showing the Number of Posi-* tions in the Executive Civil Service of the U. S., 1896. The 1939 figures (except for the postal service) are from "Federal Personnel by Types of Work Performed," *Monthly Labor Review*, June 1941. We altered the classification given in the latter source in the manner indicated in the note to Table B15. Postal service is from Table B4.

Table B17

FUNCTIONAL CLASSIFICATION OF STATE GOVERNMENT NONSCHOOL PERSONNEL NEW YORK (1900 AND 1940) AND VERMONT (1900 AND 1945)

	New York					Vermont				
	NO. OF EMPLOYEES		PERCENTAGE OF TOTAL		RELATIVE	NO. OF EMPLOYEES		PERCENTAGE OF TOTAL		RELATIVE
	1900	1940	1900	1940	1940 TO 1900	1900	1945	1900	1945	1945 TO 1900
General administrative & financial	351	3,321	4.6	6.6	9.5	11	94	3.8	4.8	8.5
Judicial	455	1,200	5.9	2.4	2.6	74	97	25.8	4.9	1.3
State police	[a]	[a]	[a]	[a]	....		60		3.0	[b]
Other protection	225	2,946	2.9	5.8	13.1	2	41	.7	2.1	20.5
Highways	351	5,819	4.6	11.5	16.6	3	709	1.0	35.9	236.3
Development & conservation of natural resources	139	706	1.8	1.4	5.1	30	174	10.5	8.8	5.8
Health	183	2,467	2.4	4.9	13.5	4	79	1.4	4.0	19.8
Hospitals	4,619	21,570	60.2	42.7	4.7	83	310	28.9	15.7	3.7
Public welfare & unemployment compensation	96	3,880	1.3	7.7	40.4		143		7.2	[b]
Correction	695	4,702	9.1	9.3	6.8	58	141	20.2	7.1	2.4
Education (excl. schools)	345	731	4.5	1.4	2.1	22	63	7.7	3.2	2.9
Recreation, parks, etc.	29	536	.4	1.1	18.5	[a]	[a]	[a]	[a]	....
Other general functions	170	1,116	2.2	2.2	6.6	[a]	[a]	[a]	[a]	....
Public enterprises	19	1,488	.2	2.9	78.3		66		3.3	[b]
Total nonschool	7,677	50,482	100.0	100.0	6.6	287	1,977	100.0	100.0	6.9
Population					1.9					1.05[c]

[a] Not shown separately.
[b] Denominator is zero.
[c] 1940 relative to 1900.

The data for New York State were classified by us using figures for individual agencies given in the annual reports of the New York State Civil Service Commission. The so-called "labor class" (who in 1922 accounted for 13 percent of the nonschool employees subject to the State Civil Service Commission) is not included in 1900. The Vermont data were prepared by the Vermont Office of Auditor of Accounts. We are indebted to David V. Anderson, Auditor of Accounts, for a copy of the figures.

Table B18

Functional Classification of Municipal Nonschool Payrolls and Personnel, 1903 and 1940 Cities with Populations of 25,000 or More

| | PAYROLLS | | | PERSONNEL | | | | | |
| | $1 million | | 1940 relative to 1903 | Number (1,000) | | 1940 relative to 1903 | | % of Total | |
	1903	1940[a]		1903	1940[a]	Direct estimate of payrolls	Est. by deflation of payrolls	1903 (est.)	1940
Administrative	13.6	67.3	5.0		31.9		2.3	8.8	5.3
Legislative	1.8	5.8	3.2		3.7		1.5	1.6	.6
Judicial	5.4	17.5	3.2		6.6		1.5	2.8	1.1
Total general control	20.8	90.6	4.4		42.2		2.0	13.2	7.0
Police	36.6	215.6	5.9	34.2[b]	94.1	2.8	2.7	22.0	15.6
Fire	21.6	159.4	7.4	20.6[b]	71.3	3.5	3.4	13.3	11.8
Highways	12.8	82.0	6.4	19.5	52.4	3.1	2.9	11.3	8.7
Sanitation	14.4	92.5	6.4		61.4		2.9	13.2	10.2
Health	2.4	28.7	11.9		16.9		5.4	2.0	2.8
Hospitals	1.9	52.0	26.8		53.1		12.2	2.7	8.8
Public welfare	1.7	33.8	20.3		23.6		9.2	1.6	3.9
Water supply	9.4	73.6	7.9		42.8		3.6	7.5	7.1
Electricity	.4	23.8	52.8		12.6		24.0	.3	2.1
All other functions	15.4	219.1	14.2		133.1		6.5	12.9	22.1
Total	137.3	1,071.1	7.8	170.3	603.5	3.5		100.0	100.0

[a] October 1940, multiplied by 12. Part-time workers are included.
[b] Excludes callmen, volunteers, substitutes, and supernumeraries.
The 1903 figures are from U. S. Census Bureau, *Bulletin 20,* "Statistics of Cities Having a Population of over 25,000, 1902 and 1903". 1940 figures are from *Public Employment and the War.* Recent issues of *Government Employment* show an Oct.

1940 total of 601 thousand, but the revision is not broken down by function. The estimate of 1940 total employment relative to 1903 is derived from the data for all cities (Table B9) adjusted for the changing importance of cities over 25,000, as measured by population. Total employment in 1903 is estimated from the ratio of 1940 to 1903 (3.544).

DATA ON GOVERNMENT CAPITAL GOODS

Sources of Information

The sources underlying the estimates of government capital goods were described in "Government-Owned Nonmilitary Capital Assets since 1900", *Studies in Income and Wealth, Volume Twelve* (National Bureau of Economic Research, 1950). Here we supplement that description to indicate changes and additions.

First, we divided the assets of federal government corporations and credit agencies into two groups: the assets of defense agencies and all other (Table C1). Exclusion of the former from our total of federal nonmilitary assets yields an estimate of nonmilitary assets substantially lower than the total including them in 1919-22 and 1942-46.

Second, we prepared rough annual estimates of total nonmilitary capital assets excluding roads and streets, in 1929 prices, for use in Chart 3 (Table C2).

Third, we added a few tables providing functional distributions of capital assets. Sources, largely compilations by the Bureau of the Census, are mentioned in notes to Tables C3-7.

Comparisons with Other Estimates

Studies in Income and Wealth, Volume Twelve included an important set of estimates of government assets for 1939 and 1946 prepared by J. E. Reeve and his associates at the Bureau of the Budget. We compared these estimates with ours in the paper cited above. Since publication of these two sets of estimates, Raymond W. Goldsmith has prepared a third, covering 1896-1949.[1]

With one major exception, our estimates are largely based on balance sheet data, while those of Reeve and Goldsmith are based on

[1] These are as yet unpublished. We are greatly obliged to Mr. Goldsmith for permission to examine his preliminary estimates and for answering questions concerning them.

cumulated net capital formation, with depreciation charges estimated by them. (The exception is roads and streets, all estimates of which are derived by the cumulated net capital formation method.) Our estimates may therefore be considered largely independent of the other two. It appears that all agree, broadly, in respect of changes. If the other estimates are accepted as the standard, our estimates for the federal government are somewhat low; for state and local governments, they are rather high. On net balance our estimates seem to overstate levels.

Table C1

ASSETS OF FEDERAL GOVERNMENT CORPORATIONS AND CREDIT AGENCIES, 1917-1946

(Unit: $1 million)

YEAR	TOTAL			DEFENSE			OTHER		
	Capital Assets	Property Held for Sale	Capital Assets and Inventories	Capital Assets	Property Held for Sale	Capital Assets and Inventories	Capital Assets	Property Held for Sale	Capital Assets and Inventories
1917	53	...		53	...		...	...	
1918	743	...		743	...		...	...	
1919	2,237	...		2,237	...		...	...	
1920	2,743	...		2,743	...		...	...	
1921	2,122	...		2,122	...		...	...	
1922	2,371	7		2,370	7		1	...	
1923	236	3		234	3		2	...	
1924	236	4		225	1		11	3	
1925	202	12		190	1		12	11	
1926	166	16		150	...		16	16	
1927	156	21		138	...		18	21	
1928	147	22		128	...		19	22	
1929	112	23		91	...		21	23	

1930	111	28		89	……	22	28
1931	106	43		79	……	27	43
1932	93	71		69	……	24	71
1933	81	86		51	……	30	86
1934	72	81		n.a.	n.a.	n.a.	n.a.
1935	125	105		48	1	77	104
1936	151	192		31	1	120	191
1937	224	500		31	1	193	499
1938	395	804		38	70	357	734
1939	439	865	1,308	37	157	402	708
1940	517	1,175	1,697	30	108	487	1,067
1941	588	1,802	2,392	37	565	551	1,237
1942	798	5,581	6,376	107	4,126	691	1,455
1943	1,600	11,039	12,582	745	9,712	855	1,327
1944	1,614	17,314	18,456	685	16,337	929	977
1945			22,619		20,262		2,357
1946			16,968		15,233		1,735

n.a.: not available.

Data are as of June 30.

For sources, see notes to columns 7-9, Table 2, pp. 540-1 of *Studies in Income and Wealth, Volume Twelve.* Defense agencies are those designated by the Treasury Department as "defense" or "World War II" agencies (see, e.g., *Annual Report of the Secretary of the Treasury,* 1944, p. 767), plus the U. S. Maritime Commission, War Shipping Administration, and predecessor agencies.

Table C2

GOVERNMENT NONMILITARY CAPITAL ASSETS, EXCLUDING ROADS AND STREETS, ANNUAL ESTIMATES

(Unit: $1 billion, 1929 prices)

YEAR	TOTAL		YEAR	TOTAL	
	Including Defense Corps.	*Excluding Defense Corps.*		*Including Defense Corps.*	*Excluding Defense Corps.*
1902	8.4	8.4	1932	28.9	28.8
1912	14.3	14.3	1933	29.4	29.4
1920	16.5	13.3	1934	29.2	29.2
1921	17.6	15.0	1935	29.9	29.9
1922	18.9	15.9	1936	30.9	30.9
1923	16.5	16.2	1937	31.7	31.6
1924	17.4	17.2	1938	32.8	32.6
1925	18.9	18.6	1939	33.8	33.6
1926	19.9	19.8	1940	35.5	35.3
1927	21.4	21.2	1941	36.3	35.6
1928	22.5	22.4	1942	40.5	36.1
1929	23.3	23.2	1943	46.5	35.9
1930	25.4	25.4	1944	52.3	35.1
1931	27.1	27.1	1945	56.4	36.1
			1946	50.9	35.8

Book-value totals given in Table C1 above and Table 1, p. 539, *Studies in Income and Wealth, Volume Twelve* (the latter slightly revised to take account of new 1946 data on education assets) were interpolated by data for the major types of government unit from Tables 2 to 5 of the *Studies* paper, with straight-line interpolations to fill the few remaining gaps. The totals thus obtained were deflated by the following price indexes: for years through 1939, an average of the price indexes underlying the second and third lines of the text table on page 534 of the *Studies;* for 1946, the price index underlying the third line; with rough interpolations for missing years derived from the indexes given in Solomon Fabricant, *Capital Consumption and Adjustment* (National Bureau of Economic Research, 1938), pp. 183, 186.

Table C3

FUNCTIONAL CLASSIFICATION OF GOVERNMENT CAPITAL ASSETS
BY TYPE OF GOVERNMENT UNIT, 1939

	FEDERAL	STATE	CITY	OTHER LOCAL	TOTAL
		Percentage Distribution			
General control, including misc. & unallocable	22	6	5	7	11
National defense	27	....	....	....	8
Public safety, other	....	1	2	....	1
Highways & waterways	18	67	26	29	32
Health & hospitals	....	8	2	4	3
Sanitation & waste removal	....	....	13	5	5
Public welfare	....	1	1	....	0.5
Correction	....	3	1	2	1
Natural resources	27	1	....	....	8
Recreation & parks	....	1	12	....	5
Schools	....	8	10	53	14
Public enterprises	5*	3	28	1	12*
Total	100	100	100	100	100
		Billions of Dollars			
Total	19	13	22	10	63

* Does not cover the Post Office, which is included in general control.

Blank spaces indicate either zero or usually (but not always) small amounts not shown separately but included most frequently in the first category. Capital assets include land, subsoil assets, construction, and equipment. The federal government figures are depreciated values in 1939 prices; the other figures are rough estimates based on classifications available for a year closest to 1939, and are usually depreciated book values, sometimes undepreciated book values. Federal data are from J. E. Reeve and associates, "Government Component in the National Wealth", *Studies in Income and Wealth, Volume Twelve.* The state and local totals, excluding highways, sewage systems, and schools, and the separate data on these three items are from "Government-Owned Nonmilitary Capital Assets since 1900" from the same volume. The state total was distributed among the several functions by the 1931 proportions (Table C5); the city total, by the 1936 proportions for large cities (Table C7); and the total for other local, on the basis of very rough estimates derived mainly from outlay data. The distribution of highways, sewage systems (included in sanitation) and schools among the three types of nonfederal government shown is exceedingly crude but sufficient to show rough relative proportions; and the estimate of the total value of sewage systems also is very crude.

Table C4

CLASSIFICATION OF FEDERAL NONMILITARY PROPERTY, BY MAIN
CATEGORY, 1902-1946

	1902	1912	1922	1929	1939	1946
			EXCLUDING DEFENSE AGENCIES			
			Percentage Distribution			
Public buildings outside D. C.	20	24	22	18	16	15
Property in D. C.ᵇ	36	27	22	17	7	6
River, harbor & other waterway improvements	42	41	46	48	36	34
Reclamation projects	0	7	10	9	9	11
Other real property outside D. C., excl. property of corporations	1	1	1	6	13	12
Govt. corp. & credit agencies: nondefense agencies						
Capital assets	0	0	ᵃ	1	7 ⎫	22
Held for sale	0	0	0	1	12 ⎭	
Total, excl. defense agencies	100	100	100	100	100	100
			Millions of Dollars			
Total	615	982	1,398	1,954	5,718	7,985

	1902	1912	1922	1929	1939	1946
			INCLUDING DEFENSE AGENCIES			
			Percentage Distribution			
Public buildings outside D. C.	20	24	8	17	15	5
Property in D. C.ᵇ	36	27	8	16	7	2
River, harbor & other waterway improvements	42	41	17	46	35	12
Reclamation projects	0	7	4	8	8	4
Other real property outside D. C., excl. property of corporations	1	1	ᵃ	6	12	4
Govt. corp. & credit agencies: nondefense agencies						
Capital assets	0	0	ᵃ	1	7 ⎫	7
Held for sale	0	0	0	1	12 ⎭	
Total, excl. defense agencies	100	100	37	96	97	34
Govt. corp.: defense agencies	0	0	63	4	3	66
Total, incl. defense agencies	100	100	100	100	100	100
			Millions of Dollars			
Total	615	982	3,775	2,045	5,912	23,218

ᵃ Less than one-half percent.
ᵇ Not including municipal government property.
From Table C1 and *Studies in Income and Wealth, Volume Twelve,* pp. 540-1.

Table C5

FUNCTIONAL CLASSIFICATION OF STATE GOVERNMENT CAPITAL
ASSETS, EXCLUDING SCHOOLS AND HIGHWAYS, 1915 AND 1931

	1915	1931
	Percentage Distribution	
General control	23.	17.
Protection to persons & property[a]	3.5	3.7
Conservation of health & sanitation[b]	0.8	2.3
Hospitals	27.	31.
Charities[c]	9.4	4.1
Correctional institutions	17.	13.
Libraries	1.2	1.4
Recreation & parks	2.0	5.1
Development & conservation of natural resources	5.9	5.4
Miscellaneous general govt.[d]	0.9	5.1
Public service enterprises	9.8	12.
Total, excl. funds	100	100
	Millions of Dollars	
Total, excl. funds	679	1,841
Capital assets held in investment funds	21	57
Capital assets held in trust funds	477	571
Total, incl. funds	1,177	2,470

[a] Mostly armories, which might be classified as national defense.

[b] Mostly tuberculosis hospitals in 1931.

[c] Includes soldiers' and sailors' homes.

[d] Includes in 1931 highway department equipment ($76 million), not shown separately in 1915.

Data are from the Census Bureau's *Financial Statistics of States, 1915* and *1931,* and relate usually to the year ending June 30. Real estate assets of trust funds in 1915 are estimated from miscellaneous assets by the 1917 ratio. The totals differ from those in the *Studies* paper, because the latter were put on a December 31 basis.

Table C6

FUNCTIONAL CLASSIFICATION OF COUNTY GOVERNMENT CAPITAL
ASSETS, EXCLUDING SCHOOLS AND ROADS, 1912

	Percentage Distribution
Courthouses	61
Charities & hospitals	19
Jails	12
All other general functions	7
Public service enterprises	0.4
Total	100
	Millions of Dollars
Total	480

From the Census Bureau's *Wealth, Debt, and Taxation, 1913*, Vol. II, p. 343.

Table C7

FUNCTIONAL CLASSIFICATION OF MUNICIPAL GOVERNMENT CAPITAL
ASSETS, EXCLUDING SCHOOLS, STREETS AND
SEWAGE SYSTEMS, 1902-1936

	CITIES OVER 25,000	CITIES OVER 30,000		CITIES OVER 100,000[a]	
	1902	1912	1930	1930	1936
			Percentage Distribution		
General control	7.1	6.2	5.9	6.6	6.2
Police	1.4	1.1	1.0	1.3	1.3
Fire	3.7	3.6	2.9	3.3	2.5
Other protection	*	.7	.7	.6	.5
Health	*	*	.9	1.3	1.3
Sanitation[b]	*	*	3.8	5.7	6.0
Charities	1.9[c]				1.3
Hospitals	.8	4.2	4.2	5.0	2.9
Correction	1.4				0.8
Recreation (incl. parks)	38.7	33.7	31.7	23.4	21.6
Highways[b]	*	*	1.3	1.6	1.1
Misc. general govt.	3.6	5.3	4.7	5.6	5.5
Water supply systems	26.9	33.8	29.8	33.2	33.5
Electric-light and power systems	.6	.9	2.7	3.8	4.3
Other public service enterprises[d]	14.0	10.4	10.5	8.7	11.1
Total, excl. investment funds	100.0	100.0	100.0	100.0	100.0
			Millions of Dollars		
Total, excl. investment funds	1,397	2,730	8,219	4,646	5,247

[a] Not including New York, Dayton, and Fort Wayne.

[b] Includes only equipment and buildings of sanitation or highway departments.
Sewage systems and streets are not included.

[c] Asylums and almshouses.

[d] Excludes transit systems owned but not operated by cities.

* Not available separately; presumably included in the miscellaneous group.

Data for 1902 are from Census *Bulletin 20;* 1912 data, from *Wealth, Debt, and Taxation* and the *Financial Statistics of Cities;* figures for other years, from various issues of *Financial Statistics of Cities.* Because the 1936 asset totals did not include New York, Dayton, and Fort Wayne, we excluded these cities from the corresponding totals for 1930 also. Real property classified as "assets of investment funds and miscellaneous investments", including certain transit systems and other public service enterprises owned but not operated by cities, is omitted. The most important of these is the New York City Transit System.

DATA ON GOVERNMENT PURCHASES, PAYROLLS, TRANSFERS, AND EXPENDITURES

This appendix describes in detail the estimates, used in summary form in the text, of government outlays on capital goods, other purchases, and payrolls (the sum of which measures government's current purchases of goods and services); of government transfers to the public, and net government interest payments (which, together with the foregoing, make up total government expenditures not including intergovernment transfers); and of functional classifications of government expenditures.

Definitions

Government expenditures are divided into five classes: Payrolls, Outlays, Other Purchases, Public to Private Transfers, and Interest. In addition, another category, Public to Public Transfers, is distinguished to insure its exclusion from government input and expenditures as we define them.

Payrolls are wage and salary payments on current account plus government contributions to pension funds or, in lieu thereof, pension payments to government workers less their contributions to pension funds. Wage and salary payments in kind are excluded from payrolls and classified as other purchases.

Outlays are expenditures on fixed plant and equipment, including land, roads and streets, improvements to waterways, etc., less sales of such property. Included is expenditure, other than payrolls, for force-account construction as well as contract construction and purchases of assets. Major alterations and replacements are also included.[1]

Other Purchases are purchases of goods and services from the pub-

---

* Prepared by Robert E. Lipsey.

[1] The earlier data of the Bureau of the Census, on which we lean heavily, were so constructed as to imply the exclusion of replacements. However, it is likely that many such replacements were in fact included.

lic other than payrolls and outlays. Included are purchases of materials, rents, payments for contract labor (other than those covered by
outlays), and payments for miscellaneous services such as telephone
and power. Because the item is calculated as a residual, the figures
often cover expenditures which should have been classified elsewhere,
but could not be identified.

Public to Private Transfers are payments to the public not in return
for any goods or services. For the federal government, they consist
mainly of veterans' pensions, subsidies to agriculture, shipping, and
other industries, work relief, and social insurance benefits. For state
and local governments, public assistance and other charity payments
are preponderant.

Interest includes the interest payments of all government agencies
to both the public and other government agencies, less the interest
receipts of all such agencies. All intra-government payments are thus
eliminated, and the interest figure becomes in effect the difference
between interest payments to the public and interest receipts from
the public.

Public to Public Transfers are payments by one government unit
to another, chiefly apportionments or grants-in-aid, and, since 1937,
shared taxes. These transfers appear as government expenditures
when the receiving government spends them.

Government Expenditures are equal to the sum of the preceding
items other than public to public transfers. Therefore, all operations
relating to the public debt and other loans and investments, except
interest payments, also are excluded.

War Expenditures on payrolls, outlays and other purchases, which
are distinguished from nonwar, include through 1939 only expenditures of the War and Navy Departments other than certain outlay
payments for river and harbor improvements, flood control, and the
Panama Canal. For 1942, the Census classification, which includes
war expenditures of all federal agencies, was used.[2]

All payments by school systems, except interest and pension payments, are included under School Expenditures. School system interest payments, including those of school districts, are included under
state or local nonschool expenditures. All other payments of school
districts, no matter how classified by the Census, are included under
school expenditures.

[2] There is one exception: expenditures of the Veterans Administration were
transferred by us to the nonwar category in keeping with the earlier classification.

Government, as defined here, covers not only general government functions but also business enterprises owned by government units and independent funds, such as trust and pension funds.

Sources

Main sources for federal expenditure data (Table D1) are the Census Bureau's *Governmental Finances in the United States: 1942* and various issues of the *Annual Report of the Secretary of the Treasury on the State of the Finances* and *The Budget of the United States Government.* Some data are from issues of the Census Bureau's *Wealth, Debt and Taxation, Financial Statistics of States* (later *State Finances* or *Compendium of State Government Finances*), and *Financial Statistics of Cities* (later *City Finances* or *Compendium of City Government Finances*), and special reports on federal subsidies and federal corporation finances.

Federal payroll data for 1929 to 1942 are from the Bureau of Labor Statistics (published currently in the *Monthly Labor Review*), and earlier data are from a variety of sources, including the United States Budget, a census of the civil service, and reports of various government departments, with the addition of some very rough interpolations.

Most of the nonschool data for state and local governments (Tables D2-3) are from the Census Bureau's annual reports on state and city finances and the decennial censuses of governments, and the recent special census studies of state and local government finances. Payroll data are from the Census Bureau's quarterly surveys of state and local government employment and payrolls, the WPA-BLS State, County, and Municipal Survey (some of the results of which were published in BLS *Serial No. R. 1732,* "Public Employment and Pay Rolls in the United States, 1929-39, and Post-War Implications", by Carol P. Brainerd), and extrapolations back from these figures, using our employment estimates and payrolls per employee from Simon Kuznets, *National Income and Its Composition* (National Bureau of Economic Research, 1941), W. I. King, *The National Income and Its Purchasing Power* (National Bureau of Economic Research, 1930), and Paul Douglas, *Real Wages in the United States* (Houghton Mifflin, 1930).

The data for schools (Table D4) are from various issues of the *Biennial Survey of Education* and the *Bulletin* and *Annual Report* of the United States Office of Education.

Deficiencies

The data suffer from two main types of deficiency: gaps in the coverage of various levels of government unit, and inconsistencies and difficulties in the classification of expenditures by type.[3]

Complete coverage of all levels of government is available from Census Bureau data only for 1903, 1932, and 1942. For 1913 there are no Census data for cities with populations under 2,500, special districts overlying these cities, and other minor civil divisions. It is not clear to what extent special independent districts, such as school, highway, and other districts, are included in the data for cities over 2,500.[4] However, as expenditures of school districts, by far the most important of these special districts, are estimated from Office of Education data, the question is probably not important.

We estimate local nonschool expenditures in 1913 by interpolation between 1903 and 1932, using expenditures of cities over 30,000 and counties. Totals for all the levels of government for which figures are available are given in the notes to Table D3. No adequate data are available for expenditures on public higher education before 1932, and no estimates are made here, but data on other education expenditures by all levels of government are available for the whole period. In 1923 and 1929, no data are available for counties, cities with populations under 30,000, and other minor civil divisions. In 1939, no

[3] The present discussion is confined to National Bureau estimates. Department of Commerce estimates for each year beginning with 1929, covering all levels of government, are described briefly below, and the DC and National Bureau estimates are compared. Reference is made there also to estimates by the National Industrial Conference Board that cover all levels of government.

[4] According to *Wealth, Debt, and Taxation, 1913*, Vol. II, p. 399, "payments for expenses of highways and schools do not include those made by independent road and school districts, the payments shown in these tables being only such as were made from municipal revenues". However, a comparison of the figures in this source for cities over 30,000 with those in the *Financial Statistics of Cities, 1912* indicates that, at least for the cities in this size group, overlying school and other districts were included in the *Wealth, Debt, and Taxation* figures and a statement in *Wealth, Debt, and Taxation, 1932* suggests that schools, at least, were included with cities of all sizes. There does not seem to be any way of knowing whether the same is true of other overlying areas in cities with populations between 2,500 and 30,000. In 1932, cities under 2,500 and townships, not including overlying areas, accounted for 7.4 percent of total expenditures for operation and outlays by local governments other than school districts. The proportion was probably higher in 1913, since about 8.9 percent of the population of the continental United States lived in incorporated places with populations under 2,500 in 1910, as compared with 7.5 percent in 1930.

data are available for counties, cities under 100,000, and other minor civil divisions.

The most serious difficulties, however, are not with the measurement of total expenditures, but rather with the breakdown of expenditures by type. The interest item is the most reliable throughout, since the figures are given in almost every case where total expenditures are shown.

The state and local outlay figures too are comparatively reliable, except for state outlays in 1902. In that year, *Wealth, Debt, and Taxation* did not contain any separate figures for state outlays, except for a small amount shown for "Buildings and Sites", and a rough — probably excessive — estimate had to be made, mainly on the basis of 1912 proportions of outlays to other expenditures (see notes to Table D2). Another possible source of error is in the distribution of state and local outlays between school and nonschool, where such a breakdown is not given in the source, as in 1932.

The federal outlay figures are less reliable than those for state and local governments. General government outlay figures, for 1923 to 1939 from United States Budgets, and for 1942 from *Governmental Finances in the United States,* are fairly accurate, but some corporation outlays in 1942 had to be estimated from changes in assets, and are probably too low because no allowance is made for the offsetting of outlays by depreciation. The 1903 and 1913 nonwar figures are merely sums of obvious outlay items from the annual reports of the Secretary of the Treasury and probably include some expenditures that were not really outlays; on the other hand, they omit a larger amount of expenditures including equipment that should be classified under outlays. The residual "other purchases" item for 1903 and 1912 is almost certainly overestimated on this account. The opposite is true of the estimates of war outlays for these two years, which are based partly on construction data that include maintenance and repairs.

The estimates for state and local public to private transfers almost always contain some items which properly should be classified elsewhere, particularly under payrolls. The upward trend in these transfers has been so strong as to be little affected by these inaccuracies. Underestimation of purchases on this account has probably increased in relative importance.[5] Federal public to private transfers are easier to estimate because they are concentrated in a few well defined cate-

[5] In 1940 cities with populations over 100,000 showed expenditures for charities other than transfers — in other words, payrolls and purchases — of $16 million (*Financial Statistics of Cities*). The October 1940 payroll figure under

gories (military pensions and benefits in the earlier years, and the same plus work relief, social insurance benefits, and subsidies in more recent years) and because administration costs are usually separated from transfer payments.

Federal public to public transfers present no important difficulties, but state and local transfer figures suffer from two defects. The less important is a change in definition in 1937 so that shared taxes, formerly considered nongovernment cost payments and receipts, came to be treated as grants by the government that levies the tax. Since such items had not been considered government cost payments, however, the other categories were not affected by the change. The second defect is an upward bias (and therefore a downward bias in the other purchase series) because transfers are more easily identified in the later years. Some transfer payments other than for schools and highways are omitted from the transfer item and included with other purchases in the earlier years.

All the school payroll figures, and the other payroll figures from 1929 on are fairly reliable. But the federal payroll figure for 1903, based partly on payroll items picked from the reports of the Post Office, State, War, and Navy Departments, probably omits some payrolls in these departments not easily identified, and the pay of some low paid employees of other departments. The purchase figure is correspondingly overestimated. Because the payroll estimates for 1913 are based partly on the 1903 payroll per employee, they too may be a bit low.

The state payroll figures for 1903, 1912, and 1923 are extremely crude, for they are derived from other estimates already quite rough. If, as is likely, part-time work has been diminishing in importance, the earlier figures are probably too high because the average salary figures used to estimate them do not seem to take full account of this trend. The estimate of total local nonschool payrolls in 1903 is subject to a similar error, and probably to a greater degree because part-time work was more important at the local level. There are fairly reliable data, however, for large-city payrolls in 1903.

Because the figures for other purchases are residuals, almost all the previously described defects of the estimates for the other categories

---

"Administration of Charities", for cities over 100,000 (*Public Employment and the War*, State and Local Government Quarterly Employment Survey, Vol. 1: No. 31A, Feb. 1942), multiplied by 12, was $30 million. The transfer figure for that year is therefore probably overestimated by something more than $14 million, or over 3 percent.

of expenditure affect them. They are also distorted by the frequent inclusion of payrolls for force-account construction under both payrolls and outlays. It would be desirable to remove completely these expenditures from the outlay item, but sufficient data are not available.[6]

Years Covered

For the federal government, the data uniformly relate to the twelve-month period ending June 30 of the year specified. For state and local governments, however, the years to which the data relate might more appropriately be called "report years" than fiscal years. Generally, Census reports on state, city, and local finances use the fiscal year ending within a given calendar year, so that the one report year may include expenditures that took place as much as two years apart. Further, the report years themselves may not coincide for the different levels of government, so that the data are spread over an even longer period. The following is a brief description of the coverage of the different report years.

1903: States and territories, counties, and other minor civil divisions including cities with populations under 8,000: fiscal years ending between July 1, 1902 and June 30, 1903 inclusive. Cities with populations over 8,000: fiscal years ending between July 1, 1903 and June 30, 1904, inclusive. Schools: school year 1902-03.

1913: States, counties, and cities with populations over 2,500: fiscal years ending between July 1, 1912 and June 30, 1913, inclusive. Schools: school year 1912-13.

1923: States: fiscal years ending during the calendar year 1923, mostly between June and December. Cities with populations over 30,000: fiscal years ending between March 1923 and January 1924, inclusive. Schools: school year 1921-22.

---

[6] We can get some idea of the error involved in this duplication. For instance, in 1903, in cities with populations of 8,000 to 25,000, payrolls included under outlays were a little over 5 percent of all outlays, about 4 percent of other payrolls, and over 6 percent of other purchases. In that same year, in cities with populations over 25,000, payrolls included under outlays were about 4 percent of total outlays, over 4 percent of other payrolls and about 8 percent of other purchases.

For the federal government, we have figures for force-account payrolls under public works, including the Corps of Engineers, the Public Works Administration, the Public Roads Administration, the United States Housing Authority, the Bureau of Reclamation, the Panama Canal, the Tennessee Valley Authority, and others, for December 1939 and June 1940. The annual total estimated from these data (which apparently do not include any purely military construction) is about 8 percent of 1939 nonwar payrolls, almost 17 percent of nonwar outlays, and over 13 percent of other nonwar purchases.

1929: States: fiscal years ending during the calendar year 1929, mostly between June and December. Cities with populations over 30,000: fiscal years ending between March 1929 and January 1930, inclusive. Schools: school year 1927-28.

1932: State and local governments: fiscal years ending between July 1, 1931 and June 30, 1932, inclusive. Schools: school year 1931-32.

1939: States: fiscal years ending during calendar year 1939, mostly June 30. Cities with populations over 100,000: fiscal years ending during calendar year 1939 or January 1940. Schools: school year 1937-38.

1942: States: fiscal years ending in the 12-month period ending with June 30, 1942; most of the fiscal years end on June 30, 1942. Cities with populations over 25,000: fiscal years ending during the calendar year 1942 or January 1943. Counties: fiscal years ending during the calendar year 1942, December 1941, or January 1943. Schools: school year 1941-42.

The picture of trends in government input and expenditures that one gets from figures for these isolated years may be distorted by the peculiarities of the particular years chosen as "key years", especially since these were chosen mainly because data were available rather than because they were in any way representative. Fortunately, except for war periods (which affect seriously only the last of the "key years"), year-to-year fluctuations appear small compared with trends for all series except outlays. For years after 1929, this is shown clearly in the text charts that reproduce Department of Commerce annual data.

For outlays, available annual series indicate the following cases where the figure for a "key year" would seem to be considerably different from, say, a five year average around that year:

1903: Total and nonwar outlays are considerably lower than in following years for two main reasons: first, 1903 was just before the beginning of large outlays on reclamation and the Panama Canal, and second, there were unusually large land sales in that year, which further reduced the figure for net outlays. Before 1903, the trend of nonwar outlays was gradually upward. For war outlays, 1903 was about the end of a steep upward trend from the very low levels of the late 1870's and early 1880's, and the beginning of something like a plateau in military outlays which lasted, with some fluctuation, until about the beginning of the first World War.

Because the Corps of Engineers is so important, especially in the earlier years, we have adjusted the outlay item to exclude it (see notes to Table D1), thus removing more than half of the duplication. The remaining 1940 payrolls under outlays were less than 4 percent of other 1939 nonwar payrolls, less than 8 percent of outlays, and a little over 6 percent of other nonwar purchases.

1913: This was an extremely low year for military outlays, lower than any later year, and any earlier year since 1898, and almost 50 percent below the average of 1903-12.

1923: Federal nonwar outlays, higher in 1923 than they had been during the war, reached a peak in 1924 and then tapered off. War outlays continued the steep postwar decline through 1925, and then started to increase again. State and city outlays in 1923 were at the end of a very sudden postwar increase, and at the beginning of a more gradual, but still considerable, rate of growth. School outlays, after a very rapid war and postwar increase, grew slowly after 1922, and reached a peak in 1925.

1929: For most of the series, 1929 was one of the years in an upward movement that went from a postwar trough in 1923-25 to a peak in 1931 or 1932, or continued through the thirties. One exception was city outlays, which remained at about the same level from 1926 to 1930 after a sharp rise from 1919-26 and then dropped off rapidly. School outlays reached a peak in 1925 and 1926, dropped gradually until 1930, and then sharply.

Comparisons with Other Estimates

Our estimates of government expenditures differ in several respects from those prepared by the National Industrial Conference Board (various issues of the *Economic Almanac*), the Department of Commerce (*Survey of Current Business,* National Income Supplement, 1951), and the Twentieth Century Fund (J. F. Dewhurst & Associates, *America's Needs and Resources,* 1947, Chapter 20).

The main differences between our figures and those of the N.I.C.B. are: 1) The National Bureau figures include all transactions of government corporations and funds with the public, while the N.I.C.B. excludes all such transactions and includes only government subsidies to enterprises. 2) The National Bureau figures exclude public to public transfers from the expenditures of the grantor government and include them in the expenditures of the grantee government when they are spent. The N.I.C.B. figures include them as expenditures of the grantor government, and subtract the amount received from the expenditures of the grantee government. 3) The National Bureau interest figure is net, subtracting total interest receipts from total payments of general government and corporations. The N.I.C.B. figures include only general interest paid. Thus the National Bureau figure is in effect interest payments to the public less interest receipts from the public, all intra-government payments being eliminated. The N.I.C.B. figure includes some payments by the government to its own agencies, and excludes some payments by government agencies to the public.

The main differences between our figures and those of the Department of Commerce are: 1) The National Bureau figures are for fiscal or report years, while the DC figures are for calendar years. 2) The National Bureau figures include work relief with public to private transfers; the DC includes it with payrolls. In Table D6 we have adjusted the DC payroll estimates to exclude work relief. 3) The National Bureau figures include all enterprise transactions with the public, while the DC includes enterprise interest payments and receipts, and outlays, but not current expenditures. The DC does include general government subsidies to enterprises, less their current surplus. 4) The National Bureau figures treat wage and salary payments in kind as other purchases, the DC treats them as part of payrolls. In the adjusted DC figures presented in Table D6 we have shifted wage and salary payments in kind by the federal government from payrolls to other purchases. 5) In the National Bureau figures, purchases from business are separated into "other purchases" and net outlays, sales of land, buildings, and equipment being subtracted from total outlay payments. Other purchases are gross. The DC separates purchases from business into new construction in the continental United States and "other purchases", which include purchases of equipment, government cash gifts and contributions abroad, and construction outside the United States. "Other purchases" are net, receipts from domestic sales of surplus consumption goods, sales of surplus property abroad, and cash and credit lend-lease being subtracted from payments. "New construction" is a gross figure. 6) The National Bureau treats unemployment insurance funds as state funds (as does the Census Bureau in *State Finances*) while the DC includes them under federal funds.

The National Bureau figures differ from those of the Twentieth Century Fund because of differences in concept, such as our exclusion of loans, and because we use later and revised data.

Adjustment for Price Changes

Trends in government input are considerably affected by price changes. To observe changes in input, free of these price changes, we deflate by appropriate price indexes, expressing input in terms of 1929 prices. Since price indexes for individual components of government input may move very differently, the deflation is applied separately to payrolls, outlays and other purchases. The deflating indexes for outlays and other purchases are only crude combinations of familiar construction cost and price indexes weighted so as to approximate roughly the average importance of the items in each component of government input over the whole period. Deflated payrolls are simply number employed multiplied by 1929 payrolls per employee.

The Department of Commerce has similarly deflated its estimates of government expenditures since 1929, but has published only the deflated total and a breakdown between payrolls and other expenditures.

Functional Classification of Government Expenditures

In Tables D7-12 we show functional breakdowns of expenditures in so far as the data permit. The totals differ from those in Tables D1-6 because lack of information prevented us from adjusting expenditures on individual functions to fit the concepts defined above. Thus the federal figures in Tables D7-8 exclude interest payments, expenditures of enterprises other than the Postal Service, and trust fund payments, but include payments by the general fund to enterprises and trust funds and public to public and public to private transfers. The state and local functional data include public to private transfers, almost all of which are in the public welfare category.

The functional classification of federal expenditures (Table D8) is extremely crude; only a few of the more easily identified functions, not including some with large changes, are shown separately. The city figures suffer from discontinuity because overlying areas, such as school and other special districts, are omitted in 1941 and later years. The main effect of this omission is that the importance of school expenditures is much reduced, but highways, sanitation, and other functions are also affected.

For some years we show no figures at all, either because no data are available, as for states in most of the years before 1915, or because changes in classification from year to year were so numerous as to make it either impossible or not worth while.

Table D1

FEDERAL GOVERNMENT EXPENDITURES, BY TYPE, 1903-1942

(Unit: $1 million)

	1903	1913	1923	1929	1932	1939	1942
War and Nonwar							
Payrolls & purchases	437	758	1,882	2,245	2,423	4,294	33,556
Payrolls	219	441	1,083	1,362	1,407	2,107	5,931
Outlays	48	103	85	202	354	1,105	10,340
Other purchases	170	214	714	682	661	1,082	17,285
Transfers							
Public to private	138	175	625	693	924	3,639	3,167
Public to public	6	10	89	118	229	1,010	837
Net interest							
payments	28	25	1,016	666	562	583	941
Nonwar							
Payrolls & purchases	251	505	1,215	1,593	1,716	3,115	3,070
Payrolls	143	315	674	955	998	1,488	1,799
Outlays	9	65	25	104	246	726	468
Other purchases	100	124	516	535	472	902	803
War							
Payrolls & purchases	185	253	667	652	707	1,179	30,486
Payrolls	76	126	409	407	410	619	4,132
Outlays	39	37	60	98	108	380	9,872
Other purchases	70	89	198	147	189	180	16,482

Totals for federal expenditures are based on the historical series published in the Treasury Department's annual reports, such as in the 1950 report, pp. 448-53. We adjusted this series in several ways so that it would be comparable over the whole period and would conform more closely to the definition of expenditures used here. The main adjustments were the addition of trust fund and enterprise expenditures where they were not included, and the elimination of transactions among government agencies, loans, and refunds.

1903: Payrolls and other purchases are total expenditures as shown by the *Annual Report of the Secretary of the Treasury*, less identifiable debt retirement, outlay, interest, and transfer items (the last consisting only of pensions and apportionments), and less expenditures of the District of Columbia. Payrolls, whenever possible, are from actual payroll data (the Postal Service, Army and Navy military pay, Navy Department civilian payrolls and the State Department). For other departments, average salaries and numbers of employees reported by the Census Bureau in "The Executive Civil Service of the United States", *Bulletin 12, 1904*, were used together with aggregate salaries of employees not reported by the census, as given in the *Annual Report of the United States Civil Service Commission, 1904*.

Outlays are net, receipts from sales of public lands having been subtracted from expenditures. These receipts were unusually large in 1903, almost $9 million. War outlays are based on the series on military and naval construction from the Census Bureau's *Historical Statistics of the United States* (1949), with the addition of outlays on equipment from the *Annual Report of the Secretary of the Navy, 1903* and the *Annual Report of the Secretary of the Treasury, 1903*. Navy outlay payrolls have been subtracted from outlays.

NOTES TO TABLE D1 (continued)

War activities of civilian departments are classified as nonwar expenditures, while civilian activities of the War Department other than rivers and harbors and the Panama Canal are classified as war expenditures. Interest payments are from the series in recent issues of the *Annual Report of the Secretary of the Treasury.*

1913: Payrolls and other purchases are total expenditures as given in the *Annual Report of the Secretary of the Treasury,* less debt retirement, District of Columbia expenditures, interest, and identifiable outlay and transfer items. Payrolls of civilian departments other than the Post Office are estimated from employment, and payroll per employee interpolated between 1903 and 1923 by annual average earnings of government employees in the District of Columbia from Paul Douglas, *Real Wages in the United States* (Houghton Mifflin, 1930). Military pay is taken directly from the annual reports of the War and Navy Departments as is civilian pay of the Navy Department. Outlay payrolls are excluded from Navy and rivers and harbors outlays. Civilian pay of the War Department (except river and harbor improvement payrolls) is estimated from employment in the same way as that of other civilian departments except the Post Office. Post Office payrolls are actual pay figures from the *Annual Report of the Postmaster General, 1913.* These payrolls are the sum of individual pay figures shown in the auditor's report, so they may be slightly underestimated if some small payroll items were not identified.

Outlays and interest are estimated in the same manner as in 1903.

1923: Payrolls and other purchases are estimated from total government expenditures by a method similar to that used in 1913, except that the classification of obligations by character and object of expenditure from *The Budget of the United States Government, 1928* was used to eliminate certain types of expenditure, and certain data on government enterprises were derived from their annual reports and from 76th Congress, 3d Session, Senate Document No. 172, *Financial Statements of Certain Government Agencies.*

Payrolls are based mainly on obligations for net personal services as reported in the 1928 Budget with the addition of other payrolls and pension payments and the separation of war and nonwar payrolls from the 1925 Budget and other minor sources.

Transfers and outlays are also based on Budget data, with some adjustments, mostly minor except for the deduction from outlays of a large amount of ship sales by the United States Shipping Board reported in its *Annual Report* for 1923.

Interest is from the Treasury series cited above, with the addition of net interest payments of enterprises, from their own reports or the *Financial Statements,* and less trust fund interest receipts, shown in the 1923 Treasury Report.

1929: Payrolls and other purchases are derived as in 1923. Total civilian payrolls are the BLS figure for calendar 1929 extrapolated to fiscal 1929 by employment (the average of our employment estimates for 1928 and 1929), plus government contributions to pension funds. War and Navy Department civilian payrolls are estimated from the total by the ratio for civilian employment. Military payrolls are Department of Commerce estimates for calendar 1929 extrapolated to fiscal 1929 by military pay, subsistence, and transportation, etc., given in the Treasury report.

Transfers, outlays, and interest are estimated as for 1923.

1932: Payrolls and other purchases, transfers, and outlays are all estimated in the same way as in 1929, with very minor exceptions. Payrolls are estimated

Notes to Table D1 (concluded)

by averaging the 1931 and 1932 calendar year figures of the BLS. Military cash pay is estimated from two Department of Commerce calendar year figures.

1939: Payrolls and other purchases are estimated as in 1929, except that the Budget classification was used only to eliminate outlays and some minor items from the total, while we used the annual reports of the Secretary of the Treasury for 1939 and 1940 to estimate transfers. Payrolls are derived from the same sources as in 1932, making use, however, of the monthly estimates of civilian payrolls which begin with January 1939.

Public to private transfers are the sum of a number of items listed in the 1939 Treasury report, chiefly WPA expenditures, agricultural subsidies, and veterans' pensions. Public to public transfers are based mainly on a special compilation in the 1940 Treasury report.

Outlays and interest are estimated as in earlier years, except that military outlay obligations are scaled down to match actual expenditures as reported by the Treasury Department.

1942: Payrolls and other purchases are the sum of federal general government and enterprise operation expenditures as reported in the Census Bureau's *Governmental Finances in the United States: 1942*, plus trust fund expenditures (other than transfers) and government contributions to civilian pension funds, and less public to private transfers classified by the Census Bureau as operation. The Census Bureau definition of war activities, wider than ours, was followed with one exception — we took veterans' care and similar items out of war and placed them under nonwar activities. Nonwar payrolls for the fiscal year are interpolated from BLS calendar year figures by monthly employment, and military pay, in the same way, by number of men in the armed forces. The war category is somewhat less inclusive than that for payrolls and other purchases so war purchases other than outlays are probably somewhat overstated.

Public to private transfers are the sum of Treasury figures for veterans' pensions and benefits, government civilian retirement pensions, work relief, Old-Age and Survivors Insurance and Railroad Retirement Benefits, and the Commodity Stamp Trust Fund and an estimate for subsidies from a special compilation by the Bureau of the Budget. Public to public transfers are the Census figure for "Aid to other governments".

General outlays are based on *Governmental Finances* with the exception that the Veterans Administration has been shifted from war to nonwar. Enterprise outlays are from corporation reports where available, and in other cases are estimated from increases in assets, as reported by the Treasury Department.

Table D2

STATE GOVERNMENT NONSCHOOL EXPENDITURES, BY TYPE
1903-1942
(Unit: $1 million)

	1903	1913	1923	1929	1932	1939	1942
Payrolls and Purchases	102	224	809	1,343	1,681	2,024	1,822
Payrolls	57	107	257	385	446	711	738
Outlays	18	43	322	618	848	699	613
Other purchases	27	74	231	340	387	614	472
Transfers							
Public to private	4	2	50	37	48	979	932
Public to public	54	87	353	367	764	1,543	1,818
Net Interest Payments	—1	—3	3	20	40	17	—47

1903: General operation and outlays were lumped together in the data for states in the Census Bureau's *Wealth, Debt, and Taxation, 1903*, except for a small item called "buildings and sites". To estimate total outlays we assumed that, for each department, expenses and outlays were in the same ratio as in 1915.

The payroll figure is the product of the National Bureau estimate of nonschool employment, and payrolls per employee, the latter roughly estimated by extrapolating the 1929 figure to 1909 by state payrolls per employee from Simon Kuznets, *National Income and Its Composition* (National Bureau of Economic Research, 1941), estimated annual pay of state and county employees, from W. I. King, *The National Income and Its Purchasing Power* (National Bureau of Economic Research, 1930), and average annual earnings of government employees in the District of Columbia, from Paul Douglas, *Real Wages in the United States* (Houghton Mifflin, 1930).

Expenditures under "common schools" were treated as public to public transfers. The figure for other public to public transfers is the sum of all local receipts from subventions and grants, less District of Columbia receipts from the federal government.

Public to private transfers are the sum of "outdoor poor relief," estimated from "charities, hospitals, and corrections" by the 1915 ratio, and "aid to special classes" other than soldiers and sailors in state institutions, estimated from "miscellaneous and general" by the 1915 ratio.

1913: Net interest consists of corporate interest payments less corporate interest receipts. Payrolls and other purchases are the sum of expenses of general departments and public service enterprises less schools, apportionments, estimated public to private transfers, and pensions.

Payrolls and public to private transfers were estimated as for 1903.

Public to public transfers are education and highway apportionments from *Wealth, Debt, and Taxation, 1913*. Apportionments for purposes other than education and highways are included in operation expenditure. No estimate for total apportionments could be derived from receipts in 1913 because of the incompleteness of the census.

1923: Public to public transfers are highway and other apportionments as shown in the Census Bureau's *Historical Review of State and Local Government Finances* (1948). For the first time this figure includes local shares of state-imposed taxes, and is therefore not comparable with the figures for earlier

NOTES TO TABLE D2 (concluded)

years. The figure for highway apportionments, comparable with those for earlier years, is $19 million, instead of $68 million. School apportionments are not affected by the change.

1929: Payrolls and purchases, outlays, and transfers are estimated as for 1913. No payments of locally shared state taxes or grants other than for highways and schools are included in public to public transfers and the transfer figure is therefore comparable with 1903 and 1913 rather than with 1923 and later years.

Payrolls are from the WPA-BLS State, County, and Municipal Survey (published in BLS *Serial No. R. 1732*, "Public Employment and Pay Rolls in the U. S., 1929-39, and Post-War Implications", by Carol P. Brainerd) shifted from calendar to fiscal 1929 by our employment estimates (using the average of calendar 1928 and calendar 1929 as fiscal 1929).

1932: Payrolls, outlays and other purchases, and transfers are estimated as for 1929, except that public to public transfers include local shares of state collected taxes and grants other than for highways and schools.

1939: Payrolls and other purchases are expenditures on general and public service enterprise operation less grants, unemployment and public assistance benefits, contributions to public service enterprises, and pensions. Payrolls are the average of calendar year figures for 1938 and 1939 from the WPA-BLS State, County, and Municipal Survey.

Public to private transfers are the sum of unemployment benefits, pension payments, and public assistance. Public to public transfers are the sum of grants, shared taxes, and shared alcoholic beverage monopoly system receipts.

1942: Payrolls and other purchases are the sum of expenditures on general and enterprise operation, administration of pension funds and workmen's compensation funds, and government contributions to state employee pension funds, less public assistance other than administration. Payrolls are wages and salaries from the Census Bureau's State and Local Government Quarterly Employment Survey plus government contributions to state employee pension funds.

Public to private transfers are the sum of public assistance less administration and unemployment compensation benefits. Public to public transfers are state aid, including shared taxes, grants by state school trust funds, and state contributions to pensions for local employees.

Net interest payments are general and public service enterprise interest payments, less general interest receipts and earnings on investments of sinking funds, pension funds, trust funds, unemployment compensation funds, and workmen's compensation funds.

Table D3

LOCAL GOVERNMENT NONSCHOOL EXPENDITURES, BY TYPE
1903-1942

(Unit: $1 million)

	1903	1913	1932	1942
Payrolls and Purchases	689	1,282	3,779	3,750
Payrolls	269	452	1,647	2,028
Outlays	212	451	1,143	519
Other purchases	208	379	990	1,204
Transfers				
Public to private	12	5	181	797
Public to public	2	n.a.	65	48
Net Interest Payments	61	145	630	505

1903: Payrolls and other purchases are the sum of: 1) county expenses, less interest payments and outdoor poor relief; 2) payments by cities over 8,000 for general and municipal service, municipal investment, public trust fund, and municipal industrial expenses, less outdoor poor relief, payments to other civil divisions, net corporate interest payments, payments of Massachusetts cities for interest and sinking funds, and receipts from refunds; and 3) total expenditures, other than interest payments and outlays, of minor civil divisions and cities under 8,000. Some public to public transfers are probably included with county other purchases and some public to private transfers with other purchases of cities under 8,000 and other minor civil divisions. Data for counties and minor civil divisions are from the Census Bureau's *Wealth, Debt, and Taxation, 1903;* data for cities with populations over 25,000, from Census *Bulletin 20* (1905); and data for cities 8,000-25,000, from Census *Bulletin 45* (1906).

Payrolls are estimated by multiplying local public employment by payroll per employee. The employment figure is the average of the 1900 and 1905 National Bureau city full-time equivalent employment figure from Table B9 plus the 1902 estimate of other local employment from Table B10. The payroll per employee figure is a very rough guess, being an extrapolation back from the WPA-BLS State, County, and Municipal Survey 1929 estimate to 1919 by "wages and salaries per city and county nonschool employee", from Simon Kuznets, *National Income and Its Composition* (National Bureau of Economic Research, 1941); to 1909, by "payrolls per employee of police and fire departments, municipal utilities, and miscellaneous civil departments", from W. I. King, *The National Income and Its Purchasing Power* (National Bureau of Economic Research, 1930); and to 1903 by average annual earnings of federal employees in the District of Columbia, from Paul Douglas, *Real Wages in the United States* (Houghton Mifflin, 1930).

School outlays of cities under 8,000 and other minor civil divisions, not shown apart from other outlays in the source, were estimated by using the ratio of school expenses to total expenses in these cities and the ratios in cities 8,000-25,000 of school expenses to total expenses and school outlays to total outlays. Receipts by cities over 8,000 from the sale of real property are subtracted from outlay payments.

Public to private transfers are outdoor poor relief payments of cities over 8,000, and county payments, estimated from expenditures for charities, hospi-

NOTES TO TABLE D3 (continued)

tals, and corrections by the ratio for cities 8,000-25,000. No estimate was made for cities under 8,000; their transfer payments are therefore included with other purchases.

Public to public transfers are payments by cities over 25,000 to other civil divisions for charities and correction.

Net interest is net corporate interest payments plus payments of Massachusetts cities for interest (see Census *Bulletin 20*), less net corporate interest receipts.

1913: All the 1913 figures in Table D3, except for payrolls, are interpolations between 1903 and 1932, via the data for cities over 30,000 and counties. Alternative figures, using all the data available for 1913, but not including cities under 2,500 or their overlying areas and possibly excluding overlying areas of some other cities, are given below.

County payrolls and other purchases in 1913 are expenses of general government departments and public service enterprises less outdoor poor relief. The data are from *Wealth, Debt, and Taxation, 1913*.

City payrolls and other purchases are expenses of general departments and public service enterprises, less outdoor poor relief estimated from charities, hospitals, and corrections, and less pension assessments estimated from receipts from gifts and pension assessments by the 1912 ratios in cities over 30,000. The data are from *Wealth, Debt, and Taxation, 1913* and the Census Bureau's *Financial Statistics of Cities, 1912*.

Payrolls are estimated as for 1903, using a figure for local employment other than municipal interpolated between 1902 and 1929 by municipal employment, and one for municipal employment interpolated between 1910 and 1915 by King's estimates.

School outlays of counties were separated from other outlays using the ratio of school operation to total operation and the 1903 ratios of school operation to total operation and school outlays to total outlays. City school outlays were estimated in a similar way, using 1912 ratios for cities over 30,000.

County interest receipts are estimated from interest and rents and earnings of government departments and public service enterprises by the 1903 ratio of interest receipts to total commercial revenue. City interest receipts were estimated from receipts of interest and rents by the 1912 ratio for cities over 30,000.

The data for cities over 30,000 in 1903 used in the interpolations are from Census *Bulletin 20*.

The figures for those units of government which were covered by the 1913 report are as follows (in millions of dollars):

Payrolls and purchases	1,135
Outlays	415
Other purchases and payrolls	720

1932: Payrolls and other purchases are operation and maintenance of general departments and public service enterprises less public to private transfers and pension assessments, the latter estimated from receipts for donations, gifts, and pension assessments by the 1931 ratio for cities over 30,000. No functional distribution is given in the source for operation expenditures of local governments other than counties in several of the states, and we assume that the operation expenditures of local governments in the missing states are distrib-

NOTES TO TABLE D3 (continued)

uted in the same way as in those for which figures are available. The following are the percentages that operation expenditures in the states for which the functional breakdown is given are to the totals in the whole country for each type of government unit:

Cities over 30,000	74.0
Cities 8,000-30,000	74.1
Cities 2,500-8,000	66.8
Cities under 2,500	59.2
Townships and towns	80.3

Most of these data are from *Wealth, Debt, and Taxation, 1932*. The 1931 ratios for cities over 30,000 are from the *Financial Statistics of Cities, 1931*. All school district expenditures are considered to be for schools; all other special districts' expenditures are treated as nonschool.

Payrolls are based on the WPA-BLS State, County, and Municipal Survey.

School outlays were estimated by assuming that, for each level of local government, the ratio of school outlays to total outlays bore the same relationship to the ratio of school operation to total operation as in cities over 30,000 in 1931. The school operation figure we use for counties excludes $65 million in apportionments to independent school districts (see the Census Bureau's *Historical Review of State and Local Government Finances, 1948*).

Public to private transfers are outdoor poor relief, estimated from charities, hospitals, and corrections by the 1931 ratio for cities over 30,000; and aid to special classes, estimated from miscellaneous expenditures by the 1931 ratio in cities over 30,000.

Public to public transfers are county apportionments to independent school districts, from the *Historical Review of State and Local Government Finances*.

Interest receipts are estimated from receipts for highway privileges, rents, and interest by the 1931 ratio in cities over 30,000.

1942: Payrolls and other purchases are general and enterprise operation plus state and local contributions to pensions for local employees, administration of pension and retirement funds and leased public service enterprises, less general relief and other public assistance, except administration.

Payrolls are wages and salaries from the Census Bureau's State and Local Government Quarterly Employment Survey plus state and local contributions to pension funds for local employees.

Outlays are general expenditures plus partly estimated public service enterprise expenditures. We estimated county enterprise outlays by assuming that, for each type of county public service enterprise, outlays in 1942 bore the same relationship to outlays in 1944 as in cities with populations over 100,000. (Out of total county outlays of about $76 million, estimated enterprise outlays were less than $1 million.) A similar method was used to estimate the enterprise outlays of cities of 25,000-100,000 population, using 1943 instead of 1944.

Public to private transfers are general relief and other public assistance excluding administration, plus pension payments to local employees.

Public to public transfers are shown as "aid paid to other governments".

Net interest payments are general interest payments plus partly estimated public service enterprise interest payments, less partly estimated general interest receipts. County enterprise interest payments are estimated from payments by five counties, interpolated between 1941 and 1944 and raised by the 1944

NOTES TO TABLE D3 (concluded)

ratio of total county enterprise interest payments to the payments of the five counties. County general interest receipts are estimated from miscellaneous receipts by the 1941 ratio for 27 counties. General interest receipts of cities 25,000-100,000 are estimated from earnings and miscellaneous receipts by the ratio for cities over 100,000. Sinking and pension fund interest receipts of local governments other than cities over 100,000 are estimated from data on fund assets from the Census Bureau's *Governmental Finances in the United States: 1942* and *Retirement Systems for State and Local Government Employees, 1941.*

Other data, except for payrolls, are from *Governmental Finances in the United States: 1942,* the *Revised Summary of State and Local Government Finances in 1942, City Finances,* 1942, 1943, and 1944, and *County Finances,* 1941, 1942, 1943, and 1944 (all Census Bureau publications).

Table D4

SCHOOL EXPENDITURES, EXCLUDING HIGHER EDUCATION, BY TYPE
1903-1942

(Unit: $1 million)

	1903	1913	1922	1928	1932	1938	1942
Payrolls and Purchases	246	509	1,537	2,092	2,034	2,117	2,213
Payrolls	176	341	985	1,339	1,451	1,442	1,571
Outlays	46	84	306	383	211	239	138
Other purchases	24	85	246	371	372	436	505

Data for higher education, for the years available, are as follows:

	1932	1938	1942
Payrolls and purchases	282	331	398
Payrolls	152	190	231
Outlays	39	41	29
Other purchases	91	100	138

1903 and 1913: Payrolls are extrapolated from 1922 by the ratio to total payments (other than outlays) of "salaries of superintendents, supervisors, principals, and teachers". Data are from issues of the *Annual Report* of the United States Office of Education.

1922 to 1942: Payrolls are salaries and per diem under general control, and salaries under instruction and operation of plant. Other purchases are supplies under general control, texts and supplies under instruction, fuel, light, and supplies under operation of plant, and maintenance, auxiliary charges, and fixed charges. Data are from various reports of the Office of Education's Biennial Survey of Education. Interest payments of school districts, school interest payments of other governments, and school pensions are included with nonschool expenditures.

Table D5

GOVERNMENT EXPENDITURES BY TYPE, IN 1929 PRICES, 1903-1942

(Unit: $1 million)

	1903	1913	1923	1929	1932	1939	1942
Federal Government, Nonwar							
Payrolls and purchases	578	1,037	1,422	1,594	1,882	3,321	3,090
Payrolls	383	674	874	955	1,041	1,577	1,839
Outlays	20	142	26	104	296	727	418
Other purchases	175	221	522	535	545	1,017	833
Federal Government, War							
Payrolls and purchases	371	452	668	652	803	1,233	29,368
Payrolls	174	242	412	407	408	589	2,932
Outlays	73	69	59	98	139	416	8,958
Other purchases	124	141	197	147	256	228	17,478
States, Nonschool							
Payrolls and purchases	188	371	794	1,343	2,094	2,271	1,755
Payrolls	117	191	295	385	454	683	683
Outlays	27	64	280	618	1,143	868	595
Other purchases	44	116	219	340	497	723	477
Local, Nonschool							
Payrolls and purchases	1,280	2,310			4,242		3,329
Payrolls	542	888			1,521		1,631
Outlays	396	828			1,449		482
Other purchases	342	594			1,272		1,216
Schools							
Payrolls and purchases	779	1,134	1,654	2,085	2,151	2,196	2,123
Payrolls	632	795	1,113	1,339	1,429	1,476	1,516
Outlays	106	190	319	383	275	261	131
Other purchases	11	149	222	363	447	459	476
Total							
Payrolls and purchases	3,196	5,304			11,172		39,665
Payrolls	1,848	2,790			4,853		8,601
Outlays	622	1,293			3,302		10,584
Other purchases	726	1,221			3,017		20,480

Data do not include expenditures on higher education. For the years available, these are as follows (in millions of dollars, 1929 prices):

	1932	1938	1942
Payrolls and purchases	310	345	380
Payrolls	150	195	223
Outlays	51	45	27
Other purchases	109	105	130

Payrolls in constant prices are measured by full time equivalent employment multiplied by the 1929 payroll per employee. Most of the 1929 estimates for payrolls per employee use the figures given in earlier tables. Local payrolls per employee in 1929 are estimated by extrapolating from 1932 to calendar 1929 via the WPA-BLS figures (see notes to Table D1), and to fiscal 1929 using Simon Kuznets' data (*National Income and its Composition,* National Bureau of Economic Research, 1941).

Federal nonwar "other purchases" were deflated by a combination of two price indexes weighted equally: an index of the cost of transportation and travel, and an index of the cost of commodities and other services. The index of the cost of transportation and travel is composed of an index of the cost per mile of railway mail, weighted three, and indexes of the cost of rail freight and rail passenger service from Harold Barger, *The Transportation Industries, 1889-1946* (National Bureau of Economic Research, 1951), each weighted one. The index of the cost of commodities and other services is a combination of four wholesale price indexes (foods, fuel and lighting, textiles, and paper) and two construction cost indexes, the American Appraisal Company (New) Index and a combination of the Engineering News-Record Construction Cost Index and the Associated General Contractors Index, each weighted one. The construction cost indexes are used to cover the cost of repairs and maintenance. Federal war "other purchases" were deflated by an index composed of the BLS wholesale food price index, weighted four, indexes of the wholesale price of fuel and lighting, textiles and the cost of transportation and travel, each weighted one, and a military construction cost index, weighted two. The travel and transportation index is the same as is used for nonwar purchases except that the cost of railway mail service is not included. The military construction cost index is an unweighted average of the George A. Fuller Company Index, the American Appraisal Company Index, the Turner Construction Company Index, and the Public Roads Administration Index. The weights used in constructing these indexes are only rough guesses as to the importance of the various items; the only item of government purchases which is available separately in every year is railway mail service which is given in the annual reports of the Postmaster General. Travel, transportation, and repairs and alterations are available for 1923 to 1939 in the United States Budgets. Other weights are based on a rough classification of the detailed distribution of commodity purchases by type of commodity given in TNEC Monograph No. 19, *Government Purchasing — An Economic Commentary* (1940).

State and local government nonschool "other purchases" were deflated by an index constructed of four wholesale price series (foods, and fuel and lighting, each weighted three; paper, and drugs and chemicals, each weighted one) and the deflator used for local outlays (see below), weighted three times. School "other purchases" were deflated by a combination of wholesale price indexes for fuel and lighting, and paper, and the American Appraisal Company Construction Cost Index, weighted in the proportions 3:3:2. A very rough idea of the type of purchases by state and local governments was obtained from the TNEC report mentioned above, while for schools, the Biennial Surveys of Education show the proportions of school expenditure for "operation of plant, fuel, supplies, etc.", "general control and instruction, texts, supplies, etc.", and "maintenance".

The price indexes used for deflating outlays were constructed mainly from those in the Department of Commerce publication, *Construction and Construction Materials,* Statistical Supplement, May 1949, most of which were extrapolated back to 1903 by the Engineering News-Record Construction Cost and Building Cost Indexes. Weights were devised for each of the several levels of government to allow for the differences in type of outlay undertaken (mainly road construction as opposed to buildings or other types of outlays).

Notes to Table D5 (concluded)

For the federal government, the index used for military outlays was the one used also by the Department of Commerce, an unweighted average of the George A. Fuller Company Index, the American Appraisal Company Index, the Turner Construction Company Index, and the Public Roads Administration Index. For nonwar federal outlays, we used an unweighted average of the American Appraisal Company Index, the Engineering News-Record Construction Cost Index, and the Associated General Contractors Index. The Department of Commerce uses the first of these for hospital, institutional, and other nonresidential building, and the latter two for conservation and development, and "all other" public construction.

For state nonschool outlays, we used an average of the Public Roads Administration Index, and the American Appraisal Company Index, weighted in the ratio of 4:1. For local nonschool outlays, we used an unweighted average of the Public Roads Administration Index for roads and streets; an average of the Engineering News-Record Construction Cost Index and the Associated General Contractors Index for sewers, water supply, etc.; and the American Appraisal Company Index for nonresidential building. For school outlays, we used the American Appraisal Company Index, also used by the Department of Commerce in the source cited above.

Table D6

ADJUSTED DEPARTMENT OF COMMERCE ESTIMATES OF GOVERNMENT PAYROLLS
AND PURCHASES, 1929-1949

(Unit: $1 million)

	1929	1930	1931	1932	1933	1934	1935	1936	193?
Federal									
Compensation of employees	900	935	942	901	1,187	1,718	1,791	3,592	3,03(
Less: work relief, wages and salaries	0	0	0	0	356	764	611	2,174	1,63(
Less: payment in kind	61	58	52	47	47	46	54	63	6:
Payrolls (adjusted)	839	877	890	854	784	908	1,126	1,355	1,32(
Outlays	155	209	271	333	334	404	467	502	52(
Purchases from business except new construction	186	195	244	186	448	830	618	656	89
Plus: net purchases from abroad	70	71	80	60	49	39	55	65	9(
Plus: payment in kind	61	58	52	47	47	46	54	63	6
Less: domestic sales of surplus consumption goods and materials	0	0	0	0	0	0	0	0	
Other purchases (adjusted)	317	324	376	293	544	915	727	784	1,05(
State and Local									
Compensation of employees	3,456	3,630	3,737	3,565	3,531	3,884	4,178	3,696	3,88(
Less: work relief, wages and salaries	0	4	46	92	341	680	791	74	4
Payrolls (adjusted)	3,456	3,626	3,691	3,473	3,190	3,204	3,387	3,622	3,84
Outlays	2,236	2,544	2,293	1,445	884	1,131	974	1,592	1,41
Other purchases	1,469	1,585	1,651	1,587	1,525	1,744	1,803	1,640	1,73

The Department of Commerce estimates of government expenditures are adjusted to bring them
into closer conformity to the National Bureau measures. The original data are from the *Survey
of Current Business,* National Income Supplement, 1951, the Department's unpublished *Technical
Notes on Sources and Methods Used in the Derivation of National Income Statistics,* Section o
Wages and Salaries and Employment, and some data received directly from the Department.

1938	1939	1940	1941	1942	1943	1944	1945	1946	1947	1948	1949
3,529	3,444	3,537	5,046	10,836	21,255	27,905	30,614	14,741	9,356	8,922	9,979
2,110	1,875	1,579	1,213	580	50	0	0	0	0	0	0
68	77	127	442	1,375	2,639	3,729	4,088	1,364	653	613	695
1,351	1,492	1,831	3,391	8,881	18,566	24,176	26,526	13,377	8,703	8,309	9,284
476	537	974	3,588	9,279	5,363	1,761	1,440	931	957	1,186	1,490
1,211	1,116	1,581	7,966	30,735	53,261	58,624	42,221	6,716	5,751	8,832	10,253
64	64	84	330	1,193	1,411	925	943	−726	13	2,225	3,834
68	77	127	442	1,375	2,639	3,729	4,088	1,364	653	613	695
0	4	6	7	16	67	209	422	716	293	143	83
1,343	1,253	1,786	8,731	33,287	57,244	63,069	46,830	6,638	6,124	11,527	14,699
4,121	4,185	4,280	4,368	4,443	4,621	4,883	5,296	6,080	7,262	8,517	9,445
8	10	10	6	2	0	0	0	0	0	0	0
4,113	4,175	4,270	4,362	4,441	4,621	4,883	5,296	6,080	7,262	8,517	9,445
1,488	1,809	1,559	1,416	1,092	672	552	652	1,431	2,539	3,721	4,913
1,861	1,917	1,924	1,997	2,162	2,114	2,082	2,092	2,459	3,027	3,338	3,768

Table D7

FUNCTIONAL CLASSIFICATION OF FEDERAL GOVERNMENT
EXPENDITURES, 1900-1949

(Unit: $1 million)

Year	Post Office Expenditures	National Defense	Veterans' Services and Benefits	International Affairs and Finance	Other Expenditures	Total Expenditures
1900	108	191	152	3	116	570
1901	116	206				589
1902	125	180				563
1903	139	202	151	3	114	609
1904	152	268				694
1905	167	244				682
1906	178	247				699
1907	190	247				726
1908	208	294				820
1909	221	308				862
1910	230	284				882
1911	238	283				894
1912	249	284		5		902
1913	262	293	192	5	199	951
1914	284	298		5		984
1915	299	297	176	5	236	1,013
1916	306	305	171	6	201	989
1917	320	602	171	891	263	2,247
1918	325	7,110	235	4,748	367	12,785
1919	363	13,548	324	3,500	458	18,193
1920	454	3,997	332	435	531	5,749
1921	621	2,581	646	83	615	4,546
1922	546	929	686	10	601	2,772
1923	557	680	747	14	607	2,605
1924	587	647	676	15	598	2,523
1925	639	591	741	15	629	2,615
1926	680	586	772	17	641	2,696
1927	715	578	786	17	652	2,748
1928	726	656	806	12	696	2,896
1929	782	696	812	14	748	3,052
1930	804	734	821	14	962	3,335
1931	803	733	1,040	16	1,015	3,607
1932	794	703	985	19	2,130	4,631
1933	700	648	863	16	2,278	4,505
1934	631	540	557	12	4,751	6,491
1935	697	711	607	19	4,294	6,328
1936	754	914	2,350	18	4,370	8,406
1937	773	937	1,137	18	4,753	7,618
1938	772	1,030	581	19	4,369	6,771
1939	785	1,074	559	19	6,327	8,764

Year	Post Office Expenditures	National Defense	Veterans' Services and Benefits	International Affairs and Finance	Other Expenditures	Total Expenditures
1940	808	1,497	551	50	5,991	8,897
1941	837	6,370	564	141	5,161	13,073
1942	874	26,847	556	633	4,863	33,773
1943	953	70,243	605	166	6,771	78,738
1944	1,069	83,736	744	244	7,999	93,792
1945	1,145	84,532	2,094	677	7,741	96,189
1946	1,354	45,103	4,414	1,462	4,750	57,083
1947	1,505	14,281	7,370	6,542	5,846	35,544
1948	1,688	10,924	6,566	4,780	5,972	29,930
1949	2,149	11,865	6,668	6,458	9,097	36,237

Post Office data are from the *Annual Report of the Secretary of the Treasury on the State of the Finances, 1945* and *1949*.

For national defense, the 1915 to 1948 data are from a special tabulation by the Division of Fiscal Analysis of the Bureau of the Budget, and the 1900 to 1914 data are from the *Congressional Record,* Volume 94, Part 2, 80th Congress, Second Session, pp. 2576-7. The 1949 and 1950 figures for national defense are from *The Budget of the United States Government, 1952,* except that expenditures of the National Advisory Committee for Aeronautics (see *The Budget of the United States Government, 1950* and *1951*) have been subtracted from the published figure to maintain comparability with earlier years.

The 1915 to 1948 figures for veterans' services and benefits are from the special tabulation referred to above, and those for 1900, 1903, and 1913 are extrapolated from 1923 via our estimates (see Table D8). *The Budget of the United States Government, 1952* is the source for the 1949 and 1950 figures.

For international affairs and finance the 1915 to 1948 data are from the special tabulation, and those for 1912 to 1914, from the issue of the *Congressional Record* referred to above. The 1900 and 1903 figures are extrapolated from 1913 via our estimates (Table D8). The 1949 and 1950 figures are from *The Budget of the United States Government, 1952.*

Total expenditures in this table are total budget expenditures other than interest payments and refunds on taxes, plus postal expenditures not included in budget expenditures, i.e., Post Office expenses payable from Post Office revenue. The special tabulation for 1915 to 1948, and *The Budget of the United States Government, 1951* give comparable figures for total budget expenditures excluding tax refunds; we subtracted interest payments on the public debt shown in the same sources and actual or estimated interest on refunds, where necessary. For 1900 to 1914, the issue of the *Congressional Record* mentioned gives budget expenditures including both interest payments and tax refunds; we subtracted interest payments, given in the same source, and tax refunds, given in various issues of the *Annual Report of the Secretary of the Treasury.*

The category "other expenditures" is the difference between "total expenditures" described above, and the sum of the items shown separately in the table.

Table D8

DETAILED FUNCTIONAL CLASSIFICATION OF FEDERAL GOVERNMENT EXPENDITURES, 1900-1949

(Unit: $1 million)

	1900	1903	1913	1923	1929	1939	1949
National Defense	170	176	247	612	681	1,075	11,865
Veterans' Services and Benefits	145	144	183	712	772	559	6,668
Veterans' pensions	141	138	175	394	425	417	2,154
Veterans' insurance				89	261	40	95
Veterans' readjustment benefits				140	.01	1	3,334
Veterans' hospitals, other services, and administrative costs	4	6	8	89	86	101	1,086
International Affairs and Finance	3	3	5	14	13	19	6,458
Conduct of foreign affairs	3	3	5	14	13	17	172
International recovery and relief						2	5,720
Foreign economic development							(45)
Foreign military assistance							414
Philippine war damage and rehabilitation							197
Social Welfare, Health, and Security	5	10	13	38	48	3,946	1,907
Retirement and dependents' insurance						110	584
Assistance to the aged and other special groups			5	6	9	657	1,041
Work relief and direct relief		3	.2	.01	.3	3,109	8
Promotion of public health	1	3	3	14	12	37	171
Crime control and correction	4	4	6	15	23	29	88
Other				3	4	5	15
Housing and Community Development					.5	(154)	282
Education and General Research	3	3	6	15	19	36	70
Promotion of education	1	1	3	9	11	25	39
Educational aid to special groups	.4	.5	1	.05	.1	1	3
Library and museum service	1	1	2	2	3	5	9
General purpose research				4	5	4	18
Labor	.2	.2	.2	3	3	70	193
Unemployment compensation and placement activities					.2	63	163
Other	.2	.2	.2	3	3	7	30

Agriculture and Agricultural Resources	3	4	15	56	63	1,198	2,512
Development and improvement of agriculture, other than financial aids and conservation	3	4	14	44	50	70	177
Loan and investment programs to aid agriculture	.....	.....	.....	11	12	285	1,965
Other financial aids	.....	.....	.....	.....	.....	815	311
Conservation and development of agricultural land and water resources	.....	.....	1	1	1	28	59
Natural Resources Not Primarily Agricultural	9	11	22	29	54	228	1,512
Development and control of atomic energy	.....	.....	.....	.....	.....	.....	622
Other conservation and development	9	11	22	29	54	228	890
Postal Service	108	139	262	557	782	785	2,149
Transportation and Communication	25	27	95	264	264	460	1,141
Promotion of the merchant marine	.....	.....	.....	78	16	43	124
Provision of navigation aids and facilities	24	26	92	76	136	157	309
Provision of highways	.....	.....	.2	80	95	178	453
Regulation of transportation and communication	.6	1	2	6	10	15	22
Other	.....	1	1	23	6	68	234
Finance, Commerce, and Industry	.....	1	2	13	18	51	120
Control of money supply and private finance	.....	.....	.....	5	6	7	7
Promotion or regulation of trade and industry	.....	1	2	8	12	17	62
Business loans and guarantees	.....	.....	.....	.....	.....	42	65
Other	.....	.....	.....	.....	.....	(14)	(14)
General Government	58	69	84	174	229	554	1,087
Legislative	10	12	9	10	13	15	34
Judicial	3	3	4	14	18	9	19
Executive direction and management	.2	.4	.2	.4	.5	1	7
Federal financial management	23	25	26	78	75	110	378
Government payments toward civilian employee general retirement systems	.....	.....	.....	.....	20	74	225
Other	22	29	46	71	103	343	424
Total	529	589	936	2,487	2,947	8,827	35,964

Excess of repayments and collections over expenditures is indicated by parentheses.

Additional notes on p. **246.**

Table D9

FUNCTIONAL CLASSIFICATION OF STATE GOVERNMENT EXPENDITURES, 1903-1949

(Unit: $1 million)

	1903	1913	1915	1916	1917	1918	1919	1923	1924	1925	1926	1927	1928	1929	1930
General control	28	44	50	53	51	56	56	86	84	95	97	111	110	130	128
Public safety	7	26	30	30	32	34	35	55	54	59	62	68	73	75	85
Highways	5	26	65	62	51	55	75	365	464	545	531	550	640	725	857
Sanitation and health	3	4	6	6	7	8	10	16	17	18	19	20	23	24	26
Hospitals and institutions for the handicapped	53	97	55	56	59	66	72	118	124	126	136	151	160	170	187
Public welfare			34	35	39	43	47	79	148	114	69	66	72	72	76
Correction			32	37	39	45	55	66	54	53	56	63	68	72	80
Schools	16	57	59	64	65	69	76	159	170	178	186	190	209	220	229
Natural resources			18	20	20	23	26	53	59	61	68	72	71	76	84
Other general expenditures	5	7	11	9	9	17	18	12	17	14	15	18	20	22	25
Total general operation and outlays	117	261	360	371	371	416	469	1,008	1,190	1,261	1,238	1,309	1,444	1,585	1,775
Public service enterprises	n.a.	21	7	3	4	4	3	13	14	11	12	23	20	15	15
Total operation, outlays, and public service enterprises	n.a.	282	367	374	375	420	472	1,021	1,204	1,272	1,250	1,332	1,464	1,600	1,790

	1931	1932	1937	1938	1939	1940	1941	1942	1943	1944	1945	1946	1947	1948	1949
General control	151	138	161	168	186	172	175	172	172	172	189	204	258	273	314
Public safety	89	92	108	125	129	127	118	131	138	135	134	147	179	212	238
Highways	972	842	849	824	835	799	813	787	660	546	531	624	1,094	1,509	1,877
Sanitation and health	28	30	34	43	48	47	52	55	58	70	96	105	113	111	115
Hospitals and institutions for the handicapped	208	186	227	236	275	262	246	258	261	278	297	338	439	566	705
Public welfare	82	128	392	453	523	527	501	527	557	578	606	681	843	962	1,312
Correction	79	86	75	84	83	85	81	79	79	81	85	95	118	150	168
Schools	238	218	224	245	280	266	259	301	324	369	368	407	608	822	975
Natural resources	84	79	82	96	109	105	123	130	125	135	148	173	227	277	333
Other general expenditures	33	34	33	69	95	80	96	90	72	64	66	157	388	894	760
Total general operation and outlays	1,963	1,833	2,186	2,344	2,562	2,470	2,466	2,531	2,445	2,427	2,521	2,934	4,267	5,776	6,799
Public service enterprises	16	n.a.	214	220	221	245	86	62	n.a.	n.a.	n.a.	n.a.	n.a.	n.a.	n.a.
Total operation, outlays and public service enterprises	1,979	n.a.	2,400	2,564	2,783	2,715	2,552	2,593	n.a.	n.a.	n.a.	n.a.	n.a.	n.a.	n.a.

The figures for public service enterprises, 1937-40, include the cost of goods sold. Figures for other years do not. Cost of goods sold by public service enterprises was $231 million in 1941 and $265 million in 1942. Outlays of alcoholic beverage monopoly systems are omitted from the 1941-42 figures for public service enterprises. Additional notes on p. 247.

NOTES TO TABLE D8

Data for 1939 and 1949 are from *The Budget of the United States Government, 1951* and *1952,* with a few adjustments from the *Annual Report of the Secretary of the Treasury* (mainly the substitution of total Post Office expenditures for the Treasury's subsidy to the Post Office), and a reclassification of certain welfare activities. All the earlier figures are from issues of the *Annual Report of the Secretary of the Treasury* arranged, as far as possible, to fit the adjusted Budget Bureau classification.

Expenditures include payrolls, current purchases, outlays, loans and investments, grants-in-aid, and transfers to the public, but exclude interest. For this reason they differ from the data in other tables in Appendix D.

The totals for 1939 and 1949 in Table D8, although from the same source as those in Table D7, differ from them because the latter have been adjusted to the basis of the Daily Treasury Statement. The figures for earlier years in the two tables are from different sources.

Some notes on the classification, including departures from the Budget Bureau, follow:

Some expenditures under the social welfare, health, and security category may have been included under general government, especially in earlier years.

Educational aid to special groups is not comparable before and after 1939. Apparently, in the 1951 classification, education for Indians was shifted to some other title.

Some of the 1923 expenditure under promotion of the merchant marine should probably be classified under national defense.

Treasury Department expenditures are classified under Federal financial management.

Other general government in 1939 and 1949 includes payments of interest on uninvested trust funds, but not interest on refunds or on the public debt.

No contributions were made by the government to the retirement funds in 1923, though the funds made payments to beneficiaries which were shown in the Treasury Report.

It was assumed that a downward revision in international affairs and finance, 1949 (shown in the 1952 Budget), was completely accounted for by the largest component, International recovery and relief.

The National Advisory Committee for Aeronautics always is included under transportation and communication rather than under national defense.

NOTES TO TABLE D9

Figures cover expenditures for operation, outlays, and public service enterprises, but do not include many of the adjustments of the original data made by us for Table D2, since these could not be broken down by function. Data for general government operation and outlays for 1903, 1915, 1919, 1923, 1927, 1932, and 1937 to 1946 are from the Census Bureau's *Historical Review of State and Local Government Finances* (1948). We have assumed here that all the 1902 outlays (which we call 1903) shown in that source are for general control. All the figures for 1913 are from the Census Bureau's *Wealth, Debt, and Taxation, 1913*. The data in that source are not given in sufficient detail to judge whether comparability with other years in the functional classification is complete, but any incomparabilities do not appear to be very substantial. We made one change in the published figures: operation expenditures for care of patients in state tuberculosis hospitals, included in "conservation of health and sanitation" in 1913, were transferred from that category to "charities, hospitals, and corrections", with the aid of detailed data for 1915.

For all the other years, the data are from various issues of the Census Bureau's *Financial Statistics of States*. The figures for expenditures on natural resources, public safety, and correction have been used as they appear in the source, but we have changed the other functional categories to match as closely as possible the classification in the *Historical Review of State and Local Government Finances*.

The first of the annual series on state finances was published for 1915. There was no report for 1920, and the 1921 report covered only 30 states. We did not use the 1922 figures because they were not given in sufficient detail for us to make the necessary adjustments in the functional classification. No reports on state finances were published in 1933-36.

Table D10

FUNCTIONAL CLASSIFICATION OF MUNICIPAL GOVERNMENT EXPENDITURES, 1902–1945 CITIES HAVING POPULATIONS OVER 100,000

(Unit: $1 million)

	1902	1912	1915	1916	1917	1918	1919	1923	1924	1925	1926	1927	1928	1929	1930
General control	30	57	67	69	76	71	74	114	118	137	146	163	168	172	188
Public safety	60	104	111	114	116	125	136	230	246	270	292	315	325	339	360
Highways	83	128	148	131	141	146	128	249	290	364	396	461	462	471	518
Sanitation		61	78	72	70	74	77	146	169	194	210	241	251	217	230
Health	5	11	8	9	9	9	10	19	19	21	21	29	30	36	35
Hospitals		16	23	21	24	29	33	49	55	61	66	67	73	76	94
Public welfare	12	15	18	22	22	24	27	37	41	45	47	52	59	58	70
Correction		7	8	9	10	11	11	16	16	18	19	21	22	23	25
Schools	74	147	176	182	188	194	213	526	598	620	645	672	687	716	746
Libraries		7	8	8	9	12	10	17	19	23	25	26	28	28	31
Recreation	23	35	29	30	28	32	33	64	78	90	85	110	120	114	110
Miscellaneous and unallocable	3	9	10	7	7	12	15	15	19	21	22	25	23	24	22
Total general operation and outlays	292	594	684	673	700	740	767	1,482	1,668	1,863	1,973	2,182	2,248	2,274	2,428
Public service enterprises	51	96	90	79	79	82	97	210	261	312	332	380	354	360	447
Total operation, outlays, and public service enterprises	343	690	774	752	779	822	864	1,692	1,929	2,175	2,305	2,562	2,602	2,634	2,875

	1931	1932	1933	1934	1935	1936	1937	1938	1939	1940	1941	1942	1943	1944	1945
General control	189	170	154	151	151	158	171	184	184	185	141	131	126	133	138
Public safety	365	338	302	304	314	340	344	361	359	362	359	369	372	376	381
Highways	413	289	201	199	184	203	225	259	272	241	168	145	126	122	133
Sanitation	206	168	125	134	141	155	169	171	169	156	129	129	124	136	143
Health	37	30	27	29	27	22	29	31	32	32	29	30			
Hospitals	101	97	84	85	90	106	118	117	119	131	103	101			
Public welfare	124	180	239	289	279	279	333	382	385	368	268	232			
Correction	29	25	20	21	21	21	23	23	24	24	18	18			
Schools	760	681	567	544	582	650	678	704	717	690	384	382	370	370	370
Libraries	31	27	22	23	24	25	25	28	29	28	22	22			
Recreation	135	105	75	91	61	75	106	94	97	117	75	68	59	63	71
Miscellaneous and unallocable	21	20	19	22	100	20	24	27	27	28	30	32	389	385	394
Total general operation and outlays	2,408	2,128	1,834	1,892	1,975	2,057	2,246	2,381	2,413	2,363	1,726	1,659	1,566	1,585	1,630
Public service enterprises	409	295	204	211	243	315	343	307	394	844	426	404	406	394	426
Total operation, outlays, and public service enterprises	2,817	2,423	2,038	2,103	2,218	2,372	2,589	2,688	2,807	3,207	2,152	2,063	1,972	1,979	2,056

City corporations only, for 1941-1945. Earlier figures include over-lying areas. The 1940 figure for General Operation and Outlays comparable to later years would be $1,813 million.

NOTES TO TABLE D10

Figures cover expenditures for operation, outlays, and public service enterprises, but do not include many of the adjustments of the original data made by us for Table D3, since these could not be broken down by function. The data for outlays after 1945 are not given in sufficient detail for us to show a functional breakdown of total operation and outlays. Data for general government operation and outlays for 1902, 1912, 1923, 1927 and 1931 to 1945 are from the Census Bureau's *Historical Review of State and Local Government Finances* (1948). For other years, and for all the public enterprise figures, the sources are various issues of the Census Bureau's *Financial Statistics of Cities* and, for 1902, Census *Bulletin 20*. The functional classification used in the *Historical Review of State and Local Government Finances* was taken as the starting point and, as far as possible, figures from the other sources were adjusted to match it.

The public enterprise figures are adjusted by us to include certain outlays in New York and Los Angeles omitted in the *Financial Statistics* but included in the Department of Commerce publication by Harold Wolkind, *Fluctuations in Capital Outlays of Municipalities* (1941). The missing items are derived by subtracting the outlays for these two cities shown in the *Financial Statistics* from the Department of Commerce figures.

The years to which the dates in the table apply are sets of overlapping fiscal years, rather than a uniform period for all cities. According to *Fluctuations in Capital Outlays of Municipalities,* p. 82, the reports for 1902, 1912, and 1923 and later years refer mainly to the same calendar year, while the reports for 1915 to 1919 refer mainly to the previous calendar year. We do not present annual data before 1915 because it was not possible to make the functional classifications sufficiently comparable to observe year to year movements. No report was published for 1920, the report for 1921 did not cover all cities over 100,000, and the 1922 report did not show expenditures in sufficient detail for us to make adjustments in the functional classification, so we show no figures for those years.

The earlier figures include some service transfer payments and payments in error, but these could not be eliminated because they are not broken down by function in the sources.

Totals are available for some of the years not shown in this table from Census *Bulletin 20* and various issues of the *Financial Statistics of Cities*. They are as follows (millions of dollars):

	1903	1904	1905	1906	1907	1908	1909
General operation and outlays	326	347	358	381	449	490	489
Public service enterprises, operation, and outlays	65	63	58	63	79	94	92

	1910	1911	1913	1946	1947	1948	1949
General operation and outlays	524	569	620	1,826	2,250	2,629	2,971
Public service enterprises, operation, and outlays	101	105	98	493	618	769	910

NOTES TO TABLE D10 (concluded)

Figures for 1941 and later years are not comparable with earlier ones because data for overlying areas are excluded from the former. The 1940 figures for operation, by function, and for total outlays comparable with later years are available, but none for outlays by function. The available data, which give some idea of the effect of the change, are as follows (millions of dollars):

	1940				1940	
	Comparable with Earlier Years	Comparable with Later Years			Comparable with Earlier Years	Comparable with Later Years
Operation				Operation		
General control	169	124		Public welfare	367	302
Public safety	351	342		Correction	22	15
Highways	109	96		Schools	631	351
Sanitation	108	103		Libraries	26	21
Health	31	27		Recreation	66	53
Hospitals	111	84		Misc. & unallocable	23	16
				Outlays	350	278

Table D11

Expenditures of Local Governments, Classified by Function and by Type of Government, 1903 and 1942

(Unit: $1 million)

YEAR	TOTAL	GENERAL CONTROL	PUBLIC SAFETY	HIGHWAYS	SANITATION AND HEALTH	HOSPITALS, PUBLIC WELFARE, CORRECTION	SCHOOLS	LIBRARIES	RECREATION	MISCELLANEOUS AND UNALLOCABLE
All Local Governments										
1903	667	138	90	112	31	53	220	....	13	10
1942	5,301	498	635	547	252	972	2,090	38	89	171
Counties										
1903	166	71	....	29	2	28	34	....	....	2
1942	1,234	249	57	244	20	514	77	5	8	61
City Corporations										
1903	325	38	79	45	26	20	99	....	13	5
1942	2,266	212	547	219	207	408	491	33	81	68
Other Local Governments (Townships, School Districts, and Special Districts)										
1903	176	28	11	39	3	6	87	....	....	2
1942	1,801	37	31	84	25	50	1,522	....	....	53

Outlays and all enterprise expenditures are excluded. Data are from the Bureau of the Census, *Historical Review of State and Local Government Finances* (1948), Table 6, p. 17.

The functional classification in this table is not the classification currently used by the Bureau of the Census in reporting operation expenditure. Sanitation has been combined with health, and hospitals, public welfare and correction have been combined in order to present historically comparable data classifications.

The source lists the 1903 figures as referring to 1902, but all except those for cities cover the period we include under 1903. The city figures are partly the same as those we call 1903, but most refer to fiscal years one year earlier.

Library expenditures in 1903 are included in operation expenditure for schools; amounts cannot be segregated.

Recreation expenditures of other local governments are included in misc. operation expenditure; amounts cannot be separated. The same is true of public safety expenditures of counties in 1903.

Cities with populations under 8,000 are included under other local governments in 1903.

Table D12

TOTAL GOVERNMENT EXPÉNDITURES CLASSIFIED BY FUNCTION, TYPE, AND
GOVERNMENT UNIT, 1942 (1939 FOR NATIONAL DEFENSE)
(Unit: $1 million)

	FEDERAL			STATE AND LOCAL		
	Operation	*Outlays*	*Total*	*Operation*	*Outlays*	*Total*
General control	438	33	471	667	19	686
National defense	799	380	1,179	......	......	......
Public safety, other	47	......	47	757	33	790
Highways	66	75	141	808	657	1,465
Natural resources	1,001	196	1,197	159	11	170
Sanitation	......	......	......	190	38	228
Health and hospitals	27	......	27	566	38	604
Public welfare	1,125	......	1,125	1,226	4	1,230
Veterans' services and benefits	556	......	556	......	......	......
Schools	23	......	23	2,365	155	2,520
Miscellaneous general operation	115	7	122	476	61	538
Public enterprises	1,576	183	1,759	604	269	873
Total	5,773	874	6,647	7,820	1,286	9,106

	CITIES			TOWNSHIPS AND TOWNS		
	Operation	*Outlays*	*Total*	*Operation*	*Outlays*	*Total*
General control	212	8	220	37	1	38
National defense	......	......	......	......	......	......
Public safety, other	547	17	564	25	3	28
Highways	219	65	284	81	8	89
Natural resources	......	......	......	......	......	......
Sanitation	166	31	197	6	2	8
Health and hospitals	154	8	162	6	......	6
Public welfare	272	.5	272	42	......	42
Veterans' services and benefits	......	......	......	......	......	......
Schools	491	19	510	55	5	60
Miscellaneous general operation	204	36	240	14	5	19
Public enterprises	507	222	729	7	3	10
Total	2,773	404	3,177	273	26	299

With the exceptions noted below, the data are from the following Census Bureau publications: *Revised Summary of State and Local Government Finances in 1942; Governmental Finances in the United States: 1942;* and various issues of *City Finances* and *State Finances.*

Data for national defense are National Bureau of Economic Research estimates (see

STATE			LOCAL			COUNTIES		
Operation	Outlays	Total	Operation	Outlays	Total	Operation	Outlays	Total
169	3	172	498	16	514	249	7	256
......	......	......	......	......	......	......	......	......
123	8	131	635	25	660	57	2	59
260	527	787	547	130	677	244	56	300
123	7	130	35	5	40	16	.1	16
			190	38	228	2	1	3
286	26	312	280	12	292	119	3	122
526	1	527	700	2	702	386	2	388
275	26	301	2,090	129	2,219	77	8	85
152	15	167	325	46	371	85	5	90
38	24	62	566	245	811	7	1	8
1,952	639	2,591	5,867	647	6,514	1,242	84	1,326

SCHOOL DISTRICTS			OTHER SPECIAL DISTRICTS			ALL GOVERNMENTS		
Operation	Outlays	Total	Operation	Outlays	Total	Operation	Outlays	Total
......	......	......	......	......	......	1,105	52	1,157
......	......	......	......	......	......	799	380	1,179
......	......	......	6	4	10	804	33	837
......	......	......	4	1	5	874	732	1,606
......	......	......	20	4	24	1,160	207	1,367
......	......	......	16	5	21	190	38	228
......	......	......	1	.3	1	593	38	631
......	......	......	......	......	......	2,351	4	2,355
						556	......	556
1,467	97	1,564	......	......	......	2,388	155	2,543
......	......	......	21	1	22	591	68	659
......	......	......	45	20	65	2,180	452	2,632
1,467	97	1,564	112	36	148	13,593	2,160	15,753

Table D1). State and local government national defense expenditures are included with other public safety.

State and local expenditures for veterans are included under public welfare.

Data for public enterprises are partly estimated (see Notes to Tables D1-3). War corporations are excluded.

Appendix E

OTHER DATA

This appendix includes two tables containing data basic to certain text tables and charts, and two tables to which reference is made in the text of Chapter 6.

Table E1

POSTAL SYSTEM, INDEXES OF OUTPUT, EMPLOYMENT, HOURS
MANHOURS, AND OUTPUT PER EMPLOYEE AND PER MANHOUR
1908-1940

(1929: 100)

Year	Total Output	Employment (full-time basis)	Output per Employee	Hours[a]	Manhours	Output per Manhour
1908	38.2	65.2	58.6	100.0	65.2	58.6
1910	44.1	68.5	64.4	100.0	68.5	64.4
1912	49.4	70.0	70.6	100.0	70.0	70.6
1926	93.1	95.2	97.8	100.0	95.2	97.8
1927	95.7	96.8	98.9	100.0	96.8	98.9
1928	96.4	98.0	98.4	100.0	98.0	98.4
1929	100.0	100.0	100.0	100.0	100.0	100.0
1930	101.2	100.7	100.5	100.0	100.7	100.5
1931	95.2	99.6	95.6	100.0	99.6	95.6
1932	85.6	98.0	87.3	91.7	89.9	95.2
1933	71.5	95.4	74.9	91.7	87.5	81.7
1934	74.3	90.2	82.4	91.7	82.7	89.8
1935	79.8	89.6	89.1	91.7	82.2	97.1
1936	84.8	94.5	89.7	83.3	78.7	107.8
1937	92.6	95.8	96.7	83.3	79.8	116.0
1938	92.7	96.3	96.3	83.3	80.2	115.6
1939	94.3	97.1	97.1	83.3	80.9	116.6
1940	98.2	98.9	99.3	83.3	82.4	119.2

[a] Not including overtime.

Source: Witt Bowden, "Technological Changes and Employment in the
United States Postal Service", Bureau of Labor Statistics, *Bulletin No. 574,*
December 1932. Bowden's indexes are supplemented by later figures compiled
in an unpublished study of the National Research Project, for which we are indebted to Alexander Gourvitch and David Weintraub. The data for the whole
period are summarized in the latter source, Part II, Chapter H, pp. 59-61.

Table E2

PER CAPITA STATE AND LOCAL GOVERNMENT EXPENDITURES FOR OPERATION
BY FUNCTION, 1903 AND 1942
STATE AND LOCAL GOVERNMENT EMPLOYMENT PER 10,000 POPULATION,
SCHOOL AND NONSCHOOL, 1942
PER CAPITA INCOME PAYMENTS, AVERAGE OF 1938-1942
DEGREE OF URBANIZATION AND DENSITY OF POPULATION, 1900 AND 1940
(48 States)

STATE	URBANIZATION 1900	DENSITY 1900	PER CAPITA STATE AND LOCAL GOVERNMENT OPERATION EXPENDITURES (DOLLARS), 1903								INCOME 1938-42	URBANIZATION 1940	DENSITY 1940
			Total	General Control	Public Safety	Highways	Schools	Health, Hospitals, & Pub. Welfare	Sanitation	Other			
Ala.	11.9	35.7	3.63	.83	.22	.51	1.44	.37	.03	.23	323	30.2	55.5
Ariz.	15.9	1.1	11.60	4.14	.58	1.00	3.76	1.02	.00	1.11	531	34.8	4.4
Ark.	8.5	25.0	4.37	1.04	.19	.85	1.77	.34	.01	.17	307	22.2	37.0
Calif.	52.3	9.5	23.64	4.20	2.39	3.05	9.95	2.35	.32	1.38	880	71.0	44.1
Colo.	48.3	5.2	21.06	5.24	1.62	2.40	8.81	1.38	.18	1.43	597	52.6	10.8
Conn.	59.9	188.5	12.66	1.80	1.69	2.42	3.97	1.53	.47	.79	938	67.8	348.9
Del.	46.4	94.0	8.96	1.74	.94	1.24	3.44	.78	.34	.49	907	52.3	134.7
Fla.	20.3	9.6	6.24	1.47	.51	.97	1.94	.66	.16	.53	506	55.1	35.0
Ga.	15.6	37.7	5.03	.82	.52	.98	1.58	.78	.12	.24	358	34.4	53.4
Idaho	6.2	1.9	12.72	4.12	.10	1.43	5.60	.78	.00	.67	518	33.7	6.3
Ill.	54.3	86.1	11.17	2.56	1.72	1.26	3.72	.93	.37	.61	782	73.6	141.2
Ind.	34.3	70.1	11.66	2.88	.90	1.56	4.65	1.09	.16	.43	613	55.1	94.7
Iowa	25.6	40.2	10.08	2.66	.52	1.63	3.14	1.48	.11	.53	557	42.7	45.3
Kans.	22.4	18.0	9.82	2.78	.59	1.19	3.71	.78	.04	.73	513	41.9	21.9
Ky.	21.8	53.4	6.81	1.34	.47	.88	2.92	.71	.10	.38	348	29.8	70.9
La.	26.5	30.4	6.59	1.41	.66	.60	1.44	.45	1.48	.55	410	41.5	52.3
Maine	33.5	23.2	10.66	2.31	1.00	1.74	3.19	1.77	.14	.51	569	40.5	27.3
Md.	49.8	119.5	9.19	1.63	1.66	1.22	2.82	.85	.35	.66	774	59.3	184.2
Mass.	86.0	349.0	24.17	3.12	3.21	3.33	4.89	3.28	1.81	4.52	821	89.4	545.9
Mich.	39.3	42.1	10.58	2.38	1.10	1.11	4.09	1.16	.20	.53	721	65.7	92.2
Minn.	34.1	21.7	12.07	2.35	1.01	2.07	4.63	.98	.15	.87	562	49.8	34.9
Miss.	7.7	33.5	3.86	.97	.20	.46	1.65	.40	.02	.16	250	19.8	46.1
Mo.	36.3	45.2	10.04	1.85	1.16	1.25	2.81	.81	.24	1.92	562	51.8	54.6
Mont.	34.7	1.7	20.46	6.28	1.58	2.14	6.58	2.16	.15	1.57	629	37.8	3.8
Nebr.	23.7	13.9	9.16	2.54	.48	1.28	3.74	.67	.04	.40	511	39.1	17.2
Nev.	17.0	.4	22.79	8.38	.14	.86	8.95	3.14	.02	1.31	947	39.3	1.0
N. H.	46.7	45.6	11.12	2.15	1.06	2.45	2.81	1.81	.16	.69	593	57.6	54.5
N. J.	70.6	250.7	12.99	2.20	2.14	1.54	4.67	1.32	.43	.69	861	81.6	553.1
N. Mex.	14.0	1.6	5.49	2.04	.24	.34	1.47	.34	.03	1.03	398	33.2	4.4
N. Y.	72.9	152.5	19.55	3.49	3.42	2.57	5.56	2.50	.95	1.06	922	82.8	281.2
N. C.	9.9	38.9	3.00	.51	.14	.54	.97	.53	.05	.25	362	27.3	72.7
N. Dak.	7.3	4.5	13.76	4.84	.23	1.15	5.58	.86	.03	1.07	458	20.6	9.2
Ohio	48.1	102.1	11.72	2.15	1.15	1.76	4.52	1.38	.26	.51	726	66.8	168.0
Okla.	7.4	11.4	5.38	1.33	.14	.58	2.68	.21	.02	.43	425	37.6	33.7
Oreg.	32.2	4.3	13.77	2.54	.68	2.35	6.23	1.01	.14	.84	676	48.8	11.3
Pa.	54.7	140.6	11.68	2.01	1.46	2.00	3.87	1.22	.33	.79	685	66.5	219.8
R. I.	88.3	401.6	14.94	1.82	2.79	3.01	4.27	1.41	.69	.97	822	91.6	674.2
S. C.	12.8	44.0	3.23	.63	.28	.49	1.12	.45	.06	.20	325	24.5	62.1
S. Dak.	10.2	5.2	11.05	3.18	.15	.76	5.60	1.00	.002	.36	471	24.6	8.4
Tenn.	16.2	48.5	3.89	.89	.33	.58	1.22	.46	.06	.35	365	35.2	69.5
Tex.	17.1	11.6	6.67	1.46	.35	.77	2.91	.59	.07	.54	473	45.4	24.3
Utah	38.1	3.4	10.30	2.85	.69	1.44	3.56	.69	.16	.91	563	55.5	6.7
Vt.	22.1	37.7	8.84	1.56	.27	2.20	3.49	.91	.02	.38	563	34.3	38.7
Va.	18.3	46.1	4.63	.92	.38	.48	1.87	.62	.14	.22	510	35.3	67.1
Wash.	40.8	7.8	17.57	3.85	1.03	3.33	7.15	1.14	.09	.98	751	53.1	25.9
W. Va.	13.1	39.9	6.28	1.10	.33	.58	3.28	.71	.04	.23	439	28.1	79.0
Wis.	38.2	37.4	11.16	2.19	1.05	1.98	3.98	1.17	.16	.63	593	53.5	57.3
Wyo.	28.8	.9	12.95	4.10	.59	1.02	4.78	1.66	.06	.73	626	37.3	2.6

Income is personal income per capita.
Urbanization is percent of population in urban areas.
Density is population per square mile.

PER CAPITA STATE AND LOCAL GOVERNMENT OPERATION EXPENDITURES (DOLLARS), 1942

Total	General Control	Police	Fire	Other Public Safety	Highways	Schools	Health & Hospitals	Public Welfare	Sanitation	Other	School	Nonschool Full- & Part-Time	Nonschool Full-Time Equivalent
25.34	2.57	1.24	.57	.39	4.52	9.71	1.41	1.98	.43	2.52	87	80	67
62.95	6.40	2.62	.96	.74	6.44	21.38	3.24	13.05	.88	7.24	102	145	130
21.36	2.20	.71	.32	.34	3.17	8.28	1.72	2.49	.14	1.99	94	73	61
80.36	6.88	4.16	2.65	2.87	6.71	25.80	6.22	15.53	1.28	8.26	92	187	171
72.23	6.22	2.04	1.39	.80	8.12	20.86	4.35	21.80	.61	6.04	122	156	139
68.31	6.75	4.23	2.57	1.89	7.63	22.11	5.77	9.35	1.63	6.38	79	171	149
54.60	5.23	3.22	1.48	1.04	5.01	20.06	5.75	4.29	1.78	6.74	107	163	145
51.24	6.21	3.38	1.48	1.32	5.96	14.18	3.90	5.95	1.56	7.30	96	168	148
28.64	3.04	1.60	.78	.39	2.93	11.00	2.29	3.46	.89	2.26	98	86	71
56.63	4.63	1.75	.69	.50	8.57	18.09	1.98	9.89	.80	9.73	119	145	117
59.88	5.73	3.54	1.62	1.17	4.26	19.41	3.95	11.65	2.67	5.88	81	135	110
52.78	4.69	2.13	1.87	.66	6.75	17.73	3.27	10.35	.97	4.63	109	126	106
56.14	4.53	1.27	.78	.53	9.23	20.07	3.93	9.67	.76	5.37	136	132	95
52.16	4.70	1.17	.96	.56	8.26	19.05	1.98	9.98	.33	5.17	153	167	120
27.03	3.09	1.09	.64	.34	3.41	10.34	1.80	3.48	.46	2.38	90	78	66
43.60	4.21	2.41	.94	1.01	4.26	14.34	4.16	7.40	1.19	3.68	111	142	127
56.16	4.18	1.69	1.69	1.21	12.22	15.43	3.51	9.22	.44	6.57	113	203	125
47.12	3.63	3.73	1.94	1.21	5.48	14.02	4.64	5.34	2.16	4.97	76	139	131
75.52	6.51	4.54	4.08	1.69	6.20	18.94	7.72	15.31	2.37	8.16	81	189	161
64.81	5.56	3.77	2.05	.92	7.63	20.19	6.39	10.64	1.99	5.67	96	178	151
58.62	4.23	1.81	1.24	1.13	8.92	19.52	4.00	11.35	1.05	5.37	119	191	131
25.39	2.90	.64	.32	.23	5.75	9.52	1.54	2.26	.31	1.92	108	87	67
43.82	4.19	2.37	1.14	.53	4.20	14.65	3.31	8.99	.67	3.77	90	116	96
67.85	6.84	2.19	.90	.95	10.45	22.63	2.96	13.12	.58	7.23	139	157	132
49.97	4.97	1.41	.87	.69	8.28	17.12	2.24	8.77	.69	4.93	139	159	117
99.77	14.41	4.81	1.59	1.71	16.41	27.47	8.92	11.81	.91	11.73	139	237	195
63.32	4.29	2.25	2.61	1.18	12.73	16.59	4.36	10.75	.80	7.76	94	276	167
71.96	7.84	5.95	3.81	1.59	5.90	23.92	8.14	5.77	2.75	6.29	88	158	135
45.14	3.58	.96	.28	1.01	6.58	18.99	2.38	4.55	.18	6.63	136	107	92
79.52	7.40	6.02	3.63	1.64	6.10	22.74	8.24	14.42	3.33	6.00	82	207	186
29.09	2.56	1.38	.55	.36	3.94	12.54	2.03	2.84	.62	2.27	100	85	72
47.84	4.52	1.19	.31	.65	6.87	19.68	2.48	8.13	.37	3.64	160	168	105
55.11	5.09	2.54	1.67	.94	7.77	18.79	3.51	9.81	1.49	3.50	98	157	127
45.12	3.99	1.54	.65	.26	5.65	16.42	2.03	11.53	.28	2.77	119	100	83
62.82	5.03	2.91	2.06	1.27	10.42	20.58	3.39	9.67	.65	6.84	125	163	135
54.05	5.51	2.92	1.46	.87	5.16	19.18	3.61	10.19	1.13	4.02	89	136	102
59.80	5.76	4.34	3.39	1.85	5.99	19.07	4.91	7.67	1.73	5.09	82	167	148
29.67	2.01	1.39	.44	.58	4.33	11.57	2.84	2.40	.63	3.48	107	88	74
54.02	5.94	1.21	.52	.40	9.32	20.55	2.68	9.01	.68	3.71	156	261	147
29.33	2.61	1.28	.83	.32	4.91	10.38	2.37	3.73	.47	2.43	102	89	77
36.33	3.97	1.46	.94	.81	5.73	13.56	1.92	4.37	.67	2.90	130	101	89
68.09	5.31	2.46	.97	1.06	6.48	25.42	3.33	16.66	.77	5.63	158	188	136
54.01	6.09	1.09	1.04	.92	12.31	16.13	3.52	7.09	.14	5.68	156	151	98
32.61	3.89	1.68	.94	.72	3.77	12.51	3.13	2.51	.78	2.68	102	116	93
74.50	5.91	2.78	2.02	3.02	7.86	22.82	4.10	19.89	1.02	5.08	110	194	168
41.42	3.16	1.38	.55	.58	5.68	17.14	2.24	7.19	.44	3.06	132	81	74
65.31	4.45	2.45	2.06	1.00	11.53	20.83	5.13	9.70	2.51	5.65	98	195	140
67.35	6.93	2.01	.68	.90	8.26	25.85	4.02	7.70	.71	10.29	171	163	130

NOTES TO TABLE E2

Expenditure figures for 1942 include operation only, but the 1903 figures include also most state government outlays, because they cannot be segregated. Expenditures by public enterprises and contributions from general government funds to public enterprises are excluded. Transfer payments to the public, other than interest on the public debt, are included. Apportionments, mainly by state governments, are entirely excluded in 1942, but included in 1903, so that expenditures in that year are overestimated, particularly for highways and education.

There are numerous differences in classification between 1903 and 1942. Wherever possible, the 1903 data were fitted into the 1942 classification. The 1903 classifications "general government" and "courts" were combined into "general government", and "military and police", "fire department", and "miscellaneous protection to life and property" were combined into "protection", though in both cases there are slight incomparabilities in the figures for the two years. "Health conservation", "charities", and "insane" were combined into "health, hospitals, and public welfare" although it is not clear whether hospitals are included in the 1903 figure. "Education" in 1903 includes libraries, which are in the miscellaneous category in 1942. In both years, the miscellaneous category probably includes some items which would be more properly classified under one of the other classifications.

Expenditure data for 1942 are from the Census Bureau's *Revised Summary of State and Local Government Finances in 1942* (1948), and the 1903 data are from the Census Bureau's *Wealth, Debt, and Taxation, 1903*.

The employment data are divided into school and nonschool workers. Full-time equivalent nonschool employment is estimated by adding one-third the number of temporary and part-time workers to the number of permanent full-time nonschool employees. The figures for school employment are from the Census Bureau's *Public Employment in the U. S.: 1941* (State and Local Government Quarterly Employment Survey, Vol. 2, No. 1, August 1941). They actually cover the school year 1939-40 and are taken by the Census Bureau from the *Biennial Survey of Education in the U. S.: 1938-40*, but, according to the Census Bureau, school employment in January 1941 was probably about the same as in 1939-40, judging from nonschool employment. The data on nonschool employment are from *Public Employment in the U. S.: January 1942* (State and Local Government Quarterly Employment Survey, Vol. 3, No. 5, December 1942).

The population data used to derive the per capita figures are for the census years 1900 and 1940, as are the figures for density and degree of urbanization. Arizona, New Mexico, and Oklahoma had not been admitted as states in 1900, but the expenditures of their territorial and local governments are included. The population figure for Oklahoma in 1900 includes Indian Territory.

The income figures are averages of income payments per capita for the five years 1938-42 from the *Survey of Current Business*, August 1949.

Table E3

STATISTICAL RELATIONS BETWEEN GOVERNMENT EXPENDITURES PER CAPITA OF THE 48 STATES AND THEIR RESPECTIVE LEVELS OF URBANIZATION AND DENSITY, 1903 AND 1942

DEPENDENT VARIABLE *Expenditure per Capita*	CONSTANT TERM	REGRESSION COEFFICIENT OF INDEPENDENT VARIABLE		COEFFICIENT OF MULTIPLE CORRELATION
		Urbanization	*Density*	
General control				
1903	3.28	.1051 (.0331)	−.0266 (.0081)	.41
1942	2.27	.0643 (.0218)	−.0032 (.0027)	.40
Public safety				
1903	−.56	.0776 (.0066)	−.0006 (.0016)	.94
1942	−1.14	.1224 (.0151)	.0011 (.0019)	.88
Highways				
1903	.67	.0858 (.0119)	−.0076 (.0029)	.78
1942	5.17	.0584 (.0323)	−.0092 (.0040)	.26
Schools				
1903	6.80	.3308 (.0679)	−.0647 (.0167)	.56
1942	9.54	.2057 (.0477)	−.0145 (.0059)	.52
Health, hospitals & public welfare				
1903	.76	.0554 (.0129)	−.0046 (.0032)	.60
1942	−.43	.3210 (.0465)	−.0224 (.0057)	.72
Sanitation				
1903	−.13	.0130 (.0061)	.0032 (.0015)	.68
1942	−.45	.0305 (.0055)	.0004 (.0007)	.80
Other				
1903	.45	.0347 (.0140)	.0001 (.0034)	.49
1942	1.93	.0836 (.0245)	−.0068 (.0030)	.42
Total expenditures				
1903	11.27	.7024 (.1175)	−.1008 (.0316)	.68
1942	16.89	.8860 (.1518)	−.0545 (.0188)	.66

NOTES TO TABLE E3

Per capita expenditure is in dollars per capita (in 1942 prices); urbanization is percentage of population in cities of 2,500 or more; density is population per square mile.

Figures in parentheses are standard errors of the coefficients.

The basic data appear in Table E2. The 1903 expenditures were put into 1942 prices by multiplying by the following ratios of 1942 to 1903 prices (see footnote 8, Ch. 6): 2.065, for nonschool functions; 3.508, for schools. The implicit price ratio for total expenditures, derived from the individual functions, is 2.584, which differs a bit from the price ratio in footnote 8, Ch. 6, 2.454, because of differences in weights.

For 1942 we have equations for the following subdivisions of two functions:

	CONSTANT TERM	REGRESSION COEFFICIENT OF INDEPENDENT VARIABLE		COEFFICIENT OF MULTIPLE CORRELATION
		Urbanization	*Density*	
Public safety				
Police	−.33	.0558 (.0087)	.0008 (.0011)	.83
Fire	−.60	.0395 (.0047)	.0013 (.0006)	.91
Other	−.22	.0271 (.0054)	−.0009 (.0007)	.65
Health, hospitals, & public welfare				
Health & hospitals	.39	.0714 (.0155)	.0001 (.0019)	.70
Public welfare	−.81	.2496 (.0413)	−.0225 (.0051)	.65

Table E4

WEIGHTED AND UNWEIGHTED AVERAGE LEVELS OF STATE AND LOCAL
GOVERNMENT EXPENDITURES PER CAPITA IN THE 48 STATES
1903 AND 1942, BY FUNCTION

STATE AND LOCAL GOVERNMENT EXPENDITURES PER CAPITA,
AVERAGE OF 48 STATES

	1903		*1942*		*Ratio, 1942 to 1903*	
	Weighted by Population	*Un-weighted*	*Weighted by Population*	*Un-weighted*	*Weighted by Population*	*Un-weighted*
General control	$2.15	$2.47	$5.07	$5.01	2.36	2.03
Public safety	1.27	.92	5.75	4.76	4.53	5.17
Schools	3.70	3.89	17.96	17.86	4.85	4.59
Highways	1.54	1.44	6.14	7.04	3.99	4.89
Sanitation	.35	.23	1.44	1.04	4.11	4.52
Health, hospitals & public welfare	1.20	1.10	13.61	12.58	11.34	11.44
Other	.81	.76	4.82	5.23	5.95	6.88
Total	11.01	10.81	54.80	53.51	4.98	4.95

Data are from same sources as in Table E2.

Index

Activities of government: factors affecting the trend, 3-9, 140-55; types of, 47-50, 61-83
Adams, Henry C., 151, 152n
American Federation of Government Employees, 85n
Anderson, H. D., 75n, 76n, 77n
Anderson, William, 97n

Barger, Harold, 236
Bergh, A. E., 7n
Berolzheimer, J., 98n, 122n
Biennial Survey of Education, 216, 234, 236, 260
Book of the States, 91n, 92n
Bowden, Witt, 86n, 99n, 257
Bowley, A. L., 151n
Brainerd, Carol P., 122n, 216, 229
Brandeis, Elizabeth, 5, 76n
Brecht, Arnold, 122n
Brookings Institution (Institute of Government Research), 105n
Buck, A. E., 95n
Bundy, McGeorge, 9n, 143n
Bureau of the Budget, 216, 218, 226-27, 236, 241, 246
Bureau of the Census, 53n, 71-2, 75n, 87-90, 107n, 109n, 110n, 120n, 161-63, 165, 169-72, 175, 188, 190, 193, 200, 203, 211, 212-14, 216-19, 223, 225, 227-33, 247, 250, 252, 254, 260
Bureau of Labor Statistics, 85n, 86n, 99n, 113n, 178-79, 184, 188, 190, 193, 200-01, 216, 226-27, 229-30, 232, 235-36, 257
Burns, Arthur F., 144

Capital assets of government: compared with government employment, 16-8; compared with total, 18-21; county, 212; description of estimates, 204-13; federal, 61, 65-6, 206-07, 209-10; functional distribution, 45-6, 61, 65-6, 209-13; growth in total, 14-6, 208; by level of government, 32-5, 209; military, 16, 206-07; municipal, 213; net investment in, 19-20; state, 211
Carson, Daniel, 162, 163n, 169-71
Centralized purchasing, 93-6
Chatters, Carl H., 47n, 53n
Citizens Budget Commission, 89n
Civil Service Commission (U.S.), 85n, 92n, 165, 178, 181, 184, 201, 225
Clark, Colin, 5n
Cleveland, Grover, 4, 7n
Colean, M. L., 105n
Colm, Gerhard, 122n, 154
Commons, John R., 5n
Congressional Joint Commission on Reclassification of Salaries, 93n
Congressional Record, 241
Construction (*see* Expenditures)
Construction and Construction Materials, 236

Density of population: influence on government expenditures and employment, 122-39, 258-62
Department of the Army, 180-81
Department of Commerce (National Income Division), 106n, 159-60, 166-67, 188, 190, 193-95, 217n, 222-24, 226, 238-39
Department of the Navy, 180-81, 225
Dewey, D., 151n
Dewhurst, J. F., 222
Douglas, Paul, 85n, 216, 226, 228, 230
Durand, John D., 169-72

Edwards, Alba M., 169
Employment by government: census data, 161-63, 168-75; compared